Gender and Religion, 2nd Edition

Also available from Continuum

Does God Hate Women? Jeremy Stangroom and Ophelia Benson
Gender, Religion & Diversity, Tina Beattie and Ursula King

Gender and Religion, 2nd Edition

The Dark Side of Scripture

Barbara Crandall M.D.

continuum

Continuum International Publishing Group

The Tower Building	80 Maiden Lane
11 York Road	Suite 704
London	New York
SE1 7NX	NY 10038

www.continuumbooks.com

British Library Cataloguing-in-Publication Data
A catalogue record for this book is available from the British Library.

ISBN: HB: 978-1-4411-4871-1
      PB: 978-1-4411-7537-3

Library of Congress Cataloging-in-Publication Data
Crandall, Barbara F.
  Gender and religion: the dark side of Scripture, 2nd ed.
      p. cm.
  Includes index.
  ISBN 978-1-4411-7537-3 (pbk.) -- ISBN 978-1-4411-4871-1 (hardback) 1. Women and religion.
2. Sex role—Religious aspects. 3. Sexism in religion. I. Title.
  BL458.C73 2011
  200.82—dc23
                              2011020069

Typeset by Fakenham Prepress Solutions, Fakenham, Norfolk NR21 8NN
Printed and bound in India

'For the great enemy of truth is very often not the lie – deliberate, contrived, and dishonest – but the myth – persistent, persuasive, and unrealistic. Too often we hold fast to the clichés of our forebears. We subject all facts to a prefabricated set of interpretations. We enjoy the comfort of opinion without the discomfort of thought.'

President Kennedy's Commencement Address at Yale University on June 11, 1962.

Contents

Preface

My interest in the subject of this book, religion's role in women's progress, came out of a long period of reflection and then about eight years of research. The topic is foreign to my background in the sciences, specifically medical science, but came out of observed differences in the treatment of women both as colleagues and those they served. This has changed over the last half century, although they still remain under-represented in the sciences. Now women are to be found in all areas of employment, including the military. They serve in government but their numbers remain small among elected representatives in nearly all nations. Despite improvements, they still hold too few high-level positions in corporations and academia, and salary differences remain between the sexes for the same type of work.

The first edition of this book appeared in 2006. I prepared this second one to provide more information on when and how patriarchy was established, to add details concerning each religion and up-to-date data concerning women's recent progress. It also seems appropriate at this time, in view of the recent threats to re-establish patriarchy in the name of religious revivals or the need for economy in government and cancellation of programs important to women.

Introduction

My interest in the role religions played in women's progress goes back a long way to my days as a medical student. Medicine at that time was clearly an occupation for men, women were relatively rare and many specialities were completely closed to them. This has changed during the last half century and currently most medical school classes have about equal numbers of men and women. I learned the reason for this gender discrimination was because women were intellectually and physically inferior, and too much learning could be harmful for them. I wondered how such a situation came about, whereby half – in fact just over half – the world's population was created inferior to the other half? Whether this occurred at Eve's birth, because a higher power decided to make something less than perfect or after a long process of evolution, this appeared nonsensical: the first seemed out of character, and by the second process, the number of females in the world would be decreasing through selection. So why and how did these myths about women's inferiority arise and why did they persist for so long?

The greater physical strength of men at a time of almost continuous tribal conflict seemed a reasonable explanation for male dominance, initially. During this period, the victors first killed off all their opponents, then kept the women they captured for labour and sexual purposes and later, when they had learned how to control male captives through more effective weapons and various forms of mutilation, they too were retained as slaves to carry out the heaviest labour (1, p. 77).

When in human history did this subjugation of women occur? In her study of patriarchy, Lerner dates this to about the third millennium BCE, before the advent of slavery and before societies developed class structures. It took time to develop, probably two to three thousand years, and occurred sometime between 3100 and 600 BCE (1, p. 8). Its goal was male control of female sexuality and their reproductive potential. Once established, patriarchy was relatively easy to maintain and enforce through laws written by men, and by denying women an education and excluding them from decision-making.

Eventually, male dominance was established in nearly every known human society and lasted for about five millennia. It still persists in more subtle forms today. What were the influences that allowed this wasteful human practice to persist for so long? The only influence present in every culture appears to have been religion. Mankind, however primitive just had to believe in some higher power(s) who controlled him, his world and the universe. Initially this took the form of female gods, prophets and healers but they were mostly replaced by males and then by a single male god.

Male dominance was the custom of the society where almost all of the major religions began. Each incorporated this belief into their literature and sacred books and eventually – at different times in the world's history – it spread to dominate most of the world's cultures.

My goal in writing this book was to identify why each of the major religions believes women are inferior and the effect this has had on their progress. To do this, I reviewed the history of each religion from its inception to the present, the scriptures and laws they enacted to enforce this practice, and the effect these scriptures have had on the different aspects of women's lives, especially in countries where each is the dominant faith, including their education, employment, inheritance, government, religious practice and family law including reproductive rights.

Recorded history began after the invention of writing in Mesopotamia in about 3000 BCE. The inscribers were men who wrote about men. Women's history is a much later event and therefore brief. Information about life on earth before that time is derived from the artifacts our ancestors left behind. Archaeologists have helped to supply some of these through the many tombs, temples, sculptures, figurines and paintings they have unearthed in different places all over the world. These inform us of some of the lives, beliefs and rituals practised by men and women who lived in prehistoric times.

There is reliable evidence that women were not always regarded as inferior: a period of goddess worship existed in Europe and the Near East for a long interval of time dating back to 7000 BCE and earlier (2, p. xix). Traces of this culture have been found as far west as the Atlantic Ocean, east into Russia and south into the Mediterranean, Mesopotamia and the Indus valley region. The focus of this goddess culture was agriculture, the raising of crops and herds, fertility and regeneration, both seasonal and long term, and it seems natural for goddesses to have been credited with the power to control such activities.

Gimbutas working in Europe and Mellaart at Catal Huyuk in Anatolia and others, found large collections of pottery pieces, frescos and sculptures made from bone, stone, clay, marble, copper and gold, some of which date back into the eighth and seventh millennia BCE (2, p. xvi). These depict females, many of them pregnant or in birthing positions, but others showing symbolic designs, trees, and female deities represented as snakes, birds, rams, hedgehogs and other animals. 'There is no trace of a father figure in any of the Paleolithic periods. The life-creating power seems to have been of the Great Goddess alone' (2, p. 316). The 'Great Goddess' was revered not just as a fertility figure but as the 'Giver of life, Wielder of death and as Regeneratrix' not only of human but of all life (2, p. xix). This art shows a 'striking absence of images of warfare and male domination, reflects a social order in which women as heads of clans or queen-princesses played a central role' (2, p. xx). This does not prove the existence of a matriarchy, then or at any time, but suggests there was a period in human history when women had much more power and were not subordinate to men.

This long-lasting culture, based on agriculture and the regeneration of life, was eventually overcome by the male-dominated Indo-Europeans in about 4000 BCE (3, p. xiii). The Great Goddess slowly disappeared from Northern Europe but lasted until about 1500 BCE in some Mediterranean regions where evidence of her is found in tombs and temples on Maltese islands and in Crete's Minoan civilization, where there was a 'balanced non-patriarchal non-matriarchal social system' (2, p. xx).

The Indo-Europeans initially occupied a region surrounded by the more thriving cultures of Eastern Europe, the Middle East and Northern India. They resided in an arid land unsuitable for agriculture and lacking rivers and waterways needed for transport. They depended on livestock for food and travelled by horse, which they raised in large numbers and domesticated. They were partly nomadic and, over time, included several different tribes such as the Scythians – 'the first great Indo-Eurasians' – the Huns, the Khazars, the Khitans (4, pp. 15–37). They had a three-class society consisting of ruler-priests, warriors and peasant-farmers. They worshipped a variety of gods – male and female – representing the sun and moon and other natural phenomena. Honed by the extremes of their climate and geography and using their horses for transport and armed with lethal weapons such as daggers, spears, bows and arrows for armour, these Indo-Europeans emerged from Southern Russia in about the fifth millennium BCE and spread over Northern India, the Middle-East and Europe (2, p. xx).

The old Goddess culture was eventually eclipsed and replaced by a patriarchal, patrilinear society but the change was slow and uneven and eventually completed around 600 BCE (2, p. 8). Some of the old traditions lingered on, and a few goddesses retained their independence such as the Egyptian Isis, the Greek Artemis and Athena, the Roman Minerva and Diana, the Celtic Brigit and the Baltic Laima; others such as Hera and Juno were replaced by gods or became the wives of gods (2, p. 110). The gods and goddesses were eventually replaced by a single all-powerful male god in the monotheistic religions. Matrilinear traditions persisted in other cultures such as the Palaeo-Indian tribes who occupied North and Mesoamerica. Some survive to this day. In Europe, remnants of the Earth Mother tradition may have persisted into the Christian era and eventually fused with the cult of the Virgin Mary (2, p. 159).

Several codes of law survive to tell us about the lives of individuals in the Middle East in the third millennium BCE and later. The best known, the Laws of Hammurabi – named for a ruler of that time – were written in about the eighteenth century BCE. A copy of this Codex, inscribed in cuneiform script on stone, is preserved in the Louvre. It lists 282 laws of which 73 are about marriage and sexual matters (1, p. 102). These reflect the practices of the Babylonian people of that time, most likely the upper class rather than the ordinary people. Society was clearly patriarchal by then: males were valued more than females and fathers decided which and how many of their daughters should live and whom each should marry. He received a bride price for each one and could then use this to purchase wives for his sons (1, p. 100). He provided each of his daughters with a dowry – after the marriage had been consummated – and although this was for her use in the event of divorce or widowhood, her husband controlled it in the meantime. Divorce was easy for men to obtain but very difficult if not impossible for women. Adultery applied only to women and her punishment was death by drowning, tied to her lover. She was after all the property of her husband. A similar or worse fate awaited a woman who tried to procure her own abortion since the foetus belonged to her husband. Inheritance was patrilinear. A woman's dowry went to her sons but if she had none, it was returned to her father. Women could not cede or own property, although no law against this appears in the Codex (5). A man controlled the entire lives of the females in his family and he could also use them to work off his debts.

This Codex informs us that patriarchy had been around for some time by the age of Hammurabi but does not explain why and when this occurred. By then, females mostly accepted this state of affairs and acquiesced, probably for their own safety and that of their children and also for their own comfort and status, which reflected their husband's.

The Codex laws seem relatively generous to women, compared to the restrictions placed on them later in different cultures and endorsed by the major religions in their scriptures and laws. Females were progressively demeaned and their subjugation was extended by denying them other rights including the custody of their children, property, financial support in widowhood, and education because of younger and younger marriage ages. By the time of Aristotle in the third century BCE, even the female body was reviled and he called her a 'malformed male devoid of the principles of soul' (1, p. 207). He belittled her contribution to reproduction, saying that semen provided the all-important ingredient and the ovum only contributed 'matter'. We now know the reverse is true; the ovum contributes both mitochondria (the power-house of cells) and its chromosome complement, the sperm only its chromosomes. Aristotle had a great influence on Christian philosophy through Augustine of Hippo about seven centuries later and even later through Thomas Aquinas: their opinions are responsible for much of the Christian teaching on sex and reproduction to this day.

The worsening attitudes to women can be seen in the histories of two ancient religions, Zoroastrianism and Vedism. Earlier on, women were quite well treated in both, they could participate in the practice of both religions, they had a say in the selection of their mates and girls received the same education as boys. By the time of Buddha and Confucius a millennium later, this had worsened and continued to decline although the rate of change varied in different regions. By the time the Abrahamic religions were established, females had no rights and counted as the chattels of their men.

Although none of the major religions were the cause of women's subjugation, they accepted the attitudes and practices around them at the time, offered excuses to condone them and then elevated their importance by including them in their scriptures. Over time these came to be accepted as sacred and immune to change and they have consequently had a monumental effect on women's progress. Not surprisingly, cultures lacking written scriptures or constitutions have been more flexible and kinder to women.

The five major religions reviewed in this book are professed by 75 per cent of the world's nearly 6.8 billion people: 2.1 billion (33 per cent) claim they are Christians, of which about half are Roman Catholics and the other half are Protestants including Evangelicals; 1.5 billion (21 per cent) are Muslims; 900 million (14 per cent) are Hindus; 376 million (6 per cent) are Buddhist; 14 million (less than 1 per cent) are Jewish and 788 million (12 per cent) are equally divided between 'non-religious' and 'other' (6).

All of the major religions promote a systemic belief in the inferiority of women, placing them on the same level as slaves and children. The scriptures of each, written long ago and almost certainly by men, reflect this attitude. Except for Islam, this occurred more than two millennia earlier and common sense dictates that laws, even religious ones, must undergo change with time; behaviour appropriate to one period of history is not necessarily appropriate in another time or place.

Vedism, the parent of Hinduism (Chapter one) is the oldest major religion and dates back to the third millennium. Buddhism (Chapter two), an offshoot of Hinduism, began about a half millennium before the Current Era (CE). The dates of Judaism (Chapter three) are uncertain, but are later than Hinduism. Christianity (Chapter four) developed out of Judaism and shares its scriptures. The Eastern Orthodox Church separated from the Church of Rome in the tenth century, as did the Protestant Churches in the sixteenth century. Islam (chapter five) began in the sixth century CE and spread rapidly through North Africa, the Middle East and Southern Europe. The last chapter describes a few of the oldest known cultures and tribal religions, some of which exist today.

Vedic women were treated as equals with regard to education and religious participation and had some say in the selection of their mates. Their society had three classes and placed priests or Brahmans in the highest position followed by ruler-warriors and merchant-artisans. The indigenous people or darker-skinned Sudras became the lowest or fourth class. Hinduism's excuse for promoting male superiority was the preservation of racial and caste purity. This became an obsession, particularly for the Brahmans and female sexuality was viewed as a threat to both. In order to control and preserve their purity, girls were isolated from an early age and married off at puberty or earlier so that their education decreased to practically none.

Starting in about 500 BCE, a slow deterioration occurred in the lives of Hindu girls and accelerated after the seventh century CE. This was enhanced by the Laws of Manu, sacred laws which declared that Hindu girls were to be forever dependent on men, first on their fathers, then on their husbands and then on their sons (7). For practical purposes, a woman's life ended with the demise of her husband and she was dispatched on a funeral pyre or eked out a miserable life as a widow.

India is now a secular country and has enacted laws to improve the education and rights of Hindu females but it takes time to change the customs of centuries. The Hindu Radical Right continues to oppose change and argues that this denies the right of Hindus to practise their religion.

Buddhism, which began in the fifth century BCE, inherited the Hindu beliefs in *karma* and reincarnation, but not its caste system. Buddha taught that all people are equal, regardless of their gender or caste. He welcomed women followers and many joined him to escape from lives of misery under Hinduism. Buddha also taught that men and women are equal with regard to their *karma*s. But before long, the first gender difference arose following the requests of female followers to join the *sangha*s or monastic communities. The Buddha balked at first but finally agreed to their admission but only if they promised to treat monks as their superiors, regardless of their experience or seniority (8, p. 283). One of the Buddha's promises was broken.

The ultimate goal of Buddhists is to achieve enlightenment. This is the responsibility of each individual and does not require the intervention of a superior force or god. At some time after the Buddha's death, religious leaders decided that male and female *karma*s were no longer equal and women were incapable of winning enlightenment in their female bodies. They must be reborn as males who had already achieved a higher plane because of their past *karma*s. Another of the Buddha's promises was broken.

In most Buddhist countries today, the state controls social issues, except for the practice of religion: the availability of the former is dependent on its economy.

At first Judaism used the same excuse as Hinduism to claim male superiority – the preservation of racial purity. A second reason was to maintain the purity of the tabernacle and Temple and this excuse persists despite their destruction in 70 CE. The Torah states that both men and women are sources of contamination and restrictions were imposed on both but eventually they were applied to women only. They were denied participation in religious rites and were segregated in the Temple. Many Jews believe Moses was also given an Oral Torah on Mount Sinai and this allowed religious leaders to adapt Jewish laws to different times and situations, providing there was agreement of the majority (9, p. 146). But the majority comprised males only; the opinion of women was never sought.

Israel is a secular country but Orthodox Judaism is the state religion and its laws apply to issues of marriage and family law. Orthodox Jewish women are reminded regularly of their inferiority by the Benediction and other well-known Talmudic verses. They are treated unfairly in divorce, inheritance, religious participation and remarriage. They are reminded each month that they are unclean.

Christianity's explanation for woman's supposed inferiority is unique in religious history and based on the order of creation, as described in the first book of the Bible, Genesis. Some Christians interpret the creation story literally, despite evolutionary and archaeological evidence to the contrary (10, Gen. 2.23). One account of this states that Eve was created out of Adam's rib, so that she was the later arrival and therefore inferior, as were all of her female descendants. If true, this creation story would have made Adam and Eve identical – at the cellular level – and Eve would have had a Y chromosome and any progeny would have been unlikely, or at best, at high risk for genetic disasters. A second strike against Eve was blame for persuading Adam to eat the forbidden fruit, the apple. Yet their creator must have decided they were both equally guilty for he punished them equally. Nevertheless, Eve is the one who is blamed for this to this day by some Christians.

Women played a very prominent and essential role in the first centuries of Christianity and became both disciples and deacons. Yet from about 400 CE, they were completely excluded from these positions and from the councils that made decisions concerning the early Church. Belief in women's inferiority persists, despite the words of early Christian leaders and Jesus himself, that men and women are equal in the eyes of God. Some Protestant Churches enacted changes in favour of women such as allowing them to be priests. The Catholic Church did not and continues to add doctrines and dogmas to its basic beliefs, none of which improved the lives of women.

Most Christian countries now observe secular laws with regard to women's rights except for those where the Roman Catholic Church is the dominant religion. Here they still control issues covered by Family Law.

Islam began about 600 years after the birth of Christianity. Its scriptures claim that men are superior and women are possessions that require protection. The Prophet improved the lives of women by giving them some financial independence in the form of a dowry and the right to an inheritance. The early Medinan society appears to have been more egalitarian and women had greater freedom at that time. All of this was lost later on in Islamic history (11, p. 263).

Overall, women in Islamic countries have made slow progress in achieving basic human rights. Girls were denied an education until the late twentieth century, and their literacy rates remain low. A few Islamic countries have abolished Sharia (religious) laws entirely; others retain it only for matters covered by Family Law; a few are governed by mullahs or a monarchy that demand complete obedience to the Sharia. Some Islamic religious leaders have called for a reinterpretation of their scriptures to make them more appropriate to the present age; others disagree and advocate that Sharia law should be the law of the land, and there should be no separation of secular and religious authorities.

These five major religions share some similarities in their early histories; all experienced an initial period of relative freedom for women when they were allowed to participate actively in their religions. This occurred in Vedic history before Brahmanism, in very early Buddhism, in early Judaism, in the first centuries of Christianity before the supremacy of Rome was established, and in early Islam. Then for varying reasons, this all changed and was replaced by a long period of increasing female subordination and almost complete male domination.

Some but not all of the ancient cultures and tribal religions escaped the patriarchy of the five major religions. Those in Europe, such as the Hellenistic-Roman cultures, overlapped the period when patriarchy was being established. Others appear to have retained aspects of the goddess culture, or were perhaps less influenced by the warrior mentality. Women maintained considerable influence in Egypt, where their achievements were similar to men in the same social stratum. Women in the Palaeo-Indian tribes of North and South America appear to hold separate but respected roles, even if not entirely equal. None of these developed into world religions and many disappeared. Was this because they lacked belief in a supreme being who promised an after-life in return for obedience (Buddhism is an exception to this); or because they lacked written scriptures which contained specific instructions concerning their beliefs and laws; or perhaps because they were mainly confined to one ethnic group?

Is it fair to blame religions for their beliefs and literature concerning women's inferiority? Almost certainly this behaviour was already well established in the society where each began. Then each tried to explain and justify these beliefs and practices in their scriptures. Those belonging to the major religions all clearly state that men are superior or women are inferior, not once but many times. With time, this literature came to be viewed as inerrant or divinely inspired. Their veracity was never questioned. 'A husband must be constantly worshipped as a god', says the Hindu law (7, v. 155). Buddhism denied women enlightenment or eternal life while in their female bodies, until they had been reborn as males. 'They are gluttonous, eavesdroppers, lazy and jealous,' says the Jewish Talmud about women (9, p. 160). The Christian New Testament Epistle to Timothy decrees, 'I permit no woman to teach or have authority over men; she is to keep silent' (10, 1 Tim. 2.11-13). And, 'Men have authority over women because God has made the one superior to the other' says the Quran (12, ch. 4, v. 34). Excerpts of these scriptures are recited regularly in religious services and, with the exception of some but not all Protestant Churches and Reform Judaism, there has been no attempt to modify them. Attempts to enact changes were condemned in the name of religious scriptures and laws.

History records very little evidence of women's opposition to their subjugation. Yet it is difficult to believe that they could tolerate this type of mistreatment so silently, for so long. Except for a few outstanding leaders and queens, the history of women is notable for its absence and those few women who did leave records were authors, sometimes writing under pseudonyms. Those who dared to speak out against these edicts are likely to have been demolished and their words were never preserved. For the majority of women, centuries of subjugation bred a sense of inferiority and submission as well as a fear of retribution in the form of starvation and homelessness, not only for themselves but also for their children. Most preferred to remain protected and secure in their inferior status. Some even joined the chorus of male voices, which rose regularly to oppose any attempt to improve the status of women. It is hard to forget the cacophony of female voices shouting down their sisters who were involved in rallying support for women's franchise. But until late in human history, women lacked two essential ingredients necessary for change, an education and a voice in government.

In the past and up to the present time, a close relationship existed between a state's religious hierarchy and its rulers. Both were dominated by men who resisted any attempted change likely to threaten their control. This reciprocal relationship is evident to this day in most Latin-American states, in Saudi Arabia and some Islamic countries, and in India under the caste system. Latin America started to free itself from the double bondage of Spain and the Roman Catholic Church in the early nineteenth century. By the end of the twentieth century, virtually all countries there had achieved a constitutional type of government, except for Cuba (13). But the Catholic Church continues to retain a strong influence over Family Law, including divorce and repro-ductive issues. In many Islamic states, Sharia law is obeyed to varying degrees and continues to impede the progress of its women. Attempts are being made in India, now a secular state, to correct this inequality and improvements are evident especially in urban areas. Little change, however, has occurred to date in villages where the majority of the population resides. In the United States, despite laws separating the powers of church and state, evangelical churches clamour for a return to the old practices of male dominance and try to influence the policies of its political parties.

Religious authorities like to argue that their scriptures and laws are sacred and therefore immune to change. This has proved to be a huge obstacle in improving the lives of women. Elizabeth Cady Stanton recognized this when she was working to enfranchise women at the end of the nineteenth century. Together with others, she published the Women's Bible for which she was strongly criticized (14).

Although they have not amended their scriptures, all the major religions have made a few changes in their laws and religious practices. Most Islamic countries have modified the punishments ordered in the Quran. Orthodox Judaism has made changes concerning divorce, polygyny and levirate marriages. The Catholic Church amended some of its practices after Vatican II, as have many Protestant Churches at different times. In most religions, decisions concerning policies and practices were made by men without the input of women, even on those issues that particularly concerned them or their children.

The antiquity of religious scriptures does not make them unassailable. Recent archaeological discoveries have provided alternate accounts and interpretations to things long accepted as religious truths. The scripture of each faith is based on an oral history, transcribed much later and then augmented by later tracts, interpretations and dogmas. If the defence against change is preservation of the original, then these later additions should be erased or at least given a secondary status. The creation story is clearly mythological and cannot be accepted as a reason for designating women as second-rate and inferior. Nor can the preservation of racial purity be a valid excuse. Such laws have been co-opted and misused by dictators and tyrants and are in any event inappropriate in present-day populations: genetic studies have shown that all the so-called races are mixtures. As for women being labelled as unclean or contaminated, surely enough scientific progress has been made so that even religious authorities are capable of understanding that menstruation and childbirth are normal physiological events.

My studies over the past eight years lead me to conclude that although the belief in women's inferiority existed prior to the origins of the major religions, all of them bear a great amount of responsibility for perpetuating, amplifying and endorsing these beliefs, and this has impeded women's progress throughout history. Despite this, it is unlikely, from a practical viewpoint, that changes will be made in religious practices, at least among the more orthodox of each faith. Women must depend on themselves and on the secular governments they help elect. Legislation has been enacted to improve the education of girls and provide for equality in employment practices, ensure their voting rights, give them greater custody rights to their children and improve their property and inheritance rights. Some religions have allowed women to become priests and empowered them to participate to a greater degree in their faiths. Despite this, many of the areas governed by Family Law are unfair to women and difficult to change because of the combined control of government and religious authorities. Religions have a right to state their approval or disapproval of a proposed change, but no right to interfere with the enactment of laws whose goal is to protect the rights of the majority of women.

More aggressive action is needed against any state that permits discrimination against women in any form. Many have already enacted legislation to separate religious and secular power and these need to be enforced to prevent religious authorities from blackmailing elected leaders from voting according to the will of the majority who have elected them. Additionally, far more women must be elected and appointed to all levels of government, local as well as national. Since they constitute at least one half of the population, this will not only ensure the future prosperity of the state but also provide a buffer against the repeated cycles of fundamentalism that beset each religion.

Science has so far done too little to educate the general population that, although men and women have different abilities in order to fulfill their differing roles, one is not inferior or superior to the other. These conclusions need to be incorporated into educational protocols, applied from an early age and included in the required instruction in both public and private schools, if they seek to obtain and maintain accreditation.

Women should have equal representation on the governing councils and synods of all religions. Religions should consider amending phrases in their scriptures that demean women, or at least state that although these may have reflected the customs of the times when they were drafted, they are no longer appropriate; further, they do not now represent the belief of that religion.

References

1   Lerner, Gerda. *The Creation of Patriarchy*. Oxford University Press. 1987.

2   Gimbutas, Marija. *The Language of the Goddess*. New York. Thames and Hudson. 2001.

3   Campbell, Joseph. *Introduction. The Language of the Goddess*. New York. Thames and Hudson. 2001.

4   Sharma, A. *Women in World Religions*. State University of New York Press. 1987.

5   King, L. W. (tr). Hammurabi Code of Laws. www.eawc.evansvillesedu/anthology/hammurabi.html

6   www. adherents.com/Religions.

7   Muller, F. Max (tr.*) Laws of Manu: Sacred Books of the East*. Ed. G. Buhler. New Delhi. Motilal. 1964.

8   Wei-hsun, Fu C. and S. Wawrrytko. (Eds.) *Buddhist Behavioural Codes and the Modern World: An International Symposium*. Westport, Connecticut. Greenwood Press. 1994.

9   Cohen, Abraham. *Everyman's Talmud*. New York. Schocken Books. 1949.

10   *The Holy Bible* (RSV). Oxford University Press. 2002.

11   Aslan, Reza. *No God but God*. New York. Random House. 2005.

12   *The Koran*. Ed. N. J. Dawood. Penguin Books. 1997.

13   Sigmund, P. E. *Religious Human Rights in Latin America*. www.lawemory.edu/EIRL/volumes/spring96

14   Stanton, Elizabeth C. *The Woman's Bible*. Mineola, New York. Dover Publications Inc. 2002.

Additional Bibliography

Matheson, Peter. *Argula von Grumbach*. Edinburgh. T. and T. Clark. 1995.
Smith, Bonnie G. *The Gender of History*. Harvard University Press. 1998.

Chapter 1

Hinduism

History

Before and During the Vedic Period: 1500 to 500 BCE

Hinduism is over 4,000 years old and is believed to be the oldest living major religion. Its history can be divided into the Vedic, Epic, Medieval and Modern periods. The name Hindu comes from the old Sanskrit word *Sindhu*, meaning one who lived on the Sindhus river, in what is now North-west India (1, vol. 11, p. 507). Here, according to archaeological evidence, there was once a fairly advanced culture – the Indus valley civilization – that peaked *circa* 2500 BCE. Excavations in this region, near Harappa and Mohenjo-Daro have unearthed the ruins of well-planned, fortified cities as well as temples and statues. Little is known about the religion of the people who lived here: the female figurines and other artifacts found here may be symbols of fertility and regeneration or may indicate the worship of goddesses (2, p. 28).

By about 2000 BCE, this civilization was in decay, possibly because of climate changes resulting in long periods of drought. Successive waves of Indo-Europeans or Aryans invaded the region between 1500 and 1000 BCE and eventually occupied the greater part of Iran and Northern India (1, vol. 12, p. 187). They came from lands near the Caspian Sea and Southern Russia and migrated over the high mountain passes, following the river valleys of the Indus and later the Ganges. They were a pastoral people and lived outside the cities established by their predecessors whom they regarded as their inferiors. They worshipped fire and its god, Agni and Soma – the extract of a sacred plant – gathered by their priests and believed to have hallucinogenic or stimulant properties (2, p. 43). The people also believed in magic and practised phallic worship, and sacrifice (3, p. 97).

The Vedic period is named for the oldest of their scriptures, the *Rigveda*. Vedic society appears to have been patriarchal but it was family-oriented, and women played some essential roles. In contrast to the Indus valley people, sons were more welcome than daughters because only men could make offerings to their ancestors and defend the community.

At some time in their history, these Aryan invaders developed a three-class social structure in which the Brahmans or priests occupied the highest order, the Kshatriyas were next and represented the rulers or warriors, and the Vaishyas made up the lowest class, and included the majority of the people or commoners, such as the farmers, merchants and artisans (4, p. 41). All three classes were 'twice-born', the second birth occurring at an initiation rite or *Upanayana*. This class structure is described in the *Rigveda* (5), the oldest of the Vedic scriptures; here the head of primeval man became the Brahman, his arms the Kshatriya and his thighs the Vaishya. The indigenous people or Sudras, were regarded with contempt and made up the fourth class, represented by his feet. They were only once born.

Eventually this four-class society evolved into the well-known caste system, becoming over time more and more complex with many secondary divisions, sects and subclasses, eventually numbering into the thousands. These divisions determined marriage partners and religious, social and labour practices. Required distances of separation were maintained between the members of the different castes. Food that was prepared by a member of one caste could not be eaten by someone belonging to another. The caste of an individual was fixed at birth and determined by that of each parent. When the mother was of lower or equal rank to the father, the child retained the latter's status. If, on the other hand, the mother's caste was higher, she was viewed as defiled by her partner and the child was treated as an outcast. Changes within a subclass or caste division could be made over time and a whole group could adopt a change, take a new name and move to a higher status.

Men and women whose work involved human and animal emissions and body parts, dead or alive, were viewed as polluted. Their occupations included midwifery, barbery, laundry, undertaking and associated trades. The lowest of all subclasses were the Untouchables whose work included street cleaning, sewage, handling dead animals and other kinds of menial labour. They and their families were denied entry into temples and schools and they lived separately away from urban areas and often worked at night. Even the sight of an Untouchable was polluting.

Caste rules were strictly observed by most Brahmans, and to a lesser degree by the Vaishyas, and even less by the Sudras. Compliance varied in different regions of the country and, as a result of Muslim influences, was less strict in Northern India. But in Bengal and its surrounding regions as well as the Tamil south, caste rules were strictly enforced.

The power and control of the Brahmans increased over time, particularly in Northern India and racial purity became more and more of an obsession. This led first of all to laws to prevent intermarriage with the indigenous people and later on, between the different classes and castes. Their main purpose was to maintain the purity of each.

Two new religions – Buddhism (see next chapter) and Jainism – began in India in the fifth century BCE (6). Both were protest movements against the power of the Brahmans, including their rituals and the misery inflicted by the caste system and animal sacrifice, which was by then practised on a large scale. Neither subscribes to a higher power or God, and both are peace-seeking faiths practising universal tolerance to other religions and people. They both believe the primary duty of man is to achieve the perfection of his soul. Jains show compassion for all living creatures and believe that all forms of life have souls (1, vol. 12, p. 846). Their Five Precepts reject violence, promote truth and honesty, oppose theft in any form, avoid sensual pleasures and oppose the possession of material things and people. Jains are vegetarians and are well known in India for maintaining animal shelters (7).

Epic or Classical Period: 500 BCE to 700 CE

The second period of Hindu history is the Epic or Classical period (500 BCE–700 CE), named for its literature including the *Mahabharata* (8, p. 105) and the *Ramayana* (2, p. 107). Sanskrit treatises dictating conduct and laws for Hindu society appeared in the early centuries of the Common Era. One of them, the *Manu Smriti*, had a major influence on every aspect of women's lives, from childhood through widowhood (9).

Alexander the Great invaded North-west India between 327 and 325 BCE and, although his period of control was brief, it had a lasting influence on the language and architecture of Hindus in the region. A period of wars and foreign invasions followed and then a time of relative peace and unity was established under the Mauryan rulers. Asoka (274–237 BCE), the third of the Mauryan kings and the greatest of Indian rulers, eventually controlled all of India except for the Tamil south (10, pp. 93ff.). Asoka converted to Buddhism after he witnessed the death and destruction sustained during a battle at Kalinga and renounced all further wars.

A period of foreign invasions from the north-west followed the Mauryan kings and was succeeded by one of the most creative periods of Indian history. This began in about 400 CE and produced Sanskrit literature, philosophy, art and science. This coincided with the Gupta dynasty uniting Northern India, Nepal, Assam and the Punjab and lasted until 550 CE (11, p. 80).

Medieval Period: 700 to 1800 CE

The Medieval Period (700–1800 CE) includes the millennium of Muslim control and most of the period of European settlements. Northern India had experienced several Arab incursions starting in the eighth century CE, but Mahmud's in the late tenth and early eleventh centuries, was one of the best known and confined mainly to the Punjab. Rival Muslim rulers contended over and finally ruled all of Northern India including Delhi. By the fourteenth century, they had penetrated Southern India, but control was not uniform and mostly confined to strongholds or garrisons. Intervening areas remained largely under Hindu control.

Babur, a descendant of Timur and Genghis Khan, invaded Northern India in 1526 and became the first of the Mogul emperors. Akbar, the greatest of them, took control in 1556 and ruled for about 50 years. He eventually ruled all of Northern India from the Deccan to Kabul including Kashmir. Although a Muslim, he was conciliatory to the Hindus and abolished the poll tax usually imposed on all non-Muslims. Akbar was followed by a number of less notable rulers of whom one, Shah Jahan is remembered for some of his great buildings, including the Taj Mahal. He also encouraged the arts and literature, and painting and calligraphy flourished. Later Mogul rulers impoverished the agricultural classes by their extravagances, excluded Hindus from office and reinstated the poll tax for non-Muslims.

Sikhism was started by Guru Nanak (1469–1539) in the late fifteenth century CE and combines both Hindu and Muslim beliefs and practices (1, vol. 20, p. 505). The Sikhs are disciples of ten gurus, and their sacred scripture is the *Granth Sahib*. Nanak was influenced both by the Hindu *Bhakti* movement and the Muslim Sufis. Sikhs oppose the worship of idols and the caste system and believe in a single God before whom all men are equal. Nanak's successors built Amritsar into a centre of pilgrimage in the sixteenth century. Their leader was persecuted and then murdered by the Mughal emperor and over time, this transformed the Sikhs into fanatical anti-Muslims.

Most upper-class Hindus continued with their traditional religious practices during the period of Muslim rule, but many Hindu images, icons and some of their temples were destroyed, especially in the north. Many higher-caste Hindu women adopted the Muslim customs of veiling and *purdah*, which confined women to their homes.

Decadence and a general deterioration in morals affected the Muslim aristocracy and their military during the seventeenth century making Northern India ripe for another uprising. One came from the Marathas and another from Nadir Shah, King of Persia. The Marathas were eventually defeated by an Afghan ruler in 1761 and control passed to local rulers and generals.

European incursions into India came by sea and included one from Portugal in the sixteenth century, for the repair and fuelling of their ships as well as trade. Their capital was Goa on the west coast from where they were active in spreading Catholicism. The Dutch followed at the end of the sixteenth century in order to protect their trading posts in the East Indies, particularly in Batavia. The English East India Company consisted initially of a small group of traders, who had bases in Bombay and then in Bengal in the early seventeenth century. French trading centres were established in the second half of the sixteenth century; their conflicts with the English led to an unofficial war, which ended with the defeat of the French in 1760.

Modern Period: 1800 to the Present

The Modern period of Hindu history started in about 1800 CE. The English East India Company initially controlled Bengal where they established local rulers; their interests and control then spread to adjacent regions. The general policy of the company was to establish law and order and the dispensation of justice, to develop a civil administration and to collect revenues but to avoid any interference in local customs and religious practices. After a number of struggles, particularly in the north, virtually all conflict ended by the early nineteenth century and the English controlled nearly all of India. Slavery was abolished and attempts were made to outlaw female infanticide and *sati* (widow immolation) with very limited success. Following the Indian Mutiny of 1857, the British crown took over control of India from the East India Company.

The Hindu Renaissance had its beginning in this period. Its goals were to promote the spiritual aspects of Hinduism, to emphasize reason and to reject icon worship, the caste system, child marriages and *sati* (4, p. 69).

British rule had a major impact on the economy, as Indians were forced to produce the raw materials – especially cotton – required for the Industrial Revolution in England. The caste system and religious customs went unchanged. There was a growing and widespread discontent over the treatment of Indians and their lack of representation in senior administrative positions, and this led to a rebellion in the Punjab and a movement of passive resistance. Mahatma Gandhi (1869–1948) was a part of this movement. Born into a Vaishya family, Gandhi studied law in London and practised in Durban, South Africa where he developed his policy of non-violent protest before he returned to India.

The Indian Nationalist Movement began in the last part of the nineteenth century, and the first Indian Nationalist Congress met in Bombay in 1885. The Muslim League was formed in 1906. The push for self-determination and control was facilitated by the more generalized use of English, which had become the language of commerce and government, and resulted in improved communications throughout the country.

Indian troops, particularly from the Punjab, participated in WWI, during and after which there were promises of self-government. Protracted discussions, uprisings and passive resistance were organized by Mahatma Gandhi and others who sought greater representation in the Governor-General's Executive Committee, none of which yielded much progress. The first general election was held in 1937, and the Congress party gained majorities in every state except Bengal and Muslims protested against their limited representation.

WWII again involved military forces from India and was followed by the Muslim League's demand for a separate state. Finally, independence was achieved in 1947 and Pakistan became a separate nation. This entailed the loss of countless Muslim, Hindu and Sikh lives as thousands exchanged their homes and businesses. The Congress party was elected to power and was led by Jawaharlal Nehru who later became its first prime minister. In 1950, India became a democratic, secular state with its own constitution.

Gandhi insisted on preserving Hindu values and lived an austere lifestyle which appealed to orthodox Hindus. He was a strong believer in the dignity of manual labour and the equality of women. For a number of years he worked to improve the lives of the Untouchables, a title that became illegal after Independence. He was assassinated shortly after this was achieved. Congress enacted legislation in 1955 and 1956 forbidding discrimination against the Untouchables who, together with other lower-caste Indians, became known as *Harijans*. They however refer to themselves as *Dalits* (the oppressed).

The social structure of India is changing slowly in the cities but very little change has occurred in rural areas where about 75 per cent of Indians reside. The population of the country now exceeds one billion people, of whom about 85 per cent are Hindus (including Buddhists, Jains and Sikhs) and 12 per cent are Muslims (12). Poverty and overpopulation remain major problems and the slum-filled cities attract a stream of migrants from rural areas. Here they face inadequate housing, little if any health care and high infant and maternal mortality rates.

About 95 per cent of Hindus reside in India but there are substantial populations elsewhere, the largest being in Pakistan and Ceylon. Other sizeable Hindu groups live in Burma, Malaysia, and South and East Africa. Both Hindu and Buddhist Indians moved to Java and Bali (Indonesia) in the first centuries of the CE and Hindu temples were built there before the Indian influence waned. The majority of present-day Indonesians are Sunni Muslims, but Hindus and Buddhists make up smaller fractions of the population, the latter particularly among the Chinese. Bali is the only Indonesian country where a majority of the people are Hindus.

Hindu migrations to the west have increased in the past 40 years, and there are sizeable populations now living in Britain and the United States.

Hindu society is strongly patriarchal and patrilinear but there are exceptions and several matrilinear cultures existed. Two of these include the Khasis of North-east India and the Nairs in the South-east part of the country. The latter had been in existence for 700 years but almost disappeared in the nineteenth century, due to the pressures of surrounding cultures, urbanization and education. Both may have derived from the Indus civilization (13, p. 196).

The mother is the main figure of authority in Khasi families, followed by her brother – the maternal uncle – and the children of her sisters. Their descendants form clans or *Kurs*. Succession is matrilinear. The youngest daughter inherits most of the family property and little goes to her siblings unless the family is wealthy. Women make all major decisions concerning property, but both parents are involved in the education of their children. Other decisions relating to careers and marriages are made by the individuals concerned. Recently, patriarchal families living nearby have provoked conflicts with the Khasis and it is not known how long these cultures will survive.

Hindu Scriptures, Literature and Women

Sacred Vedic Texts

Hinduism has no single all-important scripture or holy book, nor a single source – such as a prophet – for its beliefs (1, vol. 22, p. 930). It developed out of Vedism through an intervening period of Brahmanism, sometime between the sixth and second centuries BCE. Vedism takes its name from the Vedas or Books of Knowledge. According to legend, these were transmitted orally by seven sages to priests or Brahmans and then transcribed between the fifteenth and fifth centuries BCE.

The majority of the Vedas have been lost but those that survive are called the Samhitas and include the *Rigveda*, the *Samaveda*, the *Yajurveda*, and the *Atharvaveda*. The oldest, and the most important, the *Rigveda* is revered by all Hindus as the 'original revealed source of their religion' (3, p. 29). Its date is uncertain but was probably sometime between 1500 and 1200 BCE. It contains over one thousand hymns of praise, dedicated to the many Vedic deities, each of whom represent various naturally occurring daily or seasonal events. Agni, the god of fire was especially revered; Indra, the god of war held the highest rank; Varuna was the lord of the universe: the Ashvins were twins famed for their powers of healing. Goddesses included Ushas for dawn and Aditi, Sarasvati and others. One other was Vishnu, a giant who could bestride the earth in three steps, who later evolved into one of the main gods of Hinduism. Except for mention of the goddesses, the *Rigveda* contains few comments on women. One says, 'They sing their song like women active in their tasks ... bringing refreshment to the devotee' (5, book 1, hymn XCII, 3). Another comments, 'Indra herself hath said, the mind of woman brooks not discipline, her intellect hath little weight' (5, book VIII, hymn XXXIII, 17). The *Yajurveda* contains directions for priests to perform rituals: the *Samaveda* has an index of melodies, and the 20 books of the *Atharvaveda* contain a catalogue of domestic rituals such as prayers and spells.

In addition to the Samhitas, the divinely revealed scriptures or *Shruti* include the *Brahmana*s or commentaries, probably dating from the tenth century BCE: the *Aranyaka*s which contain tracts for forest-dwelling ascetics and date back to about 600 BCE, and the *Upanishad*s, some of which just predate Buddhism (*circa* 600 BCE). Some of these are Vedic and some are post-Vedic (4, p. 42). The *Upanishad*s describe the beliefs of the Vedic religion and are said to be 'as significant to every Indian Brahman today as the New Testament is to Christians' (14, p. 46). The *Shruti* were written in ancient Sanskrit and arranged in prose and verse. They tell the story of creation, of a supreme Brahman, and of Atman, the individual soul. The fourth Brahmana discusses women's creation. Hindu's believe the highest value is accorded to understanding the truth rather than to learning and the ultimate goal of man is to achieve union of the individual soul with Brahma. The *Shruti* do not contain any concept of heaven or hell, but the *Upanishads* do suggest an after-life: 'the souls of the righteous will go to the world of the ancestors and then to the moon'(15, p. 303).

According to the Vedas, Brahmans have three debts: to the sages through prayer and the reading of the Vedas, to the gods through sacrifice, and to the ancestors by begetting sons.

Some of their ceremonies or *Samskaras* were public and presided over by priests or Brahmans, while others were private or household rites. There were no temples and public ceremonies took place outdoors and included sacrifices mostly of animals but occasionally of humans, accompanied by chanting and the reading of passages from the Vedas. The most important Vedic rite was the initiation ceremony or *Upanayana* which took place when a child was eight or nine years old. It was preceded by instruction in the Vedas provided by gurus. Just before the ceremony, the celebrant shaved his head, bathed, made an offering to the sacred fire, completed certain rituals and then received a sacred thread to be worn over the left shoulder. This indicated the recipient was now twice born. Initially, girls were allowed to participate in the *Upanayana* but this was later restricted to boys only. The Sudras, the lowest class, were also excluded.

Vedic tradition believed a bride was analogous to earth, the groom to heaven. Semen was the source of bones, teeth and body channels; the female contributed blood, flesh and internal organs. If the groom was dominant, the result was a son; if not, a daughter. There were many religious rites including one during the third month of pregnancy to ensure the birth of a son and another immediately after birth to promote wisdom and a long life. An ear-piercing ceremony took place at seven months and, for males, the first tonsure was at 16 years. Death was followed almost immediately by cremation and the ashes were usually disposed of in a sacred river; memorial rites occurred later. Domestic or household rites took place at regular times each day and were usually presided over by the male head of the household, but in his absence, his wife could take his place. During these rites, offerings were made of milk, grain and butter, in accordance with a belief that these would help sustain dead relatives. Departed spirits resided in *Pitri-laka*, the world of the ancestors or *Preta-laka*, the world of the spirits.

By 500 BCE, Vedism was changing to Hinduism and the earlier gods were replaced by the three main deities of Hinduism: Shiva the destroyer but also the restorer of life and his female partner, the Mother Goddess Shakti – also known as Parvati, Mahadevi or Devi – and Vishnu, the preserver of life. Brahma had faded in importance. The Mother Goddess was a warrior goddess and entirely different to the benign fertility model of the Goddess era of Eastern Europe (3, p. 242). The worship of female deities was fairly well developed by 600 CE and this has continued, especially in rural India: this may derive from pre-Vedic traditions and seems to be associated with the *Purana*s and *Tantra*s and may take a benevolent or malevolent form (3, p. 249). Devi had several aspects including Durga and Kali. Vishnu's female partner was Lakshmi or Sri and Krishna was the 'human form' of Vishnu (3, p. 255ff.). Later, Radha became the female partner of Krishna. The cult of Krishna is said to be the most important although this varies in different regions. Vaishnavism and Shaivism, the cults of Vishnu and Shiva, have inspired many devotees throughout India. Certain fauna and flora are associated with each god and are protected. These include the cow and monkey, the Banyan and Pipal trees.

Aryans did not believe in reincarnation, but rather that the righteous would go to some kind of afterlife. Then, by about the first century BCE, the focus of Hindu religious practice changed from sacrifice – to placate the gods – to reincarnation. This was not Vedic in origin but may have derived from the Anaryan people they had conquered. The two basic doctrines of Hinduism, continuous reincarnation (*Samsara*) and the transmigration of soul – previously known to only a few – soon became widely accepted. For every deed or action – *Karma* – there is retribution and this explains an individual's present life situation. Later *Karma* came to mean the personal consequences that can accrue from action. Good deeds in a previous life improved one's situation in the next with the opposite effect for bad deeds. This is mentioned in the *Brahmana*s and is more fully developed in the early *Upanishad*s. Death was followed by ten days of ritual before a soul could be deified as an ancestor. Then there were two possible celestial paths for the dead: one – reserved for a blemish-free previous life – was to join the gods and the other – for everyone else – was to be reborn. The first was the ultimate reward and ended the cycle of reincarnations. The path of rebirth caused the soul to come to earth in rain where it was taken up by plants and eaten by man or animals (4, p. 44). The souls of evildoers would be reborn as insects or animals. All of this implied that each person is responsible for his or her own behaviour. Through successive rebirths, an individual strives to ascend in merit and eventually achieves liberation and union with Brahma. This is believed to be a continuous process that has not changed through 25 to 28 centuries.

For a man, a harmonious life has four stages: first as a student-initiate, when he studies with a guru at an ashram; second, as a householder when he marries and carries out duties for his family and community; third, as an ascetic or *sadhu* when he lives as a hermit or forest dweller, during which he meditates; fourth and finally, he renounces the world, becomes a mendicant and prepares for death (1, vol. 18, p. 1146). Most Hindus did not complete the last two stages.

Hindu Epic Poems

Two Hindu verse-dramas appeared in the Epic or Classical period of Hinduism (500 BCE to 800 CE) and these have had a profound effect on the lives of many Hindus. The *Mahabharata* is a poem of about one hundred thousand double verses and was written sometime between the third century BCE and the first century CE and additional changes were made during the next several hundred years. By about 1000 CE, it had evolved into two versions, one for Northern and another for Southern India and there were also regional variations (2, p. 105). The *Mahabharata* describes the war of the *Bharata*s but has many digressions including details of the moral values of Hinduism. The *Bhagavad Gita* is its best-known part and was originally a separate book (8). It relates a dialogue between Arjuna, the hero, and Krishna, his charioteer who reveals himself as the Supreme Being. The heroine is Draupadi who is married to the five Pandava brothers and is portrayed as a woman of great strength, complexity and intellect (15, p. 92). The poem deals with two main topics: the nature of God and what man should do to reach him. The *Bhagavad Gita*, its best-known part, is an episode in the sixth book. It includes the words of the Hindu god Krishna epitomizing the inclusive nature of Hinduism: 'Whatever god a man worships, it is I who answers the prayer.' (1, vol. 11, p. 507). Numerous commentaries have been written about the *Gita*, and it has been translated into many languages. Its popularity really began in the nineteenth century with the Hindu Renaissance (2, p. 124). Devout Hindus read the *Gita* every day and it is recited at their religious ceremonies.

The second epic poem is the *Ramayana*, which according to legend was written by Valmiki in about 200 BCE and there were many later additions and changes. This too has a northern and southern edition (2, p. 107). It consists of twenty-four thousand double verses and occupies seven books. It tells the story of Prince Rama who is banished to the forest by his father. Sita, his devoted wife follows him there and is kidnapped by the demon king Ravana. She manages to reject his attempts to seduce her, with the words, 'I do not value life or body. Do you imagine I would wish to live despised by the world? Do not dream that out of fear or to save my life I shall yield to you' (16, p. 84). Rama's struggles to release her are eventually successful; Ravana is killed and Sita returns, whereupon Rama first raises doubts about her fidelity and then repudiates her. The faithful but rejected Sita dies. Sita, in contrast to Draupadi, is devoted to one man and her loyalty and beauty, as well as her modest and demure behaviour, have made her a model for Hindu women to emulate.

Hindu Law

The *Smriti* contain a collection of Vedic and Hindu laws or *Dharmas* and are the sources of all Hindu law; they dictate rules for the moral and social conduct of Hindus. The *Dharma Sastra*s contain commentaries. The *Grihya-sutra*s cover domestic rites including the marriage ceremony. Others deal with household rites at birth, name giving, the initiation ceremony, and household offerings, as well as rules for ascetic life and the duties of a king.

The *Manava-dharma-sastra* or Laws of Manu is one of the earliest post-Vedic works and was probably begun *circa* 300 BCE and completed *circa* 200 CE (9). It dictates the rules for Hindu conduct and religion as well as civil and criminal law. These laws are believed by orthodox Hindus to have been revealed by Brahma to man (Manu) and include sections on marriage, the duties of women, the duties of husband and wife as well as laws concerning adultery, inheritance and partition. Included in the Duties of Women is one law that says, 'By a girl, by a young woman, or even by an aged one, nothing must be done independently, even in her own house' (v. 147). Women are to be obedient to men throughout their lives, 'In childhood a female must be subject to her father, in youth to her husband; when her lord is dead, to her sons: a woman must never be independent' (v. 148). She is reminded of this again, 'Him to whom her father may give her … she shall obey as long as he lives, and when he is dead, she must not insult his memory' (v. 151), and 'Though destitute of virtue, or seeking pleasure elsewhere, or devoid of good qualities, yet a husband must be constantly worshipped as a god by a faithful wife' (v. 155) and 'she must never mention the name of another man after her husband has died' (v. 157). She is warned of future punishment for disobedience, 'By violating her duty towards her husband, a wife is disgraced in the world; after death she enters the womb of a jackal, and is tormented by diseases, the punishment of her sin' (v. 157). Men are advised about their selection of wives, 'Let him not marry a maiden with reddish hair nor one who has a redundant member, nor one who is sickly, nor one either with no hair on the body or too much, nor one who is garrulous or who has red eyes' (iii. 8). Hindus are also reminded their wives should come from the same caste, 'for the first marriage of twice-born men, wives of equal caste are recommended' (iii. 12) and 'a Sudra woman alone can be the wife of a Sudra' (iii. 13).

Other religious writings appearing in the Classical period include the *Purana*s (antiquities) which were written between the first and tenth centuries CE. About 18 major ones survive and are still used in Hindu devotions. They describe details of creation, the Hindu gods and provide secular and religious information.

The *Tantra*s appeared sometime between the end of this period (seventh century) and the tenth century. They concern symbolic rituals such as purification, meditation and the initiation ceremony, as well as a dialogue between Shiva and the supreme female deity, Devi.

The Medieval Period

The Medieval period is known for its Hindu philosophers and theologians. Two of the most influential were Sankara (about 780–880 CE) and Ramanuja in the eleventh century (2, pp. 239, 136). Both were Brahmans who were born in Southern India. Each has had a considerable influence on religious beliefs and practices that have survived to this day. Sankara wrote commentaries on the *Upanishads*, as well as numerous other works, and established monasteries in the four corners of India. Ramanuja taught that the soul could reach salvation by meditation (*Bhakti*) and passive surrender (*Prapatti*) (3, p. 176). The *Bhakti* movement was a type of personal devotion to one deity, usually Krishna, Shiva or the Mother Goddess, which became widespread between the fifteenth and seventeenth centuries although it had its origin sometime before, probably in the Epic Period. Devotees could come from any class and were not required to have a knowledge of Sanskrit.

The diets of higher-caste Hindus changed during this period; although beef was eaten in the Vedic period and probably later, vegetarianism was well established by the eighteenth century. Bengalis avoid beef but eat other meats (3, p. 193). All Orthodox Hindus avoid alcohol.

The Modern Period

Changes in Hinduism after 1800 CE reflect the influence of Western civilization. Particularly important during this time was Ram Mohan Roy (1772–1833), a Bengali Brahman who was 'committed to improving the position of women' (17, p. 33). He studied Christianity, translated the *Upanishads* and other works and founded the *Brahmo Samaj* movement, a reform Hindu church. Another reform group was *Arya Samaj* founded by Dayanand Saraswati (1824–1883) who rejected image worship, sacrifice and polytheism. Iswar Chandra Vidyasagar (1820–1891) and Behranji Mermaji Malabar (1853–1912) were other influential Hindus (18, p. 49ff.). The *Ramakrishna* movement was started by Swami Vivekananda at the end of the eighteenth century and spread to the United States and Europe. Although he was a reformer and lawyer, Mohandas K. Gandhi (1869–1948) taught respect for Hindu values and also encouraged social service and emancipation from the caste system. He focused especially on the plight of the Untouchables (4, p. 72).

After Independence in 1947, India became a secular democracy, but about 80 per cent of its people are Hindus, and Orthodox Hindus observe the sacred laws as stated in the *Smriti*. They obey the taboos dictated by the caste system, fearing isolation in their community if they do not. Hindu mythologies are read and taught to children, pilgrimages are made, and a continuous round of festivals – each dedicated to different gods and goddesses – are celebrated. The belief in reincarnation and rebirth coupled with *karma* continues.

Many Hindus are highly superstitious and believe that nearly every aspect of their lives is under astral control. As a result, an astrologer, usually a Brahman priest, is consulted before action is taken on family or business matters.

The family remains patriarchal, and the home is the centre of religious activity and five obligatory offerings and prayers are offered each day. The *Samskara* – or life-cycle rites, which continue to be practised particularly among the Brahmans – are the *Upanayana*, marriage and funeral ceremonies (2, p. 64). Santosi Mata, a new female divinity, has appeared and grants special blessings of a practical nature such as support for the indigent, home needs and utilities (2, p. 18).

Hinduism and Women

Women in the Vedic Age

During the Vedic period, until 1500 BCE, women in India were relatively independent and their status was about equal to men, although there is no record of Vedic women rulers. Girls and boys were both taught at home by their elders and many were quite well educated. Girls learned astronomy, mathematics, history and dentistry, in addition to theology and Vedic scriptures. They had well-defined duties, both in the home and the community and were trained in the production and use of weapons. They raised crops and livestock, worked as weavers and potters and practised arts and crafts. Some became lifelong students and continued their Vedic studies in centres of education, some worked as teachers and others became poets and philosophers (18, p. 10). Girls went into business and others learned healing skills, particularly as midwives. They participated in public meetings such as the *Vidatha*, an assembly where discussions were held on secular, religious and military affairs. They took part in religious rites and festivals and recited Vedic mantras. They gathered the sacred Soma, and offered sacrifices to the gods, one of the obligations of every Hindu.

Girls were expected to complete their education before they married. 'An educated maiden is to be given in marriage to a learned man. Let her not be married during her childhood,' the *Rigveda* advises (5, iii, 55 16). Although marriage was a social and religious duty, it was not obligatory and women could remain single and continue to live at home. Their marriages were often arranged – usually by their parents – but they had some say in the selection of their mates and were usually willing brides. Most marriages were monogamous although polygyny did occur (11, p. 56).

Married women usually ran their own homes and controlled their household finances. They prepared the food for their families but did not eat until their husbands had eaten, a practice that still prevails in some Orthodox Hindu homes (11, p. 52). Couples prayed for a son to honour their ancestors and to defend their homes in times of war, but they rejoiced in the birth of a daughter and prayed she would be scholarly.

Widows could live freely in society without tonsure or other restrictions and were allowed to remarry, either by *Niyoga* (levirate marriage) or in the usual way (18, p. 143).

Vedic women could not own or inherit property, even if it had previously belonged to their husbands or families.

Women's Lives from 1500 to 500 BCE

Between 1500 and 500 BCE, the status of Hindu women started on a gradual decline, but still remained tolerable until about the sixth century BCE, after which it became much worse. This was not peculiar to Hindu society but followed a similar pattern in other Near East societies (19, p. 141). During this period, the power of the Brahmans increased steadily and the preservation of racial and caste purity became religious obsessions.

Marriages between upper-class Hindus and the lower-class Sudras had been occurring with increasing frequency as had ones between the different Hindu caste members (18, p. 345). This type of promiscuity was blamed on female sexuality, now regarded as a threat to Hindu society. Women were viewed as impure and a source of contamination because of menstruation and childbirth. To prevent this and maintain racial purity, girls were married off at younger and younger ages while they were still virgins.

As the age of brides decreased, girls had less and less time for education until none was possible. They could no longer learn Sanskrit and by 500 CE the Vedas were forbidden, first to Sudra and then to all women. Girls could no longer participate in the *Upanayana* ceremony since this required long preparation in the Vedic scriptures. They were destined to be wives and mothers for which education was unnecessary. All of this served to emphasize female inferiority and dependence.

The *Ramayana* had become popular by this time, and its heroine, Sita was held up as the ideal for Hindu women to emulate: she demonstrated the reverence and devotion women were expected to pay to their husbands. Orthodox Hindus justified their treatment of women as obedience to Vedic laws, which were eternal and unchanging. The Laws of Manu clearly dictated the role of women in Hindu society and the way they were to be treated (9).

Another reason for girls to be married at an early age was to prevent young Hindu women from joining Buddhism – which started in about 500 BCE – because it promised equality regardless of caste and an escape from Brahman control.

Women's Lives up to 1700 CE

By the first century CE, the marriage age for girls had fallen to 12 or 13 years and then decreased to eight and even younger ages in the following centuries (18, p. 60). It was believed girls should be married before their first menses, which were assumed to occur at ten years 'or their menstrual blood would go into the mouths of their departed ancestors' (3, p. 153). Earlier marriage meant earlier childbearing and wives were expected to have ten children of which hopefully the majority would be sons.

A woman's life was divided into three stages: maidenhood, marriage and widowhood. Marriage was essential and the only way for a woman to attain eternity. Marriages were irrevocable and indissoluble even after death and a wife belonged eternally to her husband. The widow's death by *sati*, and the denial of her remarriage – if she avoided this – were therefore a logical conclusion to her life and practised fairly generally by 400 CE. These strict rules of conduct were observed closely by upper-class Hindus, less so by Vaishyas and not at all by Sudra women, who were expected to work alongside their men to ensure family survival.

The millennium from 700 to 1700 CE included the period of Muslim occupation and control of Northern India. The first 500 years of this period were very oppressive, but life improved under Akbar, the greatest of the Moghul rulers. *Purdah* (the seclusion of women) was unknown until 100 BCE and only practised by a few Indian royal families. This and the veiling of women were Muslim customs that began with their rule and were only practised in Northern India. Both remained more common among high-class Indians in Bengal, Bihar and the United Provinces. *Sati* was not a Muslim practice but became more frequent among Hindus in this period. It was seen as a way to save young Indian women from being kidnapped and raped by foreign invaders.

Despite the general repression women experienced in this period, a few did still manage to obtain an education and some achieved renown as poets including the great medieval poetess, Mira Bai, a devotee of Krishna (3, p. 290). The *Bhakti* movement – a type of personal devotion to a single god – became popular at this time, especially among women. It provided them with an alternative way to practise their religion after all other public roles had been denied to them.

Courtesans and dancing girls were unique classes of women in the Classical and Medieval periods of Indian history. They enjoyed a certain status, often with royal patronage and were respected as custodians of the fine arts including music and dance. Although looked down on by high-class Indians, the company of these women was sought by many Indian men because of their knowledge and experience, compared to the immature and uneducated women they had married. Some, who were musicians, worked in temples where they provided vocal and instrumental accompaniment during religious ceremonies.

Women in the Eighteenth Century and Later

The status of Hindu women reached its lowest point by the eighteenth century CE. Warren Hastings, the Governor General of Bengal at the time, commissioned a group of Indian scholars to prepare a digest of Hindu law based on their scriptures. This included a chapter on the Laws of Manu, which he decided should now apply to all castes, not just the Brahmans (17, p. 130). All of this served to reinforce the subjugation of Indian women in the name of religion. Nevertheless, the lower castes and Untouchables generally ignored this change in the law.

A short time later, the East India Company's control was transferred to the English government who were determined to avoid interference in both the religious practices and social customs of Hindus, including their caste system. Despite this, Anglican missionaries received favourable treatment and were able to evangelize in the name of their own Protestant beliefs, while they established schools and colleges. They had competition from other sources, for by this time, Portuguese and French possessions in India had brought in Roman Catholic missionaries who were active in converting Hindus to their faith. The Portuguese colonies practised Napoleonic law, which gave Hindu women some protection from Hindu inheritance laws. At that time, English laws concerning property rights for women and divorce were even more restrictive than the Hindu ones.

The English crown enacted a number of reforms in the eighteenth century, including legislation to outlaw *sati* and child marriages, improve the treatment of widows, ban polygamy and improve the property rights and education of women. Many of these were ignored or at most had a very limited effect.

A number of Indian reformers tried to improve the lives of Hindu women in the nineteenth century. Ram Mohan Roy (1772–1833), a Bengali Brahman campaigned to abolish *sati* after he witnessed the death of his sister-in-law on a funeral pyre. He was disowned by his father for this. He also argued that Vedic law gave women the right to inherit property. Eventually, legislation to abolish *sati* was passed by Lord William Bentinck when he was the Governor General in 1929. Acknowledging its cruelty, he said, 'the practice of burning or burying alive the widows of Hindus is revolting to the feelings of human nature' (10, p. 664). Nevertheless, the practice persisted. Iswar Chandra Vidyasagar (1820–1891) focused on the misery of widows and argued that a Vedic scripture – the *Parasana Samhita* – gave them the right to remarry or to live chaste lives (17, p. 37). Behranji Merwanji (1853–1912), campaigned against child marriages, at that time occurring when a girl was ten years old or even younger. He too used the Vedic scriptures to support his reforms. Dayananda Saraswati (1824–1883), a revivalist, condemned some of the customs of Orthodox Hindus. He called for a return to the Vedas for all and argued that women should have an education and access to the scriptures to make this possible (17, p. 48 ff.). Swami Vivekananda (1863–1902), another revivalist, promoted the education of Hindu girls so that they could set their own priorities: 'Women must be put in a position to solve their own problems in their own way. No one can or ought to do this for them. And our Indian women are as capable of doing it as anyone in the world' (17, p. 51). Nevertheless, Orthodox Hindus continued to oppose all reforms, insisting they would deny the Vedic scriptures and if enacted, infringe on religious freedom.

During the twentieth century, the Indian Nationalist movement led by Mahatma Gandhi and others, including several women, focused on the plight of the lowest class, the Untouchables, as well as temple prostitution, *purdah*, child marriage and widow remarriage. Further legislation concerning divorce, remarriage, monogamy, inheritance, maternity benefits and dowries followed Independence in 1947. In addition, laws were enacted guaranteeing education for both sexes.

In 1950, India adopted a constitution declaring it to be a sovereign, democratic and secular republic. A number of Articles were ratified later; Article 14 parts III and IV applied particularly to women and concerned 'property, succession, matrimonial relief, guardianship, will-making and choice in adoption' (20, p. 3). It recognized women as a 'class' and different to men. Further, the state could make special provisions for women and discriminate in their favour. The goal of these measures was to provide a uniform civil code of law, which would apply to all its citizens. Seven categories of rights were guaranteed under the constitution, including the right to equality and prohibiting discrimination based on 'religion, caste, sex, place of birth' and promised 'opportunity in employment'. (20, p. 13). Untouchable status was abolished. Forced labour was prohibited and restrictions were placed on child labour. Women were disadvantaged by Hindu laws concerning monogamy, divorce and inheritance (20, pps. 60, 63, 77). In 1950, Pandit Nehru, India's first prime minister, expressed his concern for Hindu women when he said: 'I am quite sure that our real and basic growth will only come when women have a full chance to play their part in public life. Wherever they have had this chance they have, as a whole, done well, better if I may say than the average man. Our laws are man-made, our society dominated by men, and so most of us naturally take a very lop-sided view of this matter ... the future of India will probably depend ultimately more upon the women than the men' (20, p. 81).

The Women's Movement in India started in the nineteenth century and has a long history and some notable supporters. Ramabar Ranade (1862–1924) married a reformer when she was 11 years old and, under his tutelage, became a strong advocate for women's education and independence, despite the opposition of her mother-in-law (17, p. 55). Chimnaa-Bai, the Maharani of Baroda, and Saraj Nalini Dutt were two other notable reformers. In 1917, Annie Besant was elected president of the Indian National Congress.

The All India Women's Conference held its first meeting in the late 1920s to address the need for improved education and equal rights for Hindu women. It has met regularly thereafter. The second phase of the Women's Movement started in the 1980s and 'focused on rape, dowry harassment and domestic violence' (21, p. 177). Counselling and legal centres were set up for women all over the country, many operating independently. Legislation was passed reserving places for women in both local and national elections and additional measures focused on the rights of women to matrimonial property, promoted the registration of marriages and provided protection against domestic violence (16, p. 123ff.). Poverty has become more feminized. The number of women in the workplace has declined as men replace them and force women into more menial and poorly paid jobs. Outsourcing is a recent and expanding market, which should provide additional work for both men and women.

In the last half century, the Hindu radical right, which was initially a peaceful movement, has become more aggressive in its goal to convert India into a Hindu theocracy instead of the secular status it has maintained since Independence. It includes several different organizations, each with a women's wing who are opposed to the Women's Movement, rights for minority women and are clearly anti-Muslim. Some female members have called for the restoration of polygamy and the abolition of divorce. They defend the dowry system and widow immolation and deny the existence of conjugal rape: 'If a couple are married, how can you call it rape – this concept is alien to our culture' (22, p. 329ff.). A victim of wife beating is advised that she must 'keep in mind her husband's moods and avoid irritating him' (ibid). Education is acceptable to make women better mothers, as is their employment, if it is essential. Little is said about child marriages.

A great deal of legislation has been enacted since India became a secular democracy in 1947. Much of this affects women. But the customs of several millennia do not change overnight and while these laws have impacted the lives of urban women, very little has changed in India's villages where 75 per cent of the population lives. Education is the key to change but village girls receive a substandard quality of this commodity and many do not even attend school, although by law they should be in class until they are 14 years old.

Changes in Indian law Affecting Women

Education

The education of girls deteriorated after the Vedic age and virtually ceased by the eighth and ninth centuries CE, when females were married at nine or ten years of age. There were no schools until the fourth century, and by 1000 CE, the literacy rate for girls was less than 10 per cent (18, p. 20). They were now no better informed than the despised Sudras.

Literacy rates for Hindu girls declined further during the period of Muslim rule, and by the early nineteenth century, only one in two hundred received any education and less than one in a hundred could read. Formal education for girls began with the colonists who established missionary and other schools, which taught Western education and neglected Hindu values and traditions. Bethune College in Calcutta opened in the mid 1800s and was the first institution to provide higher education for girls. Tuition was free. Some states had a good record in female education, including Travancore where the rulers were often women. By the end of the nineteenth century, girls over the age of three years could enrol in primary school, but only 2 per cent attended secondary school (23, p. 149). Some families believed excessive education was detrimental to the nature of girls, so they were removed from school at puberty and segregated from the outside world. The Zanana educational system, a type of home schooling for small groups of girls, became popular at this time and received state funding by the end of the nineteenth century.

By 1982, there were nearly 70 girls for every 100 boys in primary school (6 to 11 years) and 30 girls for every 52 boys in secondary school (11 to 14 years) (23, p. 161). Girls accounted for about one third of the total enrolment at every grade level but their drop-out rate was higher. Female literacy was about 13 per cent in 1961, 25 per cent by 1981 and 48 per cent by 2005 (24, p. 119). Male literacy was 15 to 25 per cent higher. The rates in urban areas are about twice those in rural areas.

The number of girls enrolled in school varies in different parts of the country but has greatly improved during the past five years. Ninety-five per cent of girls are said to be enrolled in primary school but fewer than 75 per cent complete it. Family incomes are a major determining factor since girls may have to work rather than attend school and child marriage is another. About one third of the students now receiving tertiary education are women.

Employment

Women's lack of education and their high rate of illiteracy limited employment opportunities until the twentieth century. Upper-class Indian women rarely worked, although a few did enter professions such as teaching, medicine and law. Lower-class women had to work to support their families, and the caste system controlled to a large extent, the type of work they could do.

Much of the male work force is unionized and salaries are controlled, but the majority of women are self-employed and work as cleaners, vendors and piece-workers, usually without benefits and earning far less than the minimum wage. A woman's income supports her family while the husband's salary – if he has one – is in part reserved for his own use.

The 1961 census reported that there were nearly half as many women working as men and nearly 28 per cent of the women worked in spinning, weaving, marketing and crafts. The Equal Remuneration Act of 1976 required employers to pay men and women the same amount for the same work but is rarely enforced and most workers are unaware of its existence (16, p. 50). In

1990, male construction workers in Bombay were receiving 25 rupees a day compared to 22 for women (a 1990 rupee equalled about six cents).

Women are often denied the tools provided to men on the grounds they will pollute them and thereby threaten the whole project (16, p. 49). Maternity benefits are supposed to be provided for women who work in mines and factories but are easily circumvented by shifting them to lower positions, which are not covered. Employers in construction plants and factories are required to provide housing and childcare, but these are often so substandard that many women choose to take their children with them to work.

Inheritance and Property Rights

The Laws of Manu state that a widow cannot inherit or own property. She is bypassed in favour of her sons, or, if she has none, her nearest male relative. This does not include the so-called movable type of property or *stridhana* that belongs to the wife, to be returned to her upon divorce or her husband's death. Here, Hindu law was well ahead of the practices in Christian countries where a husband had rights to all his wife's possessions including her salary (21, p. 16ff.). A girl's father can claim back her *stridhana* if she dies in childbirth. Otherwise, it is usually passed on to her daughters when their mothers die. The *stridhana* does not include gifts from non-relatives or any wages the wife has earned. The husband's family members can sometimes claim the *stridhana* if they are in need. At other times a young wife may hand it over for the sake of peace.

By 400 CE, there was growing support for a more equitable distribution of property after the death of a married man, and by the end of the millennium, two legal positions became evident: the orthodox one denied the need for change, while the reformists promoted the widow's right to receive her full share of her husband's property. The reformists' position was adopted throughout the country in 1300 CE, despite greater resistance to change in Northern India. The Hindu Woman's Right to Property Act was enacted in 1937 and gave the widow her husband's share of family property (18, p. 255).

The Hindu Succession Act of 1956 gave a woman absolute ownership to property she owned at the time of the Act and sole ownership of income or property she earned, inherited or had been gifted: it met with strong resistance in Congress from members who opposed any inheritance rights for women (21, pp. 67–9). A woman could now claim a part of her inheritance, the amount to be decided by the courts, unless clearly specified in a will. The concept of two forms of widow's property (movable and immovable) was abolished and replaced by a single absolute one.

The Right to Vote

The Government of India Act was passed in 1935 and extended the voluntary franchise to six million Indian women. As a result, seats were reserved for them in every provincial legislature (23, p. 293). Mahatma Gandhi played a major role in encouraging women to participate in politics. In 1949, the voting franchise was extended to all men and women, and in 1980, 62 per cent of men voted compared to 51 per cent of women (23, p. 309). However, the number of women candidates has not changed and varies between 3.4 per cent and 6.7 per cent. In 1957, 27 of the 500-member lower house and 3 of the 245 member upper house were women (22, p. 302). By 2008, 9 per cent of both houses were women (24, p. 119). In 1982, 5 per cent of government ministers and people in positions of authority were women. The number of voting women has increased slowly with their literacy and they tend to be more conservative and more influenced by religion.

Marriage

Selection of partners
In the past, a girl's parents usually selected a husband for their daughter and this still occurs in over 90 per cent of marriages in India today (18, p. 42). Caste played a major role in this selection. Marriage between a girl of lower and a boy of higher caste – called *Anuloma* – was approved by Hindu society (23, p. 32). The opposite arrangement called *Pratiloma*, where the girl was from a higher caste, was not allowed: since women are the guardians of purity, their caste should be elevated and not lowered by marriage. Inter-caste marriages were discouraged by the tenth and forbidden by the fifteenth centuries CE: disobedience was punished by excommunication and total isolation from the community. An attempt was made to correct this in 1850 but had little effect. The Special Marriage Act of 1954 allowed girls of 18 years and older to select their own mates who could be from outside their caste, community or religion (20, p. 91). This law is more likely to be observed by families living in urban areas but has had much less effect in rural areas. One survey in 1998 found 56 per cent of the population favoured marriage to someone in the same caste (25, p. 152).

Advertisements – for both a suitable bride and groom – are quite common now and appear in national newspapers like the *Times of India*. The ones placed by a woman's family tend to emphasize her looks and domestic abilities rather than her education and employment, while the groom's advertise his education, occupation and salary (25, p. 167).

Marriage age

By 200 CE, the marriage age for girls – especially among high-caste Indians – had declined to nine or ten years and by the eighteenth century, was often eight or younger. By the fourth century, a belief was prevalent that a girl's parents could be condemned to hell if she was not married by the time she reached puberty. According to Hindu scriptures, the female body is dedicated to her husband by her 'infant' marriage at age ten and is immune to divorce or his death. *Sati* and the denial of widow remarriage were logical sequelae to fulfill these scriptures. Any attempt to raise the age of consent to 12 years violated the fundamental ritual observance of the Hindu life cycle, which required the cohabitation of husband and wife by the time she reached puberty – when she reached ten years – called the *Garbhadhan* ceremony (26, p. 195). This practice did not change until early in the twentieth century, despite legislative attempts to do so earlier.

The Civil Marriage Act of 1872 made the consummation of marriage with a girl of less than ten years illegal and punishable by life imprisonment (26, p. 194). It met with strong opposition, and the bill's application was narrowed down to a very small segment of Indian society. A later attempt to raise the age of consent, this time to twelve years, raised another storm of protest. A Bengali newspaper's protest against the government read, 'By raising the age of consent, the ruler will be interfering with the religion of the Hindus' (26, p. 226). This was contrary to the policy of the British government.

A 1921 census report found that 34 per cent of girls were married before they were ten but the actual number was probably far higher (18, p. 62). The Sarda Act in 1929 made marriage illegal before 14 years for girls and 18 for boys but again had little effect. The 1955 Hindu Marriage Act raised the minimum age for marriage to 18 for girls and 21 for boys (27, p. 185). Despite this, the 1970 census reported that 30 to 40 per cent of marriages involved child-brides (girls who were less then 18 years). Although these numbers have decreased, child marriages continue to occur. Obedience to the law varies in different states and almost certainly the published data give a rosier picture than the real situation. The National Family Health Survey found that 45 per cent of 20 to 24-year-old women surveyed were married before they were 18, 23 per cent before 16, and 3 per cent before 13 (28). The law allows girls to opt out of a marriage that occurred before she turned 16 (27, p. 185).

There are numerous accounts of the deaths of child-brides at the hands of older husbands. If they were even brought to court, English judges usually exonerated these men: their goals were to stay out of Hindu religious affairs. Many young children died or their health was severely compromised, as was that of their children. In 1890, eleven-year-old Phulmonee died after 13 hours of profuse bleeding following marital rape. Her husband was not punished (26, p. 210). A Dacca paper of 1875 reported that an 'elderly man had beaten his child wife to death when she refused to go to bed with him' (26, p. 210): the jury let him off with a light sentence. The same punishment was given to a man in 1873 who killed his eleven-year-old wife after he dragged her out by the hair and beat her' (ibid.). Medico-legal data in 1872 reported that there were 205 recorded cases of child deaths from sexual violation and this only included reported cases. An Indian doctor reported that 13 per cent of the births he handled were to mothers of less than thirteen years (26, p. 215). Another stated that 20 per cent of births in Bengal occurred to girls of 11 to 13 years (26, p. 240).

Weddings

The *Smriti* recognize eight forms of marriage and additional ones were used by lower-class Hindus (18, p. 35). The approved forms of marriage now in use all have Vedic traditions. In one, called *Brahma*, the groom is selected by the bride's father and is frequently a much older man who has been previously married. The bride, usually a child, plays an inactive role in the ceremony. Another, called *Prajapatya*, includes an injunction to the couple to remain inseparable in religion, love and wealth. In another, *Arsha*, the son-in-law makes a gift of a cow and bull to the bride's father to provide the milk used in the couple's religious offerings. Lower-caste marriages usually involved a bride price where her father was compensated for the loss of her services (21, p. 26). In Southern India, a 900-year-old ceremony involves tying the *Tali* around the neck of the bride (27, p. 57).

The wedding ceremony takes place in the bride's home on a day that is astrologically favourable. The marriage of a daughter involves considerable expense for a family since it includes her dowry (discussed in the next section). The groom is welcomed into the bride's home with a special offering of grain. He takes the hand of the bride who is appropriately attired and together they walk around the fire, take seven steps forward and then repeat their vows, invoking the name of Vishnu and indicate the irrevocability of their union. She completes certain rituals and receives directions to be tender, amiable and the mother of sons. An important part of the ceremony includes the bride's father's surrender of his rights to his daughter to the groom (27, p. 57). Following the ceremony, the couple observes three days of strict celibacy (18, p. 50).

Married women wear their hair long and have a vermillion mark at their hair parting. This is believed to be a Vedic custom and a token of a woman's happiness and joy in her husband. It is worn until his death.

After her marriage, the bride leaves her parents' home forever and is only allowed to return for festivals, illness and childbirth. Her new home is usually multi-generational and dominated by her mother-in-law and other females in her husband's family. This can be quite intimidating, especially for child-brides. Her status is usually improved with motherhood, particularly if she has sons.

The abrupt separation of a young girl from her mother is described in the autobiography of Rashsundari Debi, written in the nineteenth century: 'I went straight into my mother's arms crying mother why did you give me away to a stranger?' (26, p. 95). Rashsundari was 12 years old at the time, a little older than many brides. She was fortunate with her in-laws who treated her with kindness and consideration. She adds, 'I was caged for life … in this life there will be no escape for me. I was snatched away from my own people and given a life sentence. I eventually became a tamed bird' (26, p. 121). Rashsundari learned to read when she was 25 and wrote her autobiography when she was 59, completing it when she was 80 years old.

The Hindu Marriage Act of 1955, ruled that a husband and wife are equal under the law and have equal rights and equal obligations to each other (21, p. 83). This gave women the right to work but also meant that they had a legal obligation to support their mates, however low-paying their jobs, a concept foreign to Hindu scriptures and laws. Husbands can sue for restitution of their conjugal rights if the wife's work requires her to live outside the family home. This law was not corrected until 1975 (21, pp. 84–9).

Dowries

In the Vedic period, royal brides sometimes brought gifts of horses and jewels to their marriages, but the dowry system was generally unknown until medieval times and did not become a common practice until the nineteenth century (18, p. 66).

Dowries are a form of bribery offered to the groom by the bride's family and may include land, cash, gold and jewels. Initially, a dowry provided a kind of insurance for the bride in the event of her husband's death or some other disaster, but later it became a source of income for her husband's family. Dowries constitute a form of competitive bidding by the parents of eligible girls seeking a husband for one of their daughters. They contribute to female infanticide and, more recently, selective abortion of female foetuses since dowries frequently impose a heavy financial drain on the bride's family, especially if there are several daughters. In 1988, 'three sisters ages 21, 20 and 18 hung themselves to end their own humiliation and their father's plight' (21, p. 113). Prospectors had been demanding a dowry that was 25 times the father's monthly salary.

The groom's family sometimes makes additional financial demands on the bride's which, if refused, expose her to mistreatment, injury, and perhaps death at the hands of her in-laws. Dowry deaths are usually caused by burning or poison but are frequently blamed on accidents or suicide. With his wife's death, a husband is free to seek a new wife along with a new dowry. Many dowry deaths go unreported, and the police are often hesitant to intervene in what appears to be a family dispute.

The Dowry Prohibition Act of 1961 attempted to prevent a bridegroom from seeking a large dowry (27, p. 197). This was amended in 1984 but excluded gifts given 'without demand' (ibid.). Punishment for seeking a dowry could be imprisonment for 6 to 24 months (27, p. 94). The Indian Evidence Act of 1972 ruled that a woman's suicide or unnatural death within seven years of her marriage would be assumed to be a dowry death, especially if there was evidence of prior mistreatment (20, p. 95). Despite this, dowry deaths have increased fifteen-fold since the mid-1980s and are especially common among the lower classes (29, p.p 1–6). Three dowry-related deaths per day are believed to occur in Delhi and Bombay (21, p. 112).

The dowry system degrades women and has been a major focus of the Women's Movement in India but still continues.

Polygyny

Vedic scriptures permitted polygyny but not polyandry (27, p. 61). Polygyny occurred among rulers and the upper classes and then for a time was more common in wealthy families. It became more common during the period of Muslim rule, since Islam permits a man to have four wives, and persisted among Muslims in India. Polygyny was prohibited in Bombay in 1947 and, one year later, in Madras and is now illegal in most states in India. Recent laws require the registration of marriages, and it is hoped this will prevent it completely. In the period 1951–1960, polygyny was reported in 6.83 per cent of Hindus and 5.7 per cent of Muslims (21, p. 245).

Adultery

Adultery was permissible in the Vedic period, for both men and women; women were usually allowed back into society, provided they repented. This changed for them later, once it was decided that women were the property of their husbands, in life and death. From then on, women suspected of adultery were treated as social outcasts and either lived in poverty or turned to prostitution. In contrast, men were treated with little if any opprobrium.

Divorce

According to Vedic scriptures, women were allowed to divorce and remarry, but later on remarriage was denied to Brahman women unless their husbands had been missing for five years or longer: for Kshatriyas, the period of absence was ten months. These laws became more restrictive in the fifth century CE when women were only allowed a single marriage (21, p. 88). Lower-caste women frequently ignored these rules.

Divorce laws have changed radically for Hindus and especially for women since Independence. The Special Marriage Act of 1954 and the Hindu Marriage and Divorce Acts of 1955 with later amendments, allowed divorce for either partner on the grounds of adultery, a change in religion, cruelty, desertion, and for insanity, venereal and other diseases such as leprosy, or if one partner had become an ascetic, or if the woman was pregnant by someone else at the time of her marriage (27, p. 186). Women could divorce their husbands for rape, sodomy and bestiality, non-cohabitation after maintenance had been granted or if the wife repudiated a marriage made before she was 15 years of age. Petitions could not be filed in the first year of marriage unless one of the partners had suffered extreme hardship (ibid.). Mutual consent was added as a basis for divorce in 1976.

The Indian Divorce Act of 1869 made it possible for a wife to obtain maintenance costs or alimony and the Act of 1954 determined the amount, based on the income and property of both parties. Women were denied alimony if they were guilty of 'unchaste' behaviour.

Since Independence, successive governments have attempted to bring some uniformity to both Hindu and Muslim divorce laws, but in many cases, women have suffered economically since their rights to hold on to the money and property given to them before marriage under Hindu law, called *stridhana*, or *mahr* under Muslim law, have been denied. This is now included under the couple's joint property. Further, if the husband chooses to remain unemployed, he can claim maintenance from his wife under the concept of spousal equality, even if her job is one of the least well paid. It is hoped that future legislation will improve property division for women after divorce but in the meantime, many Indian households are headed by women and they 'live below the poverty line' (20, p. 209).

Widowhood

Until about 300 BCE, women had three choices when their husbands died: to remain single, remarry or have children by a *levir*. The latter – called *nyoga* – was common in other cultures but died out among Hindus (18, p. 143).

The immolation of widows or *sati* did not occur in Vedic times and is not mentioned in the Laws of Manu (9). Rather, the widow was invited to lie down momentarily by her dead husband and then got up and rejoined his family (18, p. 120). *Sati* started in about 400 CE, mostly among queens, then won praise by 700 CE and became common between 1400 and 1600 CE, especially among Brahmans. The practice was adopted later by the Kshatriyas, in part to protect Hindu women from foreign invaders.

Hindus believe that a woman cannot join her ancestors unless she is married, and since marriage is indissoluble in this world and the next, her death is an expression of her devotion to her husband. It also fulfilled the belief that all of a man's possessions, including his wife, should accompany him to his next life. Very shortly after a man's death, his wife, often a young woman or child

– since females were often married to much older men – put on her wedding robes, climbed on to the husband's funeral pyre, placed his head on her lap and perished. Bankimchandra, a Bengali writer of the nineteenth century, wrote 'I can see the funeral pyre alight, the chaste wife sitting at the heart of the blazing flames ... her face is joyful ... life departs and the body is reduced to ashes ... when I remember that only some time ago ... our women could die like that, then new hope arises in me and I have faith that we too, have the seeds of greatness within us... Women of Bengal! You are the true jewels of this country' (25, p. 158). The worst year was 1818 when 839 burnings were reported but there were probably many more unreported cases (10, p. 665).

The funeral pyres were sometimes assembled in pits to prevent the wife's escape, and women who resisted were dragged to the pyre. Those who did escape were treated as outcasts. Despite attempts to outlaw *sati*, it continued and still occurs although now infrequent. The practice still has supporters; a pro-*sati* group argues that the practice is based on the scriptures and its practice is a constitutional right.

By 600 CE, the remarriage of widows was discouraged, and after 1200 CE, was usually banned by higher-caste Hindus: the practice was adopted by some of the lower castes later on. Widows shaved their heads, wore unadorned dark clothes without jewellery and went barefoot. Widowhood was a dreaded existence as a second-class citizen without property or means of support, often spent in the homes of in-laws who were only too happy to get rid of them. Some widows chose to live in ashrams, devoting themselves to a religious life, or became prostitutes, to survive or escape.

Legislation to improve the plight of widows included the Widow Remarriage Act of 1856, which legalized their new marriages and made their children legitimate, the Special Marriage Act of 1954 and the Hindu Marriage Act of 1955, but overall these have had little effect. The remarriage of widows is still discouraged, particularly among upper-class Hindus.

Custody of Children

Hindu law maintains that children are minors until the age of 18 years and fathers have a superior right to their custody. This is consistent with the Hindu belief that the father contributes the determining role in a child's identity. The Hindu Minority and Guardianship Act of 1956 gave the custody of children to their mothers until they reached the age of five years, after which the fathers were given custody of boys (18, p. 315). This was later changed to 12 years. Since then the Supreme Court has ruled that the child's welfare should be the determining factor in custody disputes.

Reproductive Rights

India is believed to have been the first country to institute a national programme of population control (23, p. 235). This started in 1951 and is mostly directed at women. Several attempts to encourage vasectomy – which has been available for some time – failed because of its supposed threat to male virility. Tubal ligation became more popular after 1951 and was four times more common than vasectomy (23, p. 237).

India, the second most populous country in the world, had a birth rate of 23 per thousand population in 2003 and 22 in 2008 (31). The fertility rate (the number of children born to one woman in her lifetime) was 3.1 in 2003 and 2.4 in 2008 (31). This compares to 2.0 in Europe. Estimates suggest that 60 per cent of couples would have to practise birth control to reduce the birth rate to 20 per 1000 population (23, pp. 235ff.). One study for the period 1981–82, reported that 51 per cent of urban couples had a third child and only 27 per cent used some method of birth control; 24 per cent chose sterilization, 1 per cent IUDs, and 2 per cent some other method (23, p. 238). These numbers had nearly doubled by 2003 (31).

The Medical Termination of Pregnancy Act was passed in 1971 and made abortion legal for several reasons including the welfare of the mother and child or if the pregnancy resulted from rape or failed contraception. Despite this, nearly 100,000 Indian women die each year after unsafe abortions and childbirth. This is 100 times higher than rates in developed countries, and the number is increasing (27, p. 225).

Recently, medical technology has made it possible to determine foetal sex in mid-gestation by ultrasound and amniocentesis. Estimates indicate that between 1978 and 1983, 78,000 female foetuses were aborted (17, p. 184) and a survey in Bombay in 1986 found that all but one of 8,000 foetuses aborted after these tests were females (16, p. 115).

A society that strongly favours boys over girls is more likely to tolerate killing female infants. This is alluded to in the Vedic scriptures: 'They go to the final bath, they deposit the pots, but lift up (the vessels) for *Vayu*, therefore they deposit a daughter on birth, and a son they lift up' (27, p. 24). Female infanticide was known to occur in medieval times and was widely practised by the eighteenth century. Laws against it were passed in 1795, 1804 and 1870, with little effect.

Girls who survived to birth were further disadvantaged by inadequate breast-feeding, medical care and general nutrition. Death rates in the first five years of life were reported to be 74 per 1,000 in girls compared to 50 per 1,000 in boys (16, p. 116). Unlike every other country reporting such statistics, the ratio of females to males in India is less than 1.0. The long-term effect of a decreasing number of child-bearers on the number of hoped-for-males in later generations – not to mention the number of Hindus-in-general – appears to have been overlooked in these actions.

Rape and Domestic Violence

Rapes in India have increased, especially in regions where local governments are more feudal (23, p. 255). Between 1972 and 1979 the reported increase was 50–100 per cent, but these figures are underestimates since many rapes go unreported because a girl's loss of 'purity' is a major problem for her and her family. Seventy-eight per cent of rapes concerned girls who were 16 to 20 years of age. Rape laws have not changed and still require proof that consent was lacking. There is no law concerning marital rape and violence, since a woman is the property of her husband. Custodial and family rape and crimes by government officials are rarely reported. Recently and with encouragement from the U.N. International Women's Year, Indian women are collabourating to form study groups and promote demonstrations to focus attention on these crimes.

The buying and selling of girls of less than 18 years of age for prostitution is forbidden by the Indian penal code. Nevertheless 300,000 girls aged 9 to 20 years were transported from Nepal for this purpose (23, p. 270).

The incidence of domestic violence in India is reported to be 33–66 per cent but only about 5 per cent of cases are reported to the police (30, p. 172). Non-physical violence is more common in upper-class families while physical forms occur more often in lower socio-economic groups. It occurs less often in Buddhist and Jain than in Hindu and Muslim families.

Women in Religion

In the Vedic period, women participated in the *Upanayana* and in some of the religious rites held in the home where offerings are made at specific times. Additional rites occur during pregnancy and after birth, to ensure wisdom and a long life. Purification of the mother takes place six days after birth when there is a naming ceremony. Other rites occur when solid food is started and at the time of ear piercing.

The Laws of Manu and other *Smriti* curtailed the participation of women in many religious ceremonies, for fear of pollution. Even now, pious Brahmans will not participate in any rites where women make offerings. Hindu women cannot become priests but there are a few female gurus.

The *Bhakti* movement started in the medieval period and involves personal devotion to a single deity (3, pp. 256 ff.). It became popular for women and men of all castes in about 500 CE. The *Vrata*s are personal rites performed once a year, usually for 12 years, and only women take the vow to perform these.

In the last century, most Hindu religious activities have been transferred to the home where prayers and offerings are made in a special room reserved for this purpose or in front of an image or picture, and women participate in these. The temples are mostly used for religious instruction and festivals.

Public Health Data

Public health records reflect the respect, treatment and care given to women, especially with regard to their reproductive functions. Lack of education, child marriage, preparation for pregnancy and prenatal care all affect these figures, and long established customs supported by religious and caste practices are resistant to change by new laws, at least in the short term.

In 2003, the life expectancy of Indian women was 64 years compared to 62 years for men (31). The number of pregnancies a woman has and their spacing as well as her prenatal care, all affect maternal mortality rates; estimates indicate there were 420 maternal deaths per 100,000 live births in 2005 (32). The infant mortality rate decreased from 130 per 1,000 live births in 1981–82 to 66 in 2003 and was estimated to be 55 in 2009 (Asia's in general was 54 and Europe's was less than ten in the same period) (32).

Summary

Hinduism is believed to be the oldest living religion, and its history extends back over 4,000 years. Its earliest extant scripture was written in about 1500 BCE and contains information on a class- or caste-structured society. The priests or Brahmans occupied the highest level, the warriors or rulers (the Kshatriyas) followed and artisans (the Vaishyas) formed the third level. These three were all referred to as 'twice-borns' to distinguish them from the indigenous people, the Sudras, who were only 'once born' and became the fourth or lowest caste and the servants of the others. As time passed, these castes evolved into thousands of subclasses with long-established customs.

Hinduism has no single or central dogma but believes in a single deity, three major sub-deities and many additional ones including goddess figures. The two basic beliefs of Hinduism are the transmigration of souls and a continuous process of reincarnation, which can only be ended when perfection is achieved. The process by which an individual earns the level of his or her next existence through the good and evil deeds they commit in the present one is called *karma*.

The Hindu scriptural laws or *Smriti* were written over a period of 1,000 years, starting in about 500 BCE, and dictate the behaviour of society at all levels. These have had a monumental effect on the lives of Indian women. They clearly dictate the inferiority of women and perpetuate this by denying them an education. Strict observance of these scriptures enforced women into positions of subservience to men: first to their fathers and then to their husbands, whom they must worship as gods, and finally to their sons when they become widows, if they survive. They were united eternally with their husbands both in this world and beyond. They could never be independent and were only able to attain eternity through their husbands. Widow immolation or the prevention of their remarriage served to preserve the belief that these unions were inviolate.

There appear to have been several reasons for these repressive laws: one was the preservation of caste purity which was enforced by the increasing power of the Brahmans; another was the preservation of racial purity by preventing intermarriage with the indigenous people, the Sudras, who were considered inferior; a third was to prevent the loss of women to Buddhism, a religion that promised them equality regardless of caste or gender. Child marriage was a way to preserve the purity of females, control the threat of their sexuality and limit their freedom. The practices of the Muslim invaders also had an effect, and in Northern India particularly, women were veiled and segregated. The belief in male superiority led to actions which promoted male births, such as rites and prayers in pregnancy as well as female infanticide and later the abortion of female foetuses. This mistreatment of females of all ages was applied most rigorously by upper-class Hindus such as the Brahmans but much less by the lower classes.

It was not always so: Vedic women lived primitive but fairly free lives; except for property rights, there was little inequality between the sexes. Girls were welcome offspring, and participated in the sacred thread or initiation right with their brothers, received an education, attended and spoke at meetings and had a say in the selection of their husbands whom they married at 16 or 17 years when they had completed their educations. Then, sometime after 500 BCE, the lives of Hindu women became much worse, with occasional periods of relief, to reach a nadir in the nineteenth century. Education, historically the only certain way to achieve any improvement in the standard of their lives, was almost non-existent until the nineteenth century, despite the efforts of a few reformers.

India achieved Independence in 1947 and became a secular democracy with a constitution. Its national governments have enacted laws to improve the education and welfare of women, but their enforcement has been inconsistent and limited, particularly in rural areas where the majority live. Literacy rates for girls have improved, especially in urban areas, but remain low elsewhere. More and more women are participating in elections, but too few are elected in both local and general elections to give Indian women a strong voice in their emancipation. A Hindu fundamentalist movement, the Hindu Right, which includes a number of women, continues to call for a return to the past and extols the virtues of polgyny, female subjugation and widow immolation.

The Women's Movement in India has a long history; continued pressure from them, major efforts to provide education for all children but especially girls, improved health care including reproductive counselling and management of pregnancies, election of more women and secular governments are the major avenues for future improvements in the lives of Indian women. Recent strong economic growth promises to improve the lives of all, men and women, in the country.

References

1   *Encyclopedia Britannica.* Ed. W. Benton. Chicago University Press. 1968.
2   Flood, Gavin D. *An Introduction to Hinduism.* Cambridge University Press. 1996.
3   Chaudhuri, Nirad C. *Hinduism, a Religion to Live By.* Oxford University Press. 1979.
4   Knipe, David, M. *Hinduism.* San Francisco. Harper. 1991.
5   *Rig Veda.* Tr., R. T. H. Griffith. New York. Book of the Month Club. 1992.
6   http://en.wikipedia.org/wiki/jainism
7   www.britannica.com/EBchecked/topic/266312/hindu
8   *Bhagavad-Gita.* Tr. S. Prabhavananda, & C. Isherwood. New York. Barnes and Noble. 1995.
9   *Sacred Books of the East: Laws of Manu.* Tr. F. Max Muller. Ed. G. Buhler. New Delhi. Motilal. 1964.
10 Smith, Vincent A. *The Oxford History of India.* Oxford University Press. 1923.
11 Sengupta, Padmini. *The Story of Women in India.* New Delhi. Indian Book Company. 1974.
12 *Religions in India.* http://adaniel.tripod.com/religious.htm
13 Augustine, Celine. 'Two Images of Matriliny'. In *Recent Studies on Indian Women.* Eds. Kamal K. Misra and Janet H. Lowry. Jaipur. Rawat Publications, 2007.
14 Deussen, Paul. *The Philosophy of the Upanishads.* Tr. E. S. Geden. Edinburgh. T. and T. Clark. 1906.
15 *The Thirteen Principal Upanishads.* Tr. R. E. Humphrey Milford Hume. Oxford University Press. 1934.
16 Mitter, Sara S. *Dharma's Daughters.* Rutgers University Press. 1995.
17 Robinson, Catherine A. *Tradition and Liberation.* London. Curzon Press. 1999.
18 Altekar, Anant S. *The Position of Women in Hindu Civilization.* Delhi. Motilal. 1956.
19 Lerner, Gerda. *The Creation of Patriarchy.* Oxford University Press. 1986.
20 Aggarwal, Nomita. *Women and Law in India.* New Delhi. New Century Publications. 2002.
21 Flavia, Agnes. *Law and Gender Inequality.* Oxford University Press. 1999.
22 Anitha, Manisher S. and Vasudra, Kavitha. 'Interviews with Women' in *Women and the Hindu Right.* Eds Tanika Sarkai, and Urvashi Bivaha. N. Delhi. Kali for Women. 1995.

23   Desai, Neera. and Maithreyi, Krishnaraz. *Women and Society in India*. Delhi. Ajanta Publications. 1987.

24   Seager, Joni. *The Penguin Atlas of Women in the World*. Penguin Books. 2009.

25   Chauhan, Richa. 'Seeking a Suitable Match'. In *Recent Studies in Indian Women*. Eds. Kamal H., Kamal K. Misra and Janet Lowry. Jaipur. Rawat Publications. 2007.

26   Sarkar, Tanika. *Hindu Wife, Hindu Nation*. London. Hurst and Company. 2001.

27   Subbamma, Malladi. *Hinduism and Women*. Delhi. Ajanta Publications. 1992.

28   Raj, Anita; Saggurti, Nirajan; Balaiah, Donata; Silverman, Jay, G. *Prevalence of child marriage and its effect on fertility and fertility-control outcomes of young women in India*. Lancet, v. 373, p. 1883. 2009.

29   Hitchcock, A. *Rising Number of Dowry Deaths in India*. www.W.S.W.S.org. 1998–2004. 2005.

30   Niveditha, Menon and Michael, P. Johnson. 'Patriarchy and Paternalism in Intimate Partner Violence'. In *Recent Studies in Indian Women*. Eds Misra, Kamal K. Misra and Janet H. Lowry. Jaipur. Rawat Publications. 2007.

31   World Population Data, 2003 and 2009. Population Reference Bureau.

32   www.who.int/whosis/mme.

Additional Bibliography

Allen, M. and Mukherjee, S. N. *The Hindu View of Women in India and Nepal*. Sydney. Australian National University. 1982.

Encyclopedia of Religion. London. Macmillan Press. 1957.

Jacobson, D. and Wadley, S. S. *Women in India: Two Perspectives*. New Delhi. Manohar. 1977.

Jayal, Shakambari. *The Status of Women in the Epics*. Delhi. Motilal Banarsidass. 1966.

Kapur, R. and Cossman, B. *Subversive Sites*. New Delhi. Sage Publications. 1995.

King, N. 'Women in Contemporary India'. in *Women and Religion. The Status and Image of Women in Major Religious Traditions*. New Delhi. Manohar. 1975.

Martin, M. E. R. *Women in Ancient India*. Varanasi. 1964.

Moreland, William H. and Chatterjee, A. C. *A Short History of India*. Oxford University Press. 1953.

Ray-Chaudhuri, Hemchandra C. *Political History of Ancient India*. Delhi. Motilal. 1953.

Sharma, Arvind. *Women in World Religions*. Albany. State University of New York Press. 1987.

Shastri, S. R. *Women in the Sacred Laws*. Bombay. Bharatiya Vidya Bhavan. 1959.

Upadhyaya, B. S. *Women in Rig-Veda*. New Delhi. S. Chand & Company. 1974.

Zaehner, R. C. *Hindu Scriptures*. London. Everyman's Library. 1984.

Chapter 2

Buddhism

History

The Buddha's Life and Teaching

The Buddha Dharma (Way of the Buddha) or Buddhism, is the religion of about 400 million people in the world today. It began in North-east India in a region that is now Nepal, around 500 BCE. It reached its peak in India in the third and second centuries of the same era, and then decreased there while spreading to China, Japan, Tibet and Korea. It is now the faith of the majority of people in South-east Asia except for Malaysia and Indonesia.

Buddhism's founder was Siddartha Gautama, later called Gautama Buddha because a Buddha is an awakened or enlightened one. He was born into great wealth, in about 563 BCE. His father was a chief, or king of the *Shakya* clan, hence his name *Shakyamuni* or sage of the *Shakya*. His mother died when he was a young child. He had little contact with the outside world while he was growing up, married when he was 16 years old and then lived with his wife and son in his father's palace (1, p. 1).

The Buddha is said to have made a number of excursions from the palace during which he witnessed four 'sights': one was an old man who showed the sufferings of age, another the effects of sickness, and another, of death. While searching for the reasons for these unavoidable stages of human suffering, he saw his fourth 'sight', a holy man or *Sadhu* who was on the street with his alms bowl, begging. Believing this mendicant might provide him with answers, he left his young wife and son and set out to try and find what they were (2, p. 18). He was then 29 years old.

The Buddha became in turn an ascetic, a forest dweller, a member of a *sangha* or monastic community and a *yogi*. He starved and mistreated himself and then after about five years of privation, finally achieved understanding and enlightenment. This is said to have occurred in about 528 BCE while he was sitting motionless and in a meditative state under a Pipal tree by a river in Bodhi Gaya (3, p. 22). His path to enlightenment or *nirvana* evolved through recognition of the Four Noble Truths and obedience to the Eight-fold Path (4, p. 19).

The Buddha's first sermon was preached at Sarnath – about 100 miles from Bodhi Gaya – near Benares (now Varanasi) and this was later called the First Turning of the Wheel of Dharma or the Deer Park Sermon. Here he explained to his followers that pain and suffering resulted from a focus on one-self and our unfulfilled desires and cravings. The cure to all of this is the denial of self.

The prevailing religion in India at that time was Hinduism, the oldest established faith that had evolved out of Vedism and Brahmanism during the previous millennium. Hinduism promoted a four-class society in which the priests or Brahmans held the highest position, the warriors were next, followed by the majority of the people or artisans. The indigenous people occupied the fourth and lowest place. The Brahmans were obsessed with racial and class purity, and over time, developed a rigid caste system with numerous subclasses that bound each man and woman from birth to death into a fixed and unchangeable place and in many cases, a life of misery. Over a period of several centuries, the Brahmans gained greater and greater control, demanding obedience to their laws, and restricting the lives of other caste members.

Hindus believe in a perpetual cycle of reincarnations and rebirths until perfection is eventually achieved, allowing escape and union with ancestors. An individual's earthly existence is determined by the way that person's previous life was lived. This process of cause and effect is called *karma*. The Buddha did not change this belief. Hindus believe in a Supreme Being or God and many secondary gods. The Buddha denied the need for a supreme being and preached instead that each individual has the ability to achieve salvation on his own. He did not propose changing the caste system but instead offered a way to survive it by liberating oneself from its miseries. He sought a Middle Way between the self-indulgence and power of the Brahmans, and the extremes of asceticism, whereby each individual retained responsibility for his/her own life (5, p. 5).

In contrast to Hinduism, Buddhism does not subscribe to an *atman* or immortal self or soul. This doctrine of *anatman* is central to Buddhism: self or personality is only transitory and constituted by form, sensation, perception, mental formations and unconsciousness, together called *skandha*s which are the cause of suffering (4, p. 20). An individual's final goal should be enlightenment, a state of separation and elevation, which can be acquired through obedience to precepts, meditation, prayer, and control of consciousness. This might take several lifetimes to achieve but good deeds accrued merits toward this goal and rebirth made this progression possible. The Buddha's way was open to all without the restrictions of caste or gender. He made it clear that he was not divine, although he came to be regarded as a sage or savior by his disciples and their successors.

The Sangha

The Buddha travelled widely in Northern India for about 45 years and attracted many followers, both male and female. He founded an order of monks or *bhikshu*s that was open to men of all castes, providing they were free of mental or physical ailments and had no criminal record. Minors wishing to join the order had to have parental permission. Each community of monks was called a *sangha*. A monk's duties included daily rounds for alms, meditation, prayer and instruction from senior monks. In the rainy season, they were required to preach to lay people and attend a ceremony of confession twice a month. They owned no possessions except for a robe, alms bowl and a few personal items. At his ordination, a monk recites the Threefold Refuge three times: 'I go to the Buddha as refuge, I go to the Dharma as refuge, I go to the *sangha* as refuge' (4, p. 22). He promises to obey the ten precepts which are to cause no harm to living things, nor steal, commit sexual misconduct, lie or gossip, eat solid food after noon, take alcohol, seek entertainment, wear adornments, sleep on high beds or accept gifts such as gold or silver (3, p. 8). Monks must also obey the rules laid down in the *Vinaya* or *Book of Discipline*, which is part of the Buddhist scripture.

The Buddha welcomed all – men and women – to join him and listen to his teaching. His followers included many women who were seeking an escape from the restrictions placed on them as high-caste Hindus. Yet the Buddha ruled that only men could become monks: women were excluded. His female followers, including his stepmother, Maha-pagapati, and his wife, protested and pleaded with him to be allowed to join (4, p. 29). After several pleadings, we are told the Buddha relented, due to the intervention of his closest and oldest disciple, Ananda (ibid.). Women could now become nuns or *bhikshuni*s but only under special conditions: they would receive the same education and training as monks but had to obey eight additional rules and defer to and accept all monks as their superiors, regardless of their youth and inexperience (6, p. 283). In addition to monastics, Buddhism included laymen, both men and women, whose duty was to obey the *dharma* and support the *sangha*s. Some lay people became novices and served in the *sangha*s for varying periods of time.

The Buddha died in about 483 BCE, in his eightieth year. He was surrounded by his disciples, monks and laymen to whom he gave instructions concerning his cremation and the disposal of his relics. *Stupa*s or shrines containing these were built in many parts of India during the next several centuries. The Buddha's teaching was memorized by his followers and passed on in the oral tradition of many early religions. The first written scriptures did not appear until the first century BCE, after being transcribed by monks into Pali, the ancient dialect of Northern India. These were taken to Sri Lanka where they were stored.

The Buddhist Councils and Schools of Buddhism

The first Buddhist council met in 480 BCE, shortly after the Buddha's death and was attended by a number of his disciples including Ananda. Its goal was to decide on the essential parts of his teaching and the cornerstone of their faith. A second council was held about 100 years later at Versali, to reach agreement on a code of discipline for Buddhist monks (7, p. 46). Disputes had arisen over the interpretation of their ten precepts: some monks had stored salt, some had eaten after midday and others had accepted gold and other gifts. The Buddha had allowed monks some discretion in following local customs in matters of diet but the other liberties were rejected. A number of divisions had occurred in the interpretation and practice of Buddhism and the council recognized 18 of these.

Eventually two main schools of Buddhism emerged and a third, Vajrayana – the Diamond Vehicle – developed much later, mainly in Northern India (8, p. 20). The more liberal of the first schools became known as the Great Vehicle to Enlightenment or Mahayana. The more conservative one, the Hinayana or Lesser Vehicle, became known later as the Theraveda School, a Pali term meaning the School of the Elders. Their differences mainly concerned rules for monks and the steps needed for an individual to reach the level of an *arhat* or saint. The Theraveda School focused especially on the monastic lifestyle and *sangha*s and on each individual's effort to become an *arhat*. This school believed in and obeyed the teaching or *dharma* of a single historic Buddha in whom it had absolute trust. The Mahayana school honours many Buddhas from different times and places, including one for the future called the Maitreya Buddha. They offer devotions not only to these Buddhas but also to *bodhisattva*s – who are individuals on the path to Buddhahood.

Buddhism in India

Buddhism reached its peak in India in the third and second centuries BCE, shortly after the great Indian king Asoka became a convert from Hinduism. It then spread to Bactria, a Greek state in North-west India, to Southern India and Sri Lanka. After Asoka's death, Hinduism experienced a revival and once again became the state religion of India. Buddhism continued to spread for a time in Northern India and then declined. Many of its temples and *stupa*s were abandoned, some decayed and others were replaced by Hindu shrines. The reason for its decline in India is not known; one explanation may have been the revival of Hinduism with its many gods and rituals and another may have been Buddhism's schisms. The third major sect, Vajrayana Buddhism, appeared in the seventh century CE and influenced both Buddhism and Hinduism, and was probably an additional reason. It involves contemplative and yogic practices, usually with instruction by a teacher who utilizes information attributed to gods and goddesses expressed with gestures, icons, and other symbols of lingam or phallic worship. These practices varied in different locales but some brought disapproval to Buddhism in India (9, vol. 21, p. 670). Finally, the Muslim invasions in the twelfth century caused it to nearly disappear in North-west India.

At about this time, Mongols and later Kublai Khan converted to Buddhism and this helped pacify their tribes. Their conversion to Islam came later. Meanwhile Buddhism had spread to other Asian countries and was becoming one of the world's great missionary religions.

Buddhism in China

Buddhism reached China shortly after the beginning of the Common Era, coming mostly overland through Central Asia but a smaller contingent travelled by sea. Confucianism and Taoism were well established in China by then (10, p. 36). There were sizeable Buddhist communities here by the fourth century, mostly in the south but also in the east and north of the country. An order of nuns was established in China a short time later and 'has survived as an unbroken tradition to the present' (11, p. 123). These nuns lived by the same codes as in ancient India.

There were essentially two schools of Buddhism in China: one the Dhyana or School of Deep Meditation was similar to Hinayana. The second called Prajna followed the Mahayana and eventually became the standard school of Buddhism in China. It incorporated filial piety from Confucianism and had a close relationship with neo-Taoism. Buddhist monks of this period had established fairly close ties with the aristocracy and Emperor Hsiao-Wu (373–396) became a Buddhist layman (10, p. 80). Military service and taxes could be avoided by joining a *sangha* and many of those who joined were illiterate and came from the agricultural class. The state suffered in three ways: loss of productive land, fewer potential workers for the land and military and less income from taxes. Estimates suggest there were by then about 1,786 Buddhist temples and 24,000 monks and nuns in China (10, p. 85). Repression followed and before long the *sangha*s were accused of moral laxity as well as interference in state government.

After a period of persecution, Buddhism recovered and reached its peak in the Sui and Tang dynasties (618–907). By that time, the *sangha*s were well endowed with both land and money and by the mid ninth century, the number of monastics had reached over a quarter of a million people, all living at state expense (10, p. 235). The economic drain on the country was substantial and suppression of Buddhism followed: many monks and nuns were defrocked and temples were closed or destroyed. By the end of this period, the Chinese *Tripitaka* – consisting of 55 volumes – had been assembled and a number of *Sutras* including the *Lotus Sutra* had been translated (10, p. 376).

The modern period of Buddhism in China began in 1911 when the Manchu dynasty ended and China became a republic. Taxes were then levied on the *sangha*s and temples and there was an organized movement to convert them to schools (10, p. 455). In 1949, the People's Republic confronted Buddhism with its own atheistic beliefs (10, p. 460). Monks and nuns were required to work or be reeducated, temples were deprived of their landholdings and these were redistributed to the people, and temples and shrines were converted into recreational sites.

The Buddhist Association of China was organized in 1953 and serves as an agent of the government. Students were allowed to graduate as religious workers, preachers and scholars, but the Cultural Revolution brought further losses (10, p. 462). Estimates suggest that about 17 per cent of the Chinese population practises Buddhism.

The Nationalist Government of China and its supporters moved to Taiwan where Buddhism has had a strong and growing presence. Taiwan is the main stronghold of *bhikshuni*s and there are believed to be more than 5,000 nuns living there.

Buddhism in Korea

The ancient Korean spiritual tradition is Shamanism, an animistic nature-worshipping belief that dates back to the Neolithic age and is still practised by the common people (9, vol. 13, p. 458). Buddhism, of the Mahayana school, spread to Korea from China in the fourth century and became the state religion between 400 and 1000 CE, reaching its peak in the Koryo period (932–1392) when the Tripitaka Koreana was completed. Then, during the Chosen dynasty (1342–1910), Confucianism mostly replaced Buddhism.

The Japanese annexed Korea in 1910 after which there was a return to Buddhism and Korean Buddhists sought to merge with the Soto (Zen) sect in Japan. A number of reformers appeared; one was Kongun (1879–1944) who led a movement that promoted independence from Japan. He encouraged monasteries to be self-sufficient and raise silk, crops and other commodities. Education improved for both the religious and non-religious population. Buddhist priests were allowed to marry although this was clearly prohibited in the *Vinaya*. The government later rescinded this rule but in 1926, due to Japanese pressure, the prohibition against married clergy was repealed. Furthermore, only married priests could hold monastic offices and since many had families to support by then, they were in need of additional income. About 23 per cent of the population of South Korea and 65 per cent of North Korea are Buddhist (12).

Buddhism in Japan

The indigenous religion of Japan is Shintoism whose origins are not known (9, vol. 20. p. 395). Buddhism came to Japan from Korea in the mid-sixth century C E with the arrival of monastics and Buddhist scriptures (7, p. 94). It spread fairly rapidly and Empress Suiko (592–628) became a convert and then a nun. Buddhism flourished under her successor but remained more or less confined to the rulers and aristocracy, while the rest of the population continued its Shintoist practices.

A number of Japanese schools of Buddhism were recognized during the following periods, and some incorporated Shinto practices, but in general they conformed to the Chinese Mahayana school of Buddhism. They worshipped a number of different Buddhas and *bodhisattvas* and some were female. Most of the Buddhist monks in Japan are married.

The Zen or Meditation school came from China in the twelfth century and comprised two main branches but Soto Zen had a larger following. Both stressed self-reliance through meditative practices but Soto was more involved with teaching. After periods of political and social upheaval, Buddhism was re-established during the Tokugawa period (1600–1868) when temples and shrines were repaired and rededicated. Then Buddhism was disestablished in 1861 and Shintoism became the national religion. Buddhist temples were destroyed and their priests were given the option of converting to Shintoism or being defrocked. Finally, the constitution of 1889 gave religious freedom to all. In 1945, at the end of WWII, Shintoism was disestablished in Japan when the emperor's divine origin was denied.

Many new religious sects have appeared in Japan in the last 40 years and some of these combine beliefs derived from Buddhist, Shinto, Confucian and Christian faiths, plus some old folklore. Buddhist and Shintoist traits persist and many Japanese homes contain a Shinto shrine and a Buddhist altar. Shintoist rites are often used for marriage ceremonies while Buddhist practices are observed at funerals. In general, religion is peripheral to the lives of most Japanese but the ethical influences of Confucianism persist.

Japanese Buddhism was much influenced by the religious practices in China and Korea, but there are differences. Chinese Buddhism shows strong Hinayana influences while Mahayana is dominant in Japan. The former conforms to monastic rules and regulations and the latter has a more secular and social structure with greater laity participation in temple rites. Chinese Buddhism evolved through Confucian morality, somewhat akin to Puritanism (6, p. 260). Shintoist values and beliefs remain very much in evidence in Japan. Depending on the criteria, between 44 per cent and 96 per cent of the population is Buddhist (12).

Buddhism in Tibet

The indigenous religion of Tibet is Bon, which involved animal and sometimes human sacrifice and believed in a divine kingship and oracular priests (9, vol. 21, p. 1118). Many of these practices were absorbed into Buddhism, established here in the seventh century CE. Progress was very slow until the Indian missionary, Padmasambhava, arrived in the eighth century. Bon supported a belief in demons and gods of sky and earth who had to be appeased. Padmasambhava was called in to make peace with these demons and has since been revered as a Tibetan saint (13, p. 155).

The first Tibetan monastery was built in the eighth century when the first of seven monks was ordained. Several Tibetan schools of Buddhism developed, each with oral and written scriptures. Each school constructed its own monastery with its own chief lama. Buddhist scriptures including commentaries were translated from Sanskrit and completed in the thirteenth century. Tibetan Buddhists have a special system to reincarnate their lamas who are reborn in a child. The Dalai Lama is the supreme head of Tibetan Buddhism but monasteries appoint their own superiors who are usually the sons of a lama or his male relative.

Tibetan Buddhists recognize three paths to the highest goal of enlightenment: the Hinayana path through discipline and meditation, the Mahayana's by saving others and Tantrayana's (Vajrayana or Tantric Buddhism) through meditation and magical rites. *Bardo*, a state between death and rebirth, is peculiar to Tibetan Buddhism and teaches that an individual's last thoughts can lead to their liberation and rebirth.

In 1950, the Chinese invaded Tibet. Before the study and teaching of Buddhism was outlawed, 20 per cent of the population had belonged to a clerical order (9, v. 21, p. 1110). Their rebellion of 1959 was put down, the Dalai Lama fled to India and many monasteries were destroyed and monks and nuns were imprisoned.

Buddhism in South-east Asia

Except for Vietnam, Theraveda Buddhism predominates in South-east Asia. Sixty-four per cent of Sri Lankans are Buddhists as are over 85 per cent of the people of Myanmar, Thailand, Laos and Cambodia. The influence of the Indian caste system is evident only in the *sangha*s of Sri Lanka. Theraveda *sangha*s are male-dominated and there are no fully ordained nuns. Ordained nuns who came from Western or Mahayana *sangha*s were denied recognition here. Buddhism is the established religion of Thailand, Laos and Cambodia and influences every aspect of daily life including business and politics. Everyone, monk and layperson travels in the path of the Buddha.

There are two major ethnic groups in Sri Lanka, the Sinhalese who came from Northern India in 550 BCE and the Tamils. The Sinhalese are mostly

Buddhist, the Tamils mainly Hindu. Buddhism arrived from India in the third century BCE with the monk Mahinda, King Asoka's son. Many Sinhalese regard Sri Lanka as a sacred Buddhist island with the oldest continuous Theravedan tradition (14, p. 280).

Theravedism was well established in Myanmar by the eleventh century CE. Most of the people are Buddhist, but it is not the state religion (15, p. 12). The nuns here are less than bhikshunis. Monks are the spiritual heads of villages where the *sangha*s provide most of the schooling. Villagers go there regularly for instruction and prayers.

Hinayana Buddhism came to Thailand in the sixth century, Theravedism became the state religion in the thirteenth century and the king is recognized as its supreme head. The Thai state budget provides financial support for monks and monasteries. There are more than 20,000 temple-monasteries or *wat*s and monks have a unique status in Thai society. The *wat* serves as a community centre, school and hospital in villages, but in larger towns, its function is mainly religious. There is a close relationship between laypeople and the *wat*. By supporting the *sangha* and providing alms, they are able to earn merits for their *karma*s. Many monks are poorly educated with only four to six years of education before their ordination. They are celibate and observe dietary rules.

The Buddhist population of India has grown during the last 50 years, due mostly to the conversion of the *Dalit* (the Untouchables) led by Dr. B. R. Ambedkai, who served as Minister of Law after Independence (14, p. 247). A second factor has been the influx of Tibetan exiles following the Chinese invasion of their country.

Buddhism in Vietnam is Mahayana. The society here is patriarchal and maintains a clan structure and each person is descended from a single ancestor. Seventy-five per cent of the Vietnamese belong to one of 12 main clans.

Cambodia and Laos are both Theravedan countries and the king is the supreme authority in Cambodia. Indonesia, Malaysia and the Philippines all have Buddhist communities, whose origins are mainly Chinese.

The Indian monk, Padmasambhasa brought Buddhism to the Himalayan countries and the people there mostly observe Tantric practices.

During the past two centuries, Buddhist societies of both the Theravedan and Mahayanan schools have developed in the United Kingdom. Buddhist centres also exist in the United States, particularly on the west coast and in Hawaii where there are sizeable Asian communities. Zen Buddhism became popular after WWII and more recently Tibetan Buddhism has achieved a larger following.

Buddhist Scriptures and Women

The Buddha's insights and knowledge were passed down by word of mouth through several generations of monks and transcribed much later (16, 17).

These include the most important Buddhist beliefs, the Four Noble Truths and the Eight-fold Path. The Four Noble Truths explain that we are all faced with the inevitable events of life such as birth, old age, sickness and death which bring no fulfilment or satisfaction; second, that the cause of our pain and suffering is a craving for or an unfulfilled selfish desire for achievement or sensual pleasure which binds us to the cycle of existence; third, that the cure requires removal of this craving; and fourth, the prescription for cure is the Eightfold Path of Right Living or the Middle Way (4, p. 62ff.). These eight requirements are to have: the right view or understanding, free of superstition and delusion; the right goals worthy of an intelligent, earnest man; the right speech, avoiding lies, slander and gossip; the right conduct which is peaceful, honest and pure; the right livelihood avoiding work which is harmful to living things; the right effort which cultivates self-control and wholesome acts; the right mindfulness to control feelings and thoughts; the right concentration through meditation to achieve a special state of consciousness in preparation for *nirvana*. The first two are acts of wisdom, the next three are acts of morality and the last three are acts of concentration (4, p. 64). *Nirvana* is the final state of enlightenment and is attained by overcoming desire, hatred and delusion, permitting entrance into another mode of existence without the need to pass through further reincarnations.

Pali Scriptures

The Pali canon is the earliest extant collection of the Buddha's discourses and was recorded in Sri Lanka in about 43 BCE, probably by monks, 400 years or more after his death (3, pp. 61ff.). This is called the *Tripitaka* or three baskets and consists of 32 books in three sections. The first basket or Pitaka is the *Vinaya* or Book of Discipline and contains 227 rules for monastics including details of misbehaviour and punishment. The four most serious misdeeds are any form of sexual activity, theft, killing and false claims concerning Buddhism: these require expulsion from the *Sangha*. Another 13 may lead to suspension and a further 90 to unfavourable rebirth if the misdeeds are not repented.

The second basket contains the *Sutras* or Discourses of the Buddha, comprising 36 volumes in the Pali edition including: one with 34 long discourses which cover the spiritual training of monks and aspects of religious life in India in the fifth century BCE; a second contains 150 medium-length sermons about the Buddha's struggles and includes the Eight-fold Path; the third has 56 sections with many discourses covering many subjects; the fourth includes additional discourses grouped under several headings. These four *Nikaya*s are the oldest canons. A fifth, contains some early and some later material of varying lengths including the *Dharmapada* – sayings of Gautama Buddha – one of the best-known tracts of Buddhist literature comprising 26 chapters and 423 verses. It includes the ten *Shila*s or precepts for monastics:

to refrain from harming a living or sentient being; stealing – defined as taking what is not given; sexual misconduct; unjust or false speech; imbibing intoxicants; eating solid food after noon; participating in entertainment such as music, dance or song; the use of perfume or the wearing of ornamental jewellery; sleeping in high beds; contact with money or other valuables. This includes the only comment on women: 'the stain of woman is misconduct', meaning a transgression for which she would be expelled by her husband and family and forced to wander in great misery ever after (18, p. 284). Also included in this *Nikaya* are the Jataka tales, often used in sermons. These are chants and stories of the Buddha's previous lives. They describe the ten virtues or perfections necessary to achieve Buddhahood: generosity – the most important, morality, renunciation, energy, patience, truthfulness, resolution, loving-kindness, calm benevolent behaviour and wisdom (3, p. 62).

The third basket is the special teachings basket, and includes non-canonical texts containing historical, metaphysical and philosophical commentaries. One of the best known is an account of the questions put to the monk Nagasena by the king of the Greek state of Bactria, King Milinda (16, pp. 146–161).

The Pali canon is the scripture of the Theraveda School of Buddhism. Theravedans believe the Buddha is a single human being who achieved *nirvana*. It emphasizes the monastic life and the path to become an *arhat* or saint who is exempt from further rebirths.

Mahayana Scriptures

The Mahayana School of Buddhism developed out of several other existing schools sometime between 150 BCE and 100 CE. Each had its own *Sutras* attributed to the Buddha (8, p. 75). The Mahayana canons were written in Sanskrit. One of the most familiar and revered of these is the *Lotus of the True Dharma* or *Lotus Sutra*, believed to have been preached by the Buddha over a period of eight years, and then repeated by Ananda and transmitted orally. It was written down in about 200 CE and many commentaries were added later. It contains 25 chapters in prose and verse and describes a dragon girl who became a Buddha despite being denied this on the basis of her sex (19, p. 189). It instructs *bodhisattva*s – those working toward *nirvana* – not to talk to unmarried women, widows or young girls nor go near 'unmanly' men – individuals who are impotent or show sexual deviancy, nor have intimate dealings with women. Another chapter gives instructions to women who want to have a son.

Another well-known *Sutra*, second only in importance to the *Lotus Sutra* in Mahayana scriptures, is the *Vimalakirti Sutra*. This was written for laymen and is the story of a rich merchant by the same name who lived in Northern India. It offers eight rules for Buddhists with an emphasis on compassion: to strive to benefit the people of the world without seeking a reward; to take on the sufferings of all living beings; to transfer all earned merits to others; to look on all others as equals and behave humbly before them without distinction; to look on all *bodhisattva*s as Buddhas; to avoid regarding unfamiliar *Sutra*s with suspicion or arguing with Hinayana Buddhists; to reflect on personal errors rather than the faults of others; to maintain at all times a loving heart; to strive to attain merits of all kinds (8, p. 10).

Several beliefs are peculiar to Mahayana Buddhists and include a greater emphasis on secular rather than monastic life and support for *bodhisattva*s – especially those who delay their own sainthood while assisting others to achieve the same (16, p. 164). This path is open to both layman and monk.

Vajrayana Scriptures

Vajrayana or Tantric Buddhism developed out of the Mahayana school and incorporated certain Hindu practices. This is the school practised in Tibet and some of the Himalayan countries. Their scriptures include the *Kangyur* – 108 volumes – believed to be discourses attributed to the Buddha and the *Tengyur* – 225 volumes of commentaries and other works written in Tibetan (3, p. 81). In addition, a large body of Mahayana literature survived in Tibet. Rather than *bodhisattva*s, the ideal of Vajrayana is the *siddha* who has unlimited powers and unconventional morality.

The Buddhist scriptures are massive and complex. They contain no doctrines or dogmas but rather discourses or parables (*Sutra*s) attributed to the Buddha as well as commentaries (*Shastra*s), describing the way to enlightenment and rules of conduct for both monastics and laypersons.

Buddhist Societies

The Buddhist concept of a correct society consists of two groups, laypersons and monastics who include monks, nuns and novices, both male and female. Laypersons may include former novices. These groups interact frequently and have obligations to and depend on the contributions of the others (20, p. 56). The Buddhist layperson is encouraged to seek wealth, honour, long life and rebirth into the heavens (5, p. 116).

Most homes contain shrines and in addition there are public structures such as temples and *stupa*s. Women give daily offerings of food to the monks and household spirits and attend prayer and meditation sessions at the *sangha* four times a month. The devotions of householders often occur in the morning and evening while attendance at temples can be at any time but especially on specified days and festivals. Individuals bow and repeat the three refuges, 'I go for refuge to the Buddha; I go for refuge to the Dharma; I go for refuge to the *sangha*' (3, p. 5). These words are usually repeated three times. They may listen to or chant several *Sutra*s. Family members quite commonly make pilgrimages to sites associated with the Buddha. Lay people also donate alms and support for monastics and this earns them merits toward their own *karma*s. They vow to obey the first five Buddhist precepts: not to destroy life, steal, practise sexual misconduct, lie or use alcohol. On special days they include three additional ones: to refrain from solid food after noon, to refrain from music, dance or other forms of entertainment or to wear perfume, garlands or ornamental jewellery. Monks, nuns and novices observe two more precepts: not to sleep on high beds or have contact with money and other valuables. Merits are lost if precepts are broken but to be counted as a demerit, the act must be deliberate and not accidental. Boys receive their early education in the *sangha* and serve in the temple. Most of them become novices between the ages of 10 and 18 years but they usually join the *sangha* for short periods of three to six months, often before marriage, and fewer than 40 per cent remain there for life.

Buddhist scriptures offer words of advice to prospective brides and married women, 'take whatever husbands our parents shall give us, anxious for our good since they are seeking our happiness' (5, p. 123). The Buddha's advice for married women was to 'get up before him, retire after him, willingly do what he asks, be lovely in your way and gentle in speech, not being one to anger him, to honour all whom your husband respects, whether relative, monk or Brahman, to be deft and nimble in your husband's home-crafts such as weaving'. 'She watches over servants and work people with care and kindness. She looks after the wealth of her husband. Possessed of these five qualities, women, on the breaking up of the body after dying, arise among the divas of lovely form' (ibid.).

The monastic community or *sangha* includes monks, nuns and novices. It differs from its Christian counterpart in not taking lifetime vows, nor for the most part living segregated existences. Monks and nuns usually shave their heads at ordination but there are exceptions to this practice in Japanese Buddhism. Celibacy is a general rule but Japanese, Korean and Tibetan monks may marry as do some of the nuns. Buddhism encourages monastics to integrate into and contribute to the local community. The purpose of alms seeking in a community is both to instill humility but also to insure interaction. Monks were initially forbidden to work but this changed later and depends on the customs of individual Buddhist communities. Confucianism, for instance, instilled a belief in the importance of labour into Chinese and, to some degree, into Japanese monks. Nuns were frequently forced to work in order to support themselves and their *sangha*s.

The role of the *sangha* in the local community was to provide sermons, prayers and education for boys. Up until the twentieth century and especially in South-east Asia, the *sangha* was the only source of education in villages, except for missionary schools.

The practice of temporary or short- and long-term novices varies according to local customs, particularly in South-east Asia. The monk's code of discipline, the Patimokkha is chanted on special days and the number of rules for them varies from 150 to nearly 300 in different communities. There are even more rules for nuns. These are arranged according to their importance, as are the punishments for disobedience. They include the ten precepts required for novices as well as monks and nuns.

Buddhism and Women

Women in Early Buddhism and the Sangha

Hinduism was the predominant religion in India when the Buddha was born in the fifth century BCE. It had a four-class social structure in which the priests or Brahmans held the highest place. They had an obsession with the preservation of racial and class purity and enacted rules to ensure this. These became more and more rigid with time. Breakdowns in social barriers were blamed on women's sexuality. To control this and maintain their purity, girls were married off at puberty or earlier, to partners who had been selected by their fathers, many of them much older men. They were denied any education and most were illiterate. Females had to be subject to male control for their entire lives, first to their fathers, then to their husbands and later to their sons. They had to show eternal respect for their husbands and could only achieve immortality through them. They were inferior to men and had been born female because of their bad *karma*s. Male children were essential, first for religious purposes and later on to avoid the dowry payments required for daughters. Female infanticide and the mistreatment of girls were common. Childless women were denigrated and often divorced. Widows were denied remarriage and either died by immolation or eked out a miserable existence.

The Buddha did not change the Hindu caste system or the belief in the continuous cycle of rebirths. Instead he offered individuals a way to achieve personal control of their lives and escape from the inevitability of rebirths, through meditation and mind control, so they could achieve enlightenment or *nirvana*. Everyone was welcome to join him and no restrictions were imposed because of caste or gender. Furthermore, men and women were equal with regard to their past *karma*s and both had the potential to achieve spiritual enlightenment:

> And be it woman, be it man for whom
> Such chariot doth wait, by that same car
> Into Nirvana's presence shall they come (21, p. 49).

During his travels, mostly in North-east India, the Buddha attracted a large number of followers, including many women. This was not surprising considering the societal alternatives confronting them at that time.

The first sign of sexual bias came after the Buddha established the *sangha*s or communities for monks. His female followers, especially his stepmother and his wife, begged him to be allowed to join. The Buddha refused. Ananda, his closest disciple, felt compassion for the women because of their loyalty and suffering – many had travelled barefoot over long distances wearing their renunciate robes – and he interceded on their behalf (21, p. 32). The Buddha again refused. We are told that he yielded after Ananda's third pleading. Maha-pagapati, his stepmother, was the first woman admitted to the *sangha*. The Buddha is said to have told Ananda that since women had joined the 'holy life', it would only survive for half as long, 500 instead of 1000 years (5, p. 10). The Buddha warned monks to be 'vigilant' in the presence of women. Ananda asked how monks should behave with regard to womankind. The Buddha answered, 'Don't see them, Ananda.' 'But if we should see them, what are we to do?' asked Ananda. 'Abstain from speech, Ananda,' the Buddha answered. 'But if they should speak to us, Lord, what are we to do?' persisted Ananda. 'Keep wide awake, Ananda' was the Buddha's reply (22, p. 86). These words, attributed to the Buddha, were passed down orally but no written account of them appeared until some 400 years later. Although they are included in the Budddhist scriptures, they seem to be inconsistent with the Buddha's early egalitarian goals (11, p. 107).

The Buddha allowed women to join the *sangha*s but only if they agreed to eight additional conditions (1, p. 86). 'A *bhikshuni* (nun), even if of 100 years' standing, shall make salutation to, shall rise up in the presence of, shall bow down before and shall perform all proper duties towards a *bhikshu* (monk) even if he is only just initiated: a *bhikshuni* is not to spend the rainy season in a district in which there is no *bhikshu*: every half month, a *bhikshuni* is to await from the *bhikshu sangha* two things, the asking of the *Uposadha* ceremony and when the *bhikshu* will come to give the exhortation: after keeping the rainy season, the *bhikshuni* is to enquire whether any fault can be found to her charges before both the *sangha*s with respect to three matters; what has been seen and what has been heard and what has been suspected: a *bhikshuni* who has been found guilty of a serious offence is to undergo discipline before both *sangha*s (the nun's and the monk's): when a novice *bhikshuni* has been trained for two years in the six rules, she is to ask leave for her *Upasampada* (initiation) from both *sangha*s: a *bhikshuni* is on no pretext to revile or abuse a *bhikshu*: from henceforth the official admonition by a *bhikshuni* of a *bhikshu* is forbidden, whereas official admonition of *bhikshuni* by *bhikshu* is not forbidden' (6, p. 283). Nuns could be expelled for four additional offences, 'sensual intent, touching a man anywhere between collar bone and knee, going to a rendezvous with him, not making known that another nun had broken a rule entailing expulsion, persistently imitating a monk suspected of bad behaviour' (ibid.).

The *bhikshuni sangha* was open to both married and unmarried women and novices. Nuns were supposed to receive the same education and training as monks. Female novices required five years of training before they could become eligible for ordination. After they had completed this in their own *sangha*, final ordination was required in the *bhikshu sangha*, after the monks had given their approval of each candidate. Males and females had the same duties and these included daily rounds to collect alms in the community, meditation, prayer and instruction from preceptors who were usually senior nuns and monks.

There was much less difference in the treatment of monks and nuns by Buddhist laypeople, except that it was harder for nuns to collect alms and the male *sangha*s received more generous contributions in both money and land. It was in the *sangha*s that the unequal treatment of Buddhist men and women became really obvious; however senior, devout or knowledgeable she was, a nun was always inferior to a monk. She had to stand up when he approached, bow to him and could never correct him. According to extant literature, this contrasting treatment appears to have been ordered by the Buddha himself.

Buddhist Women and Enlightenment

A second major difference in the treatment of Buddhist women concerned their ability to achieve enlightenment. In his first sermon in the Deer Park, the Buddha is reported to have said, 'It is impossible, and it cannot come to pass that a woman perfected can become a fully self-awakened one' (22, p. 87). And yet, in answer to Ananda's question 'Are they (women) capable of realizing the fruit of conversion, or of the second path, or of the third path, or of *arahatship* (sainthood) without the need for further rebirths,' the Buddha's response was 'they are capable Ananda' (17, *Khandhaka* Xth. 1, 3).

Sometime between 300 BCE and 200 CE, a doctrinal crisis appears to have occurred in Buddhism during which the spirituality of women was questioned and attempts were made to prove their inferiority, at least theologically (11, p. 114). This especially affected the Theraveda School and coincided with the beginning of Mahayana Buddhism. This misogynist attitude was not confined to Buddhism but appears to have been part of a strong movement of patriarchy affecting Hinduism, other religions and women in general in the Near East and Asia, which had started some time earlier (23, p. 22).

One of the major disagreements between the Mahayana and Theraveda schools concerned this question of enlightenment. Some Theravedans maintained that women could become *arhat*s but could not attain full enlightenment. Others regarded women as incapable of achieving *arhatship*. Women were born women because of their past *karma*s, hence their inferior state. Maleness on the other hand, was a reward for past *karma*s. Therefore women would have to accumulate enough merits to be reborn as males before they could achieve full enlightenment. Yet early Buddhist texts cite examples of women achieving full enlightenment in a female body (19, p. 188). Mahayana

*Sutra*s, usually of a later date, give accounts of women achieving full enlightenment after being reborn as men, while others claimed gender was irrelevant. The five hindrances or obstacles said to be faced by women who strive for this are: their evil and impure natures; their unbridled lust; their arrogance; their 84 bad qualities; their hatred, ignorance, attachment to the mundane and bad *karma*s make enlightenment unachievable in their female bodies (20, p. 129).

In summary, the limit to a woman's achievement while in her female body according to the Theraveda School, is one of the lower states (of which there are 9) below full enlightenment. The goal for her in the Mahayana school is a *bodhisattva*, the step below a Buddha. All Buddhas to date have been male (20, p. 123). In both schools, enlightenment is denied to women unless they are reborn into male bodies and this requires the accumulation of good *karma*s. Buddhist women's devotions are said to include a prayer that they will be born again as males in a future existence. Tibetan and Himalayan Buddhists, who follow the Vajrayana School, recognize a female Buddha and revere female *bodhisattva*s.

Despite the restrictions placed on women who joined the Buddhist order, they flocked to the Buddha, converted and became lay devotees or pleaded to become nuns. Some joined because the Buddha's teaching offered a positive alternative to an arranged marriage. Some joined because they were attracted by the Buddha's message and some because they were repulsed by the world. Some of the first nuns described their relief at escaping from their traditional women's roles in the *Therigatha* or Songs of the Sisters.

> I'm free, totally free in freedom
> From those three hideous shapes:
> My grindstone, my pestle,
> And my hunch-backed husband.
> I'm free from birth and death –
> My ties to life are broken (24, p. 53).

Theraveda Buddhism in South-east Asia

Theraveda Buddhism is the form of the religion practised in Sri Lanka, Thailand, Myanmar, Cambodia and Laos. Here there are no fully ordained nuns nor do the *sangha*s recognize or accept nuns who have been ordained elsewhere by Mahayana *sangha*s. Sri Lanka has the oldest Buddhist tradition and was at one time the only Theravedan country with a *bhikshuni* order, but this died out in the tenth century, and no more women of this order were ordained. Much later – in the 1900s – an order of lay nuns was established here and operated without the supervision of the male *sangha*. They are not full *bhikshuni*s since the laws of the *Vinaya* require a quorum of Theraveda nuns to re-establish their *sangha*.

There are no fully ordained nuns in Thailand but instead there are *de facto* or pre-ordained ones called *maechi*s (14, p. 23). These girls must be at least 16 years old to join the *sangha*. Their education used to be very limited but has improved recently (14, p. 48). The preliminary ordination of *maechi*s is attended by monks and other *maechi*s but the male *sangha*s continue to oppose the full ordination of these women. Earlier, two Thai nuns who were fully ordained in Taiwan and India, were denied recognition by their own *sangha* here.

*Maechi*s observe the eight precepts including celibacy and the bans on beautification and entertainment. They collect alms, attend morning and evening chants, meditate and study the Dharma. They live in separate quarters, usually in nunneries or temples. Once a girl has become a novice, her status is irreversible and she indicates her intention of remaining celibate by shaving her head. She must observe the required subservience to monks as in the *sangha*s. The government provides no financial support for *maechi*s, only for monks. Because of this, *maechi*s usually have to work to support themselves and often live at home.

Buddhist laymen and women usually obey the five precepts and may continue to practice as laypersons or become novices. Religion permeates all levels of Thai society and the local *wat* is the social hub of the community except in major urban areas. Village headmen are elected and, together with the monks and elders, provide leadership locally. Nearly all males spend some period of time in the *sangha*s and then return to their families. Thai society believes that men acquire maturity by becoming novices and this gives their families some status while women achieve this through marriage and childbirth.

Thai society shows great respect for older family members and ancestors. Village women play prominent roles at festivals and are accorded a relatively high position in their culture. They have authority in their own homes but tend to behave submissively in public.

Theravedan Buddhism is practised by a majority of the population of Cambodia. Earlier, women who wanted to join *sangha*s usually did so after raising their children but this has changed recently and younger women are now joining (20, p. 10).

There are no fully ordained nuns in Myanmar, Cambodia or Laos. Preordained nuns may preach in private homes and in nunneries but monks perform the rites at all other religious ceremonies. Here too, monks attract greater financial and non-financial support because of their superior status. A woman who wants to participate in a religious life can become a *yogini* – a Tantric practitioner – who observes the eight precepts, meditates and prays.

Mahayana Buddhism in East Asia

Mahayana Buddhism is practised in China, Japan and Korea but each country reflects the influences of older religious and social customs. The *bhikshuni sangha* established in South China in the fifth century mostly attracted upper class, educated women (11, p. 123ff.). It provided the nuns with some degree of independence from their families and yet allowed them to gain respect in the community.

The Ch'an School (Zen in Japan) began in the sixth century and soon became the dominant school. It emphasized discipline with less reliance on the scriptures and believed that enlightenment could be achieved in one lifetime through intensive meditation. Women were allowed to be teachers and they achieved some degree of equality (11, p. 126).

Confucianism continued to maintain a great deal of influence on social customs and women in a Chinese family were subjected to three obediences: their fathers, their husbands and their sons (25, pp. 140ff.). By the late seventeenth century and eighteenth century, Chinese monastic institutions were in physical and moral decay and many families prevented their daughters from joining a *sangha*. Those who did tended to be widows because of poverty, while others were concubines or courtesans. Others came to find refuge from an unhappy marriage. By the end of the Imperial age in the mid-nineteenth century, girls in China still had their feet bound and female infanticide was common. By the late nineteenth and early twentieth centuries, the status of women in China was at an all time low.

The Nationalist government maintained Confucianist traditions while adopting Western technologies. This changed in 1949 with communism, when loyalty to the state replaced loyalty to the family.

Modern-day Chinese women associate Confucianism with repression and Mao Tse Tung used this to gain their support during the communist takeover (25, p. 158). The authority of the father has diminished since that time and arranged marriages have mostly disappeared. Buddhist temples and shrines have been converted and monastery lands redistributed. Monks and nuns were re-educated and directed to other work. Later, the Cultural Revolution further decreased the number of monastics. The Chinese communist party views women and men as equals.

Like China, Taiwan practises Mahayana Buddhism and this appears to be gaining in popularity and nuns now exceed monks by a ratio of five to one (20, p. 15).

The first Buddhist monastics in Japan were three monks and a nun who had been ordained in Korea and arrived in Japan in the late sixth century. During the next 200 years, few women joined the *sangha*s and those that did, generally lived reclusive lives.

The monk Dogen who founded the branch of Zen called Soto Zen, believed in the equality of men and women and allowed nuns to practise in the same way as monks (14, p. 119). This practice spread to other schools in Japan. Then, during the social upheavals of the next 300 years, society became more militaristic and the status of Japanese women, including nuns, deteriorated. In 1867, Shintoism became the state religion and this lasted until a constitutional amendment in the same year gave religious freedom to all.

Reforms in temple education took place in the nineteenth century and monastic schools were established and trained women in Buddhism (20, p. 120). But despite the Buddha's promise of an equal education for monks and nuns, there were major disparities. In addition, some monks enjoyed a lifestyle of greater luxury and were able to marry, father children, support a family and drink alcohol, all contrary to the rules of the *Vinaya*. The Meiji regime abolished celibacy for monks but in contrast, most nuns lived a Spartan lifestyle, although some schools permitted unshaven heads and allowed them to marry.

Nuns in Korea can be fully ordained and there are about the same number of nuns and monks. The Zen school in Korea has master and scholar nuns and their *sangha*s are financially independent.

Vajrayana Buddhism in Tibet and the Himalayan Countries

Vajrayana Buddhism is practised in Tibet. Before the Chinese invasion in 1950, it was a feudal society. Women who are full-time religious practitioners can be perpetual novices or *yogini*s – someone between a nun and a layperson – who often wander around the country freely and may not be celibate (21, p. 87). There were no fully ordained nuns until after the Dalai Lama's exile, when Western women belonging to his Gelug School were able to receive full ordination. Here too, it is believed that women cannot achieve enlightenment unless they are reborn as males.

Himalayan countries such as Nepal, Sikkim and Bhutan also practise Vajrayana Buddhism. Their cultures are hierarchical but they do not have caste systems. Female children are viewed as mixed blessings and girls are not encouraged to become nuns. Monks receive more generous support than their female counterparts (20, p. 170).

Women in Buddhist Countries

Education

Education in most Asian countries is now controlled by secular governments. Earlier, this was one of the roles of the *sangha*s and available only to males. In Japan, the 1872 Comprehensive Education Code set up primary, middle and university education for both girls and boys and made primary school education compulsory for all children. Prior to WWII, Japanese schoolgirls were taught in segregated classes and very few received a higher education. After the war, state schools became coeducational with the same standards for boys and girls. Later laws required nine years of compulsory education (6 years of primary and three years of junior high school) for all children and established three years of high school as well as two to four years of university-level education (26). Japan now has one of the highest literacy rates in the world.

In Korea, education was mostly left up to families until the Japanese annexation in 1910 after which about one in three Korean children attended primary school. Rapid changes in both primary and secondary education followed WWII and education is now universal through public, private and missionary schools. In 2005, literacy rates in South Korea were reported to be 99 per cent for both girls and boys (27, p. 119).

Radical changes in education occurred in China after the communists came to power. It was decentralized and communes became responsible for local schools. School enrolment increased dramatically at all levels. In 2005, literacy rates were reported to be 87 per cent for girls compared to 99 per cent for boys (27, p. 117).

Ninety-five per cent of children in Taiwan were reported to have a primary school education but only 20 per cent attended secondary school and 4 per cent obtained a higher education. This has since improved, so that now at least 85 per cent receive a secondary education and 46 per cent a higher education.

Sri Lanka provides compulsory and free education from age six years through university. Literacy rates have improved and are now acknowledged to be among the highest in Asia; in 2005 these were 89 per cent for girls and 92 per cent for boys (27, p. 123).

Except for the daughters of nobles, girls in Thailand were denied any education until the early twentieth century and were mostly illiterate. In 1932, education was made compulsory for girls and four years of primary school was required. This was increased to six years in 1978 and nine years in 1994. The number of women receiving a tertiary education there now exceeds men (28, pp. 1–15). Literacy rates in 2005 were reported to be 91 per cent for girls and 95 per cent for boys (27, p. 123).

Universal education was provided in Myanmar after WWII and literacy rates were reported to be 81 per cent for girls and 89 per cent for boys (29).

Vietnam improved its educational system after 1975 and nearly all children now receive five years of primary education which is free and compulsory. Fewer go on to secondary school and in 2005, about 47 per cent were expected to receive a higher education (30).

Employment

New labour laws controlling the working conditions of women and children were enacted in Japan in 1916. A new constitution was passed in 1947 requiring equal pay for equal work and the right to work; nevertheless, Japanese women were paid 77 per cent of the salaries paid to men in the same positions in 2002 (27, p. 63). This number was 68 per cent in South Korea and 93 per cent in Sri Lanka (ibid). In Thailand, women account for nearly half the work-force: 40 per cent are in agriculture; 19 per cent in manufacturing; 18 per cent in commerce and 16 per cent in services, but they usually occupy lower rung positions, although there are exceptions (31). Between 1995 and 2005, 15 per cent of women in Cambodia were employed in service-type work, 25 per cent in Sri Lanka, 74 per cent in South Korea and 77 per cent in Japan (27).

The Right to Vote

Men and women were enfranchised in Thailand after the overthrow of absolute monarchy in 1932 but no woman won election until 1949 (32). By 1997, about 6 per cent of the legislature was female. Women won the right to vote in Myanmar in 1935 and six women were elected to the legislature in 1957 (ibid.). A military coup occurred in 1962 and shortly after, all political parties were disbanded, except for the socialists. The elected political party has not been permitted to assume power and its leader, Aung San Suu Kyi has remained under house arrest until very recently. Sri Lanka allowed women to vote in 1931 and in 1960, Mrs. Bandranaika became the world's first female prime minister (ibid.). Women gained the right to vote in Japan in 1947: South Korea and then China followed two years later (32, 33). Very few women are elected to serve in government: 6 per cent in Sri Lanka in 2008, 9 per cent in Japan and 14 per cent in South Korea (27).

Marriage

The Buddha had some words of wisdom for married couples including advice to a husband to treat his wife with respect, and to be courteous and faithful, to give her authority in the home and provide her with ornaments. She should be hospitable to their kin and faithful, watchful of the goods her husband brought to the home and industrious in discharging his business (3, p. 123).

Buddhism does not regard marriage as a sacrament but rather as a secular contract for which there are legal requirements in most countries. Monks and sometimes nuns may provide blessings at marriage ceremonies but some families arrange more elabourate rites, with greater religious involvement. There is no dowry system.

Marriages used to be arranged in China and women had to swear absolute loyalty to their husbands, alive or dead. This remnant of Confucianism more or less ended with the communist takeover in 1949. Marriages were usually arranged on the basis of class or economic status in Japan and Korea, but this changed after WWII and is now much less common, especially in urban areas.

Paternal authority remains strong in Vietnam where many of the marriages are arranged. Virginity is essential for Thai girls and most marriages are monogamous although polygamy was quite common until 1935 (14, p. 50). There is considerable sexual freedom in Tibet and sex before marriage is discouraged but not condemned. Polyandry was quite common here, usually with the brothers of the first husband.

Most Asian girls marry when they are between 18 and 25 years and even later in recent years. The legal age for marriage in Sri Lanka is 21 for men and women: since 1987 it has been 17 in Thailand (34). On average, girls in Japan marry later than in the United States and in 2000, the mean age there was 27 years.

Divorce

Buddhism allowed divorce for transgressions such as killing, lying or sexual misconduct, or where the suffering engendered by continuing a marriage would be alleviated by divorce. Mutual consent was made a reason for divorce in China and Taiwan in 1930 (9, vol. 7, p. 570). In Japan, divorce has been permissible – mostly for men – from 1896, because of mutual consent, absence for three years or longer and imprisonment for serious crimes. This changed in 1947, to include adultery and desertion and divorce was made more easily available for women. Divorce rates have increased and the majority of applicants are now women. Thailand's legal system is patriarchal and divorce was formally permitted for men only. Now, most Buddhist countries permit divorce for either party. Women in Myanmar were more advanced than their sisters elsewhere and free, independent and especially privileged. They had equal rights to men in divorce until the country came under British control when the restrictive English laws of that period were enforced. Buddhism makes no restrictions on the remarriage of widows or divorcees.

Child Custody

The custody of children is usually awarded to a single parent – the mother – in Japan and Korea, and the father in China, unless there is some mental or social reason to rule diffently. Sri Lanka decides according to Islamic law.

Rape and Violence to Women

In 2005, violence by a male partner was reported in 15, 30, 38 and 41 per cent of Japanese, Chinese, South Korean and Bangkok women, respectively (27).

Reproductive Rights

Male children are generally favoured over females because of the need to maintain property and farms and to provide support for parents. Infanticide is a crime as is rape. However, spousal rape is viewed differently.

Buddhism does not oppose birth control although its availability is limited in many South-east Asian countries, for financial reasons. Buddhism does not approve of abortion since it involves the killing of a 'sentient' being, but the practice varies in different Asian countries, depending on their secular laws. Sri Lanka allows abortion only if the mother's life is at risk. China instituted a one-child policy under communism, which made abortion common. Japan has liberal abortion laws.

Public Health Data in East and South-east Asian Countries

Female life expectancy exceeded males in all Buddhist countries and varied between 75 years in China and 86 in Japan (35). Maternal mortality (deaths per 100,000 livebirths) in 2005 was 6 in Japan, 14 in South Korea, 45 in China, 58 in Sri Lanka, 110 in Thailand and 154 in Vietnam (36, pp. 1311–19). Infant mortality estimates for 2009 (deaths per 1,000 livebirths) was 3 in Japan, 4 in South Korea, 15 in Sri Lanka, 7 in Thailand and 21 in China (35). Fertility (per woman) for the same period was 1.4 in Japan, 1.2 in South Korea, 1.6 in China, 1.8 in Thailand and 2.4 in Sri Lanka (35).

Summary

Buddhism began as a protest movement against the power of the Brahmans and the misery inflicted by the Hindu caste system. It did not change this or the Hindu belief in continuous reincarnation. The Buddha welcomed all regardless of caste or gender and preached about a Middle Way between the extremes of self-indulgence and asceticism, providing explanations for suffering and a prescription for survival. He denied the existence of a supreme being or god, but promoted the belief that each person has the ability to control his or her life. This must have been very welcome news to Hindu women whose lives by that time were deteriorating to almost complete subjugation. They joined him in large numbers.

The Buddha established a monastic community, the *sangha*, but this was for men only. The promise of equality, regardless of gender, was eroding already. We are told that after much pleading from his senior disciple, the Buddha relented, to a degree. Women were allowed to join a *sangha* but they had to first accept certain conditions. In the *sangha*s they were always inferior to monks regardless of their seniority, experience and knowledge.

A second mark of a woman's inferiority concerned her ability to attain full enlightenment, the ultimate goal of every professing Buddhist. Women were women because of errors in previous lives and they would first have to be reborn as males – if their *karma*s were good enough – in order to achieve this status.

Between 300 and 500 years after the Buddha's death, Buddhism split into two major groups, Hinayana later called Theraveda, the School of the Elders, and Mahayana, the Great Vehicle to Enlightenment. A third school, Vajrayana developed later out of the Mahayana School.

Buddhist societies consist of laypersons and monastics. Specific rules were laid down for both groups and there were few gender differences among the former. This is in stark contrast to the *sangha*s that have been described as symbols of sexism. The Theraveda School has not recognized any fully ordained nuns since the tenth century although there is evidence of some recent change. Only in China, Korea and Taiwan where Mahayana prevails, are there fully ordained Buddhist nuns. Nuns are discriminated against in Japan where they have the status of novices. Monks on the other hand have considerable latitude there with regard to their lifestyle, which exceeds that allowed in the *Vinaya*.

Buddhism places few restrictions on either the family, civic or political lives of its followers. Several Buddhist countries accorded property and inheritance rights to women, long before this occurred in the democracies of the West. Myanmar was notable in this respect and extended this to divorce. Previously, the *sangha*s provided nearly all of the education for boys, particularly in the villages, but excluded girls. Now, virtually all Buddhist countries have state-supported public education for both sexes and many have achieved high or improved literacy rates in a relatively short time. Women can vote in all of these countries but as yet, rather few have been elected to office. Although employment opportunities for women have improved, the majority of them still have lower-level positions. Divorce laws are generally determined by the state. Birth control is permissible although economic factors often limit its availability. Buddhism does not approve of abortion but most countries follow local secular laws in this regard.

The same cannot be said for *sangha*s where nuns, novices and other religious women are treated as second- or third-class citizens. A major goal for Buddhist women is to promote equality for monks and nuns in all *sangha*s, the re-establishment of Theraveda *sangha*s for nuns, and full ordination of their nuns. This is on the agenda of Sakyadhite, the International Association of Buddhist Women. As to the enlightenment issue, scientific evidence – including DNA – demonstrates women are not inferior to men – physically or intellectually – but there are no known ways to measure spiritual differences. Nor is there any evidence that women are inferior in this respect.

References

1   Armstrong, Karen. *Buddha*. New York. Penguin Putnam Incorporated. 1994.
2   Harvey, Peter. *An Introduction to Buddhism: Teachings, History and Practices*. Cambridge University Press. 1990.
3   Erricker, Clive. *Buddhism*. Chicago. NTC Contemporary Publishing. 1975.
4   Bercholz, Seymour and C. Kohn Sherab. *An Introduction to the Buddha and his Teaching*. New York. Barnes and Noble. 1993.
5   Coomaraswamy, Ananda and I. B. Horner, *The Living Thoughts of Gautama the Buddha*. Boston. Dover Publishers Inc. 2000.
6   Wei-hsun Fu, C. and S. Wawrytko, eds. *Buddhist Behavioural Codes and the Modern World: an International Symposium*. Westport, CT. Greenwood Press. 1994.
7   Saunders, E. Dale. *Buddhism in Japan*. Philadelphia. University of Pennsylvania Press. 1964.
8   Ikeda, D. and B. Watson, trs. *Buddhism in the First Millennium*. Kodansha Institute Ltd. Tokyo, Japan1977.
9   *Encyclopedia Britannica*. Ed. W. Benton. Chicago. University of Chicago. 1968.
10   Chen, Kenneth K. S. *Buddhism in China*. Princeton University Press. 1972.
11   Schuster Barnes, Nancy. Buddhism. In *Women in World Religions*. Ed. A. Sharma. Albany. State University of New York Press. 1987.
12   EnWikipedia.org/wiki/Buddhism_by_country.
13   Severy, M, ed. *Great Religions of the World*. National Geographic Society. Washington, DC. 1971.
14   Findly, E. B. *Women's Buddhism, Buddhism's Women*. Boston. Wisdom Publications. 2000.
15   Lester, Robert. C. *Theraveda Buddhism in Southeast Asia*. Ann Arbor. University of Michigan Press. 1973.
16   Conze, Edward, tr. *Buddhist Scriptures*. London. Penguin Classics. 1959.
17   Rhys-Davids, T. W, tr. *Sacred Books of the East*. Vols. XXXV and XXXVI. Oxford. Clarendon Press. 1964.
18   Carter, John R. and Mahinda Palihawadana, trs. *Sacred Writings on Buddhism: the Dhammapada*. Ed. J. Pelikan. Oxford University Press. 2000.
19   Watson, B, tr. *The Lotus Sutra*. New York. Columbia University Press. 1993.
20   Tsomo, S, ed. *Buddhist Women across Cultures*. Princeton. State University of New York Press. 1999.
21   Gross, Rita M. *Buddhism after Patriarchy*. State University of New York Press. 1993.

22 Sharma, Arvind. *Spokes of the Wheel*. New York. Books and Books. 1985.
23 Lerner, Gerda. *The Creation of Patriarchy*. New York. Oxford University Press. 1956.
24 Rhys-Davids, C. A. F. *Psalms of the Sisters*. London. Pali Text Society. 1909. Reprinted as *Poems of Early Buddhist Nuns (Theregatha)*. Rhys-David, C. A. F. and J. L. Norman. Oxford. Pali Text Society. 1989.
25 Kelleher, Theresa. 'Confucianism' in *Women in World Religions*. Ed. Arvind Sharma. Albany. State University of New York Press. 1987.
26 Amano, M. *The Perpetual Gender Track in Education*. Yokohama. YWACN newsletter. www.womencity
27 Seager, Joni. *The Penguin Atlas of Women in the World*. 4th edition. Penguin Books. New York. 2009.
28 *Exploring the History of Women's Education and Activism in Thailand*. LeeRay Costa. http://www2.hawaiedu
29 UNESCO. http://www.unstats.un.org
30 *Educational Literacy in Vietnam*. Asianinfo.org.
31 *Gender and Development in Thailand. 2000. Socio-economic status of women*. www.unifemesasian.org
32 Time and World Chronology. *Women's Suffrage*. IPU study No.28. 1997.
33 Peck, E. H. *History of Women's Suffrage*. Grolier's Encyclopedia Americana. Danbury, CT. 2005.
34 *Education in Thailand*. Thailand National Identity Office. 2000.
35 *Life Expectancy*. www. prb.org 2009 World Population Data Sheet.
36 Hill, Kenneth, *et al. Estimates of Maternal Mortality 1990-2005*. Lancet. V. 370, 2007

Additional bibliography

Barnes, N. S. *Striking a Balance. Women and Images of Women in Early Chinese Buddhism*. Haddad, Y. and E. Findley, eds. 'Buddhism'. In *Women, Religion and Social Change*. Albany. State University of New York Press, Albany. NY. 1987
Carmody, D. L. *Women and World Religions*. Upper Saddle River. Prentice-Hall Incorporated. 1989.
Coleman, J. W. *The New Buddhism*. Oxford University Press. 2001.
Falk, N. A. *Women and Religion in India*. Kalamazoo, Michigan. New Issues Press. 1994.
Horner, I. B. *Women under Primitive Buddhism: Lay Women and Alms Women*. Delhi. Motilal Barnarsidass. 1930.
Legge, J. *The Works of Mencius*. Boston. Dover Publications Incorporated. 1970.

Morgan, K. S, ed. *The Path of the Buddha: Buddhism Interpreted by Buddhists.* New Delhi. Ronald Press. 1986.

Paul, Diana L. *Women in Buddhism: Images of the Feminine in Mahayana Tradition.* Berkeley. Asian Humanities Press. 1979.

Reed, B. E. 'Taoism'. In *Women in World Religions.* Ed. A. Sharma. Albany. State University of New York Press. 1987.

Reischauer, E. O. *The Japanese.* Cambridge, MA: Belknap Press Harvard University. 1977.

Totman, C. *Japan before Perry.* Berkeley. University of California Press. 1981.

Tripet, S. *Women in Ancient India 320-1200.* New Delhi. ESS Publishers. 1987.

Weber, M. *The Religion of India.* Tr. H. H. Gerth and D. Martindale. Glencoe, IL. The Free Press. 1958.

Willis, T. D. 'Nuns and Benefactresses: The Role of Women in the Development of Buddhism'. In *Women, Religion and Social Change.* Eds. Y. Haddad and E. Findly. Albany. State University of New York Press. 1985.

Chapter 3

Judaism

History

Biblical Period 2000 up to 400 BCE

Judaism is the religion of the Jewish people who they now number about 14 million people worldwide. Their history extends back over several millennia to Abram, the first of the Jewish patriarchs. He is said to have migrated to Canaan, sometime after 1750 BCE, in the approximate region of modern-day Israel and Lebanon (1, p. 28). According to the Tanakh – the Jewish Holy Scripture – God made a covenant with Abram saying 'You shall be the father of a multitude of nations.' 'And you shall no longer be called Abram, but your name shall be Abraham' (2, Gen. 17.3-5). To seal this covenant, every male should be circumcised on the eighth day of life (ibid. 12).

Abraham and his descendants were shepherds who grazed their flocks all over the region, wherever there were verdant pastures. Joseph – his great-grandson – settled later in the Nile delta region of Egypt where he prospered, and in time was appointed grand vizier to the Pharaoh. Egypt thrived under his guidance. Some time later Joseph's father Jacob and his brothers and their families joined him in Egypt, and the population of Israelites multiplied over the succeeding generations. By the twelfth century, they were well established there (3, p. 35).

A later Pharaoh turned on the Israelites and made them into slave labourers. Escape from the country was difficult, because the Egyptians had built a series of forts along the frontier of their land. The Israelites did eventually manage to leave Egypt, probably at different times between 750 and 650 BCE, suggesting the Exodus was not one major event but occurred over a period of time (1, p. 68).

Jewish history indicates that at sometime during their return, Moses received the Ten Commandments on Mount Sinai, together with laws concerning prayer, purity and diet. These were inscribed on stone tablets that were eventually placed with their most sacred relics in the Ark of the Covenant.

For a time, the Israelites occupied Amorite lands east of the Dead Sea on the border of Canaan. Moses died before they reached the Promised Land and Joshua became their leader and eventually overcame the Canaanites – a civilized people from whom the Israelites learned a great deal (4, p. 40).

The first king of Israel was Saul whose rule started shortly before 1000 BCE. David followed him and achieved fame in a war against the Philistines. He united his own tribe of Judah with Israel and made Jerusalem his capital. David's successor, Solomon, built the first Temple in 950 BCE. Then, after Solomon's death, the kingdom split again into two states, Israel with its ten tribes in the north, and Judah and its two tribes in the south. Jerusalem was the capital of Judah.

In 722 BCE, the Assyrians overcame Israel and carried its people into exile. Judah continued to prosper for the next 190 years, until it was conquered by Nebuchadnezzar King of Babylon. Some of the people escaped to Egypt where they built a temple in Elephantine where they worshipped Yahweh and two other gods, one male and one female (3, p. 154). Most of the population was exiled to Babylon. Jerusalem was razed to the ground and the first Temple was destroyed (1, p. 44).

This Jewish exile ended after about 50 years when Cyrus, King of Persia captured Babylon, Egypt and much of the intervening territory. The first wave of returnees moved back to their former land and was followed by a second a century later. Nehemiah was appointed governor of Judah and organized the rebuilding of the walls of Jerusalem and the Second Temple, which was completed in 516 BCE (3, p. 157). The returning Judeans were aided by the Samaritans and other non-Jewish tribes living in the region. Nehemiah enacted social and religious reforms and appointed a scribe, Ezra, to set up a theocratic state to be ruled by the high priests. The Jewish scripture – the Torah – became the law of the land. The Judeans were ordered to 'separate your selves from the peoples of the land and from the foreign women' (2, Ezra 10.11). From now on, mixed marriages were prohibited. Anyone who was not fully Jewish was banished from the region.

Hellenistic Period 400 BCE up to 200 CE

The second period of Jewish history is the Hellenistic period (fourth to the first century BCE). Alexander the Great had conquered the Eastern Mediterranean lands, founded the city of Alexandria and made it his capital. In time it grew into a centre of trade and culture. Nearly half the population was Jewish and many of them spoke Greek rather than Hebrew.

After Alexander's death in 323 BCE, the territory he had conquered was divided up among his generals. Palestine came under the control of Ptolemy and his descendents who were followed by the Seleucid kings. During much of this time, Jews lived relatively free lives and their high priests enjoyed considerable power and wealth, until one of the later Seleucid kings attempted to impose a pseudo-Grecian culture on them. The Temple was looted, a Roman shrine to Zeus was installed and the Jewish religion was outlawed (5, p. 21). This provoked a revolt, led by Judas, also known as the 'Maccabee'. Jerusalem was captured in 165 BCE and the Temple was cleansed and rededicated. This victory is celebrated at Hanukkah and is believed to be the first occasion on which the rabbinic law to abstain from any labour on the Sabbath was ignored. Judas was killed and succeeded by his brothers who in turn became high priests. This period of Jewish control of Jerusalem lasted until about 76 BCE.

During the period of the Second Temple (516–70 CE), the two major religious parties in Judea were the Sadducees and the Pharisees. The Sadducees were the wealthy supporters of the high priest, their uncrowned king. They included the aristocratic families and merchants who controlled the Sanhedrin – the highest court in Jerusalem – and adhered strictly to the letter of the law. The Pharisees were the non-priestly teachers or 'dissenters', mostly scholars who attempted to free the religion from the rigid control exercised by the high priests.

At least three other Jewish sects existed at that time. One of them, the Essenes, was an ascetic brotherhood living in monastic communities in the northern Dead Sea region of Qumran (6, p. 47). All of them perished in about 68 CE when Roman legions led by Vespasian attacked their settlement (6, p. 18). Their 800 manuscripts remained in the caves of Qumran until discovered in 1947 (6, p. 66). The Zealots were a small, radical sect who promoted rebellion. They refused to pay taxes to the Romans. The Sicarii or Assassins were yet another small group who carried daggers and were finally overcome in 73 CE.

War erupted between the Pharisees and the Sadducees and the Roman general Pompey intervened, captured Jerusalem in 63 BCE, and inflicted heavy loss of life. Shortly after, Julius Caesar became the Roman ruler and appointed Herod as King of Judea. The Second Temple was rebuilt during his reign, as were many other buildings. Uprisings occurred during the rule of Herod's descendants who were then banished by Rome and Pontius Pilate was appointed procurator. The unrest continued and was eventually suppressed by Vespasian. Jerusalem was captured in 70 CE and the Second Temple was destroyed and never rebuilt: the Wailing Wall remains as its only vestige. This conflict ended the authority of the Sadducees. Vespasian – now Emperor of Rome – allowed the Jewish institution at Jabneh (modern day Jamnia) to remain intact, ensuring the survival of at least one centre of Judaism. An academy was established there, as well as a seat for the Sanhedrin – a council of priests and laymen presided over by the high priest (7, p. xlii). Meanwhile, Emperor Hadrian ordered an edifice to Jupiter to be built in Jerusalem on Temple Mount. New laws were enacted, including one forbidding bodily mutilation, intended to outlaw circumcision. Jews were finally banished from Jerusalem, after another revolt in about 132 CE.

Rabbinic Period 200 up to 1000 CE

The third period of Jewish history is the Rabbinic period, which lasted until the tenth century CE. After their expulsion from Jerusalem, the Jewish spirit of rebellion subsided, and guided by the Tannaim (the rabbis of this period), the focus of Jewish activity became the study of their scriptures, prayer and learning (8). Jabneh and Babylon became the two main centres of Jewish culture and rabbinical schools opened in both. These became centres of learning when Europe was still in the Dark Ages. Jewish courts were set up to interpret Rabbinic laws but these were strongly opposed by a branch of Judaism called Karaitism who called the new laws fabrications. They advocated obedience to the old Mosaic Law and a return to Palestine. The influence of Karaitism reached its peak between the ninth and twelfth centuries and involved several notable Jewish scholars. Small groups survive to this day.

Muhammad was born in 570 CE and within 60 years the tribal communities of Arabia were converted to the new faith, Islam. This had some similarity to Judaism; both claimed descent from Abraham, Islam through Ishmael, Abraham's concubine Hagar's son: both were monotheistic faiths and observed dietary laws, formal prayers and festivals. By the early eighth century, Islam had conquered North Africa and much of Spain and the Umayyad rulers there welcomed the Jews for their experience in finance, linguistic skills and knowledge of the sciences and philosophy of ancient Greece.

Jews had migrated throughout the Middle East and to Greece, Rome, Spain and the Rhinelands after the destruction of the Second Temple. They were allowed to become Roman citizens and many held positions of privilege in the Empire. When Christianity became the religion of Rome in the fourth century, attitudes changed: Judaism was suppressed and construction of synagogues was forbidden. The Edict of Milan in 313 CE restricted social interaction with Christians, and Jews were denied positions in the European community. In the east, as Persia converted to Zoroastrianism, it too turned on the Jews.

Many of the early Jewish settlers in Europe had been farmers, but prior ownership of land here and later the feudal system, limited their access and from then on, they mostly resided in urban areas. By the time of Charlemagne (768-824), Jews had lost their citizenship rights and survived at the will of the local ruler in walled quarters or *ghettos*, usually situated close to the ruler's palace (5, p. 95). Here they were mostly autonomous, and followed their own system of law, government, education – which was usually compulsory except for girls – and philanthropy. They were slowly forced out of most trades but allowed to engage in banking and money lending which made them especially useful to the local ruler.

Medieval Period 1000 up to 1800 CE: the Jewish Enlightenment

By the fourth period of Jewish history – the Medieval period (1000–1800 CE), European Jews comprised two major groups, based on geography, customs and language and there was very little assimilation between them. The Ashkenazim lived mainly in Germany, practised monogamy and spoke Yiddish, a mixture of German and Hebrew. The Sephardim lived in Spain where some had settled in King Solomon's time and many more came after 70 CE. Then in the seventh and eighth centuries, Arabs invaded Spain, bringing Islam with them and the Jews here integrated well into the local culture and flourished under the protection and support of the Umayyads. Cordoba, Seville and Granada became centres of learning. This period is remembered as the Golden Age of Hebrew culture and lasted from 1000 to 1145 CE. Sephardic Jews spoke Landino, a dialect derived from Spanish and Hebrew. Their religious practices are similar to Orthodox Jews but they have different prayers, feasts and foods.

Oriental Jews are a third branch of Judaism and form a more diverse group than the other two. They are descended from people who migrated after the Assyrian, Babylonian and Roman conquests. They settled all over the Middle East including Yemen, Ethiopia, India, Persia and China and their customs and languages vary according to their host countries.

In 1179 and again in 1215, all European Jews were ordered to wear identifying badges and attend Christian sermons. Jewish scriptures were forbidden to them. The Christian 'faithful' were ordered not to live alongside Jews, who were denied positions of authority over Christians (5, pp. 98–103). Edward I expelled all Jews from England in 1290 and they were not allowed to return until the time of Oliver Cromwell and the Protectorate in the seventeenth century. During this same period, Jews were expelled from France and driven out of Western Europe. They migrated east into Poland and Eastern Europe where they prospered, at least for a time. They were initially tolerated in Spain until the fourteenth century when their persecution became rampant and they were finally expelled in 1478. By the sixteenth century – except for scattered regions of Germany, Northern Italy and the Papal States – Western Europe had closed its doors to Jews (5, p. 101). The Ottoman sultans welcomed them and before long, Constantinople – a city captured by the Turks in 1453 – had the largest Jewish population in Europe. Large numbers of Jews also resided in Russia; others lived in the Balkans, then under the control of the Ottoman Empire.

Jewish resettlement in Western Europe began in the seventeenth century, shortly before the Age of Enlightenment whose leaders – men like Voltaire, Diderot and Rousseau – sought less control by the Christian Church and greater tolerance for all minorities including Jews. The French Revolution led to the Declaration of the Rights of Man in 1791, which states that all men are equal: Jews were then enfranchised and given full citizenship rights. Napoleon also ordered equal rights for Jews in all the lands he conquered, as well as their assimilation into French culture. All churches, Catholic and Protestant, as well as synagogues, had to answer to him.

In the same spirit of tolerance, Jews were encouraged to settle in the American colonies in the seventeenth and eighteenth centuries, where the Constitution gave them the full rights of citizenship. During this period, Jews also moved back into Holland, Denmark and England. But several pockets of anti-Semitism remained, and in 1745 Bavaria threatened Jews with banishment.

The United States has experienced three major waves of Jewish migration (9, vol. 12. p. 198). The first, which started in 1654 and continued until 1830, consisted of conservative Spanish Jews who were mostly Sephardic. The second, starting in 1830, was Ashkenazi; they came from Germany and brought Reform Judaism with them. The third group began in the 1880s and came from Russia, Poland and Romania.

Eastern European Jews were still experiencing many hardships: Ukrainian Cossacks, who were Orthodox Christians, rose up against their Polish rulers in 1648 and an estimated 100,000 Jews perished in these rebellions. Russian rulers organized massacres and pogroms against Jews, denying them citizenship and an education (5, p. 122). These hardships persisted in Russia until Jews were finally emancipated in the early twentieth century.

A new branch of Judaism began during this period of despair in Poland, in protest against scholarly rabbis, by poor, uneducated Jews. This pietist movement called Hasidism, practised devotion to a holy man rather than the Torah and the rigid, legalistic orthodoxy of the rabbis (5, p. 122 ff.). Their rabbi or *zaddick* is all-important and acts as an intermediary between God and the community and receives absolute obedience. Women may not participate in prayer or in the study or interpretation of Jewish law, but have been active in establishing outreach programmes in their own communities. Hasidism spread quickly in Eastern Europe and then declined in the nineteenth century. Rather few Hasidic groups remain in Europe but there are several well-known ones in the United States such as the Lubavitcher and Bostoner Hasidics; each has its own rabbi and conforms to strictly Orthodox practices.

The Jewish Enlightenment began in the second half of the eighteenth century and its goal was to westernize European Jews and encourage their assimilation. Its first leader was Moses Mendelssohn (1729–1786), who recommended Jews retain their own laws and rituals but modernize their traditional synagogue practices. He encouraged Jews to participate in European customs, using tolerance, reason, morality and a secular education (5, p. 117). Although realizing the advantages of the German language, he recommended the retention of Hebrew for communication, and wrote a modern biblical commentary in Hebrew.

The Eastern Enlightenment, the *Haskalah*, occurred a little later and was directed more to the establishment of a Jewish homeland than their assimilation. These two differing goals reflect the much worse situation of the Eastern Jews who formed the majority. By the end of the eighteenth century, Poland – with the largest Jewish population – had been partitioned three times. The Treaty of Berlin in 1878 was an attempt to protect the civil and political rights of minorities, but had only limited success and Jews in Eastern Europe continued to struggle. Leon Gordon, a poet of the Eastern Enlightenment, was denounced by Jewish Orthodoxy for writing '*The Tittle of the Yod*', a plea for the rights of Jewish women (9, vol. 13. p. 114).

Modern Period 1800 CE up to the Present

The Modern Period of Jewish history began in 1800 CE. By the end of the nineteenth century, Jews had achieved equal rights in most Central and Western European states: Lord Rothschild took his seat in the English House of Lords in 1885, and Disraeli – who had been baptized as a child – was enjoying power and prestige as Queen Victoria's prime minister and became one of her favourites. Conversion and secular Judaism were alternative paths followed by a number of European Jews. Others preferred to integrate but maintain their own culture, and this led to the Reform movement in European Judaism.

Reform Judaism started in Hamburg, Germany and spread to other regions of Germany and Austria and then to England (5, p. 127 ff.). German replaced Hebrew as the language of the liturgy. Confirmation replaced the Bar Mitzvah, and music and choir singing were introduced into services. Men and women were no longer segregated in the synagogue and instead, families sat together. Judaism was viewed as a continually evolving religion in which some older traditions and dietary laws were abandoned while moral laws were maintained. There was strong opposition from Hasidic and Orthodox Jews. Reform Judaism slowly decreased in Germany but became firmly established in the United States where the first Reform Society of Israelites began in Charleston, South Carolina in 1824. A revised prayer book was issued in 1894. Through the years, the beliefs of Reform Judaism have changed to promote the 'integration of Jews into American culture' (9, vol. 13, p. 115).

Conservative Judaism began as a compromise between the Reform and Orthodox groups. It accepts the Torah as binding but believes the *Halakhah* (Jewish Law) is a living force, open to change if it is supported by a majority of the people, and there is a historical basis for the change. It preserves most aspects of traditional Judaism, including its dietary laws but accepts the need for changes in interpreting the Talmud.

Reconstructionism is a branch of Conservative Judaism that views Judaism as a culture rather than a religion and emphasizes Jewish customs and symbols for secular Jews. Jewish laws and rituals are retained only if they foster loyalty and support self-fulfilment. Women are accepted as peers.

Orthodox Judaism follows classical Jewish traditions without concern for Western civilization and maintains unchanged religious practices. The laws of God – as prescribed in the Jewish scriptures – are viewed as immutable and therefore cannot be reinterpreted. Family and home rank higher than the individual and strict codes of behaviour are prescribed for both sexes. Most Jews in Europe are Orthodox.

The religious practices of many Sephardic Jews remain unchanged and they continue to observe the commandments unless these are time-dependent. Social interaction between the sexes is discouraged.

The Zionist movement began at the end of the nineteenth century, in response to anti-Semitism, which had resurfaced at about this time. The first Zionist congress was organized by Theodor Heizl and met in Basel in 1897. Its goal was to promote Zionism. Although the planners came from the West, the most enthusiastic response was from Jews in Russia and Eastern Europe. Women played a major role in this movement but their contributions – although recognized in England – were ignored elsewhere, especially in Eastern Europe (10, p. 45). Most women who joined the movement did so because of an interest in social service and to promote Jewish, feminist and social welfare interests. After WWI, England became the centre of Zionism.

After Hitler gained control in Germany in the 1930s, and later in Austria and the countries he conquered in WWII, he instigated a programme to exterminate Jews and almost succeeded by the end of the war. At that time, their largest population lived in Russia.

The Balfour Declaration – calling for a Jewish homeland in Palestine – was published in 1917, shortly before the end of WWI. Although it became a mandate for the victors, no action was taken until after WWII. Then the state of Israel was established in 1948 after the British mandate of Palestine ended and the country was handed over to the United Nations. About 300,000 Jews were moved to the new state from refugee camps in Germany and Italy and about the same number moved to the United States, Latin America and Australia. More recently, larger migrations have taken place from Russia and later from Eastern Europe. Generous financial support from established countries, including the United States, ensures the survival and prosperity of Israel, despite opposition from most Arab countries, who currently refuse to recognize it.

Today, Israel has a population of about 7.5 million, of whom about 80 per cent are Jews, 15 per cent Muslim, 2 per cent Christian and 3 per cent other religions (11). Orthodox Judaism is the official religion, but the majority of Jews there are secular. Israel has an elected parliament, the Knesset, with a prime minister – who is the leader of the majority party – and a president. Outside Israel, the largest Jewish populations are to be found in the United States and Russia. Smaller communities exist in Iran and other Arabic states, Europe, Central and South America (11).

Jewish Scriptures and Women

The Torah

According to Jewish scriptures, there is only one God who made a covenant with Abraham and conveyed his laws through Moses. These laws are contained in their sacred books, the Torah and the Talmud. The Torah consists of the Pentateuch, or five books of Moses: Genesis, Exodus, Leviticus, Numbers and Deuteronomy. These narrate the history of the people of Israel, from the creation of man up to Moses' farewell to them. It includes the story of the flood, the Exodus from Egypt and Moses' receipt of the Law on Mount Sinai. The multiple and differing versions of the creation, the flood and other episodes of this history, suggest there were at least four sources for the Torah and these were patched together at some later date (3, p. 53). The earliest was written between the seventh and sixth centuries BCE (1, p. 11). Scholars have questioned Moses' involvement in the Pentateuch; Deuteronomy, for instance describes his death and must therefore have been written at some later time (ibid. p. 6).

In addition to the Pentateuch, the Hebrew Bible includes 34 more books. The first group, the Prophets – early and late – was written over a span of 350 years lasting to the end of the fifth century BCE and tells the story of the conquest of Canaan up to the defeat and exile of the Israelites. The second, the Hagiographia, which includes the Psalms, Proverbs and Book of Job, as well as the Songs of Solomon, Books of Ruth and Esther, Lamentations, Ecclesiastes, Prophesies of Daniel, and History – Chronicles, Ezra and Nehemiah – were compiled much later, from the fifth to the second centuries (1, p. 6).

The Bible was mostly written in Hebrew, with some later additions in Aramaic, which replaced Hebrew in the sixth century BCE. The Pentateuch was translated into Greek in the mid third century in Alexandria by 72 'wise men' from Jerusalem, six from each tribe of Israel. The translation of the other books followed in the second century BCE (12, p. 302). Copies of much of this literature were found among the Dead Sea Scrolls in the caves of Qumran near Jericho, in 1947 (6, p. 3).

According to Jewish tradition, the Mosaic laws were written on stone tablets, later preserved in the Ark of the Covenant. These became their sacred standard (1, p. 9). They were handed down to Joshua, Moses' successor, and from Joshua to each of the ruling bodies of Israel down to the men of the Great Assembly, consisting of 120 members whose guiding principle was 'to be deliberate in judgment, raise up many disciples, [and] make a fence around the Torah' (7, p. 125). The Great Assembly ceased to exist sometime in the mid third century and was replaced by the Sanhedrin whose role was to interpret the Law.

The Written Torah contains 613 precepts (7, p. 149) and in addition there are 42 enactments in the Oral Torah, believed by many Jews to have been received by Moses at Sinai. The Oral Torah is said to allow flexibility in Jewish law, although any change in its interpretation required a majority decision (7, p. 148). The Sadducees denied the validity of the Oral Torah and would not accept any law not included in the Written Torah. By contrast, the Pharisees believed that oral law had evolved over time through the teaching of the prophets and allowed for change or reinterpretation. Hillel was a strong supporter of this concept, since it made it possible for the Torah to be 'adaptable to varying circumstances' (7, p. xl). The Oral Torah is included in the Talmud.

Two schools of law existed in the early first century: one was led by Hillel and the other by Shammai (12, p. 470). Over a period of time, Hillel's more liberal school prevailed. He introduced the principle of intention: an act committed without intent to break the law, does not count as an act of law breaking. This concept was passed down orally by his disciples, transcribed later and is included in the Mishnah – the collection of laws compiled in the Rabbinic period.

The Talmud

The Talmud is second only to the Torah in importance and includes the Mishnah and the Gemara, a commentary, paired with a supplement, the Tosifta. The Mishnah was in part the work of Akiba – who was killed by the Romans in 132 CE – and completed by Judah the Prince (175–220). It contains a collection of laws covering all aspects of Jewish life. Its goal was to regulate relations between man and God and between men; it was subdivided according to subject matter and consists of six sections or orders, each one with a number of tractates (63 in all) and chapters (523 in all). Each chapter is accompanied by an appropriate commentary in the Gemara, and together they form the Halakhah, the whole body of Jewish law. In addition, the Talmud contains the Haggadah, a non-legal section that includes lectures and the opinions of rabbis, compiled from the fifth to the twelfth centuries CE (7, p. liv).

The first order of the Mishnah, the Zeraim (seeds), deals with benedictions, agricultural rules and regulations, offerings to the priests and gifts to the poor. The second order, Moed (festivals), covers Sabbath law, fast days, taxes to maintain the Temple and their collection. The third order, Nashim (women) covers the laws applying to dowries and marriage settlements, incest, infidelity, divorce, levirate marriage, adultery and special vows. The fourth order, Nazikin (torts) deals with damages and injuries, theft, robbery, property, usury and the sale and purchase of movable and immovable property, inheritance, criminal law, punishment and testimony. The fifth order, Kodashim (sanctities), contains laws covering sacrifice, first-borns and temple offerings. The sixth order, Taharoth (purities), deals with purity laws relating to women.

There are two alternate forms of the Gemara; one, the Palestinian or Jerusalem edition was completed in the fourth century CE, and consists of 39 tractates. The other, the Babylonian edition, completed at the end of the fifth century CE, has 37 tractates but is considerably longer.

The Tosifta contains material that is not included in the Mishnah, and an additional tractate – the Baraitoth – has some alternate or obsolete laws. Both provide additional details of the history and social life of the Jews (7, p. xlviii).

Overall, the Talmud dictates laws for virtually every kind of human act and behaviour. Laws beginning 'thou shalt' are positive commandments and must be performed at a specific time or date; these include the wearing of the four-cornered garment, the recitation of the *Shema* (Jewish statement of faith), the blowing of the *shofar* (ram's horn), inclusion in the Minyan, and study of the Torah. Women were excused from these activities since they could interfere with their primary duties, to serve their husbands and care for their families and children. They were not excused from positive laws that were independent of time, such as the one to 'honour thy parents'. Nor were they excused from laws beginning 'thou shalt not' or negative laws, whether or not they are time-bound (13, p. 12). Apart from these and a few other exceptions, men and women were on an equal footing with regard to the laws of the Torah (13, p. 40). Three laws applied specifically to women: to observe the requirements of Niddah (rules for the menstruant), to keep the Hallah (the burning of one-tenth part of the dough, a tithe or offering to God) and lighting of the Sabbath candles.

General Attitude to Women

The ideal woman is described in Prov. 31.12–26: 'She is good to him (her husband), never bad … supplies provisions for her household … her mouth is full of wisdom.' Another proverb reads 'women are light-minded' (7, p. 161), but another contradicts this, saying: 'God endowed women with more intelligence than men' (ibid.). Women are derided repeatedly in Hebrew scriptures: they are described as 'gluttonous, eavesdroppers, lazy and jealous'; they are also labelled as 'querulous and garrulous' (7, p. 160). 'Her thought is only for her beauty' one proverb criticizes (7, p. 161). The Benediction, which is offered three times a day by Jewish men, gives thanks that the speaker is an Israelite but not a woman or a boor, and in the prayer book, women are coupled with heathens and slaves (7, p. 159). Nevertheless, the Torah includes the books of two women, Ruth and Esther, and seven prophetesses are honoured for speaking prophecies for Israel. Women are revered for several other roles: as mourners (2, Jer. 9.17), as temple singers (2, Ezra 2.65), and as nurses (2, Ruth 4.16). These citations suggest that while Jews revered individual women in their history, they viewed women collectively as inferior. There is no record of a female rabbi in their scriptures, although there is no law saying women cannot serve in this capacity. Female judges existed at the time of the tribes but disappeared some time later (3, p. 36).

The Talmud attaches supreme importance to filial piety, and Exod. 20.12 dictates 'honour thy father and mother' (2). However, when there is a conflict of interest here, the father is to be given preference over the mother (7, p. 181).

Laws Involving Women

Issues concerning women and marriage are covered fairly extensively in the order *Nashim* (women), which addresses forbidden or incestuous unions, marriage and the marriage contract, the duties of men and women to each other, infertility, birth control and abortion, infidelity and adultery, divorce and Levirate marriage. These very explicit laws reflect the prime importance of families and children in Jewish culture.

Early marriage was recommended and it was the father's duty to procure a husband for his daughter. The recommended marriage age for girls was 12 and a half years – a girl ceased to be a minor at 12 – and 13 years for boys, but earlier marriages did occur (13, p. 66). A girl who was married at a younger age could repudiate her vow later. The girl was expected to be a virgin, which was usually assured by her young age. If it was discovered later that this was not the case, she could be stoned to death: 'then the girl shall be brought out to the entrance of her father's house, and the men of her town shall stone her to death; for she did a shameful thing in Israel' (2, Deut. 22.21–22). A man was forbidden from taking a wife without seeing her first (7, p. 164). A girl was supposed to give her consent to her marriage but her silence was accepted as agreement. When she married, a girl became the property of her husband and from that time she was forbidden to other men until she was divorced or widowed. The Talmud contains advice on the selection of wives; daughters of a learned man should be sought after, and tall men should avoid tall women lest their children be 'lanky' (7, p. 64), while short men should avoid short girls lest their children be dwarfs (ibid.).

In biblical times, a wife was purchased by the groom's family to compensate the girl's father for the loss of her services. By the Rabbinic period, marriage had become more of a business transaction: the contract, or *Ketubah*, spelled out a man's financial obligations to his wife (13, p. 6). This stated the amount of the *Mohar*, or purchase price, the *Mattau*, or compensation to a girl's father, and the dowry – the property or money a girl received from her father that was supposed to remain her personal property after marriage. By the second century BCE, a woman's dowry had become the property of her husband, although she could demand its return if the couple divorced. At the Kiddushim or espousal ceremony, the man declared that the girl was to be set aside for him alone and promised to provide her with food, clothing, medical care in sickness, ransom if she was abducted, marital satisfaction and burial costs. The girl vowed to supply her husband's physical and sexual needs, bear and rear children, prepare food, make clothing and run the home. Most importantly, she had to ensure that he would be able to study the Torah. A wife was allowed to retain title to any property she owned at the time of the marriage, although her husband could claim the profits it yielded. She however controlled the sale of her property and he had to comply with her wishes in this matter.

Procreation was a positive command to Jewish families; 'Be fertile and increase, fill the earth and master it' (2, Gen. 1.28). This fulfilled the need to establish a family and community, and curbed unlawful sexual temptation. Jewish men had a duty to have children and to ensure this, there were laws to prevent the waste of sperm – the 'spilling of seed' or Onan's sin (2, Gen. 38.9). Other laws dictated the frequency of sex; this could be daily for men of independent means or much less often for others who were away for long periods of time, such as camel drivers (13, p. 129).

Sons were valued over daughters, both to support a man in his old age and so that the son might become 'a scholar of renown'. By contrast, a daughter was considered 'a vain treasure to her father' (7, p. 171).

Infertility was usually blamed on the wife and a man was required to divorce his wife if their infertility lasted for ten years or longer, since he had not fulfilled his duty to procreate. The wife could then remarry, but her second husband could not divorce her for the same reason until another ten years had elapsed.

Polyandry was illegal but polygyny was permitted according to the Talmud, although it was probably infrequent. The law could be interpreted in several ways and allow up to four wives or an unlimited number. The high priest usually had only one. Polygyny was prohibited for European Jews by the tenth century, but continued in Sephardic and some Oriental Jewish communities.

The Pentateuch orders Jews to 'be fruitful', but the Talmud recognizes the need for abstinence or birth control in emergencies such as famines (7, p. 171). Only women were allowed to use a contraceptive, an absorbent cloth or *mokh*. Three groups of women were ordered to use this: girls under the age of 12, since a pregnancy might prove fatal to them; pregnant women, because a second pregnancy could result in a miscarriage; nursing mothers, in case a new pregnancy resulted in premature weaning and the death of their infant. For other women, it is not clear whether the *mokh* was required or recommended or whether it should be used before or after intercourse (13, p. 203).

The Talmud also addresses abortion and miscarriage. If a miscarriage resulted from injury to a pregnant woman in the course of some conflict, financial compensation had to be paid to her husband. If the conflict resulted in the death of a pregnant woman, the penalty was death for the perpetrator (2, Exod. 21.22–25). The foetus was considered to be 'formless' until the fortieth day of pregnancy. Abortion prior to this time was not a crime, since there was no victim. If the mother's life was in danger, the foetus could be destroyed 'until the greater part had emerged' (13, p. 221), meaning – presumably – until half its body had emerged. An abortion could also be ordered when a pregnant woman was under sentence of death.

Much of Talmudic law is directed to the protection of the family, so it is not surprising that so much attention is given to adultery and the avoidance of sexual passions likely to incite infidelity. 'Gossip with women ... [walking] behind a woman along the road ... [crossing] a stream behind a woman' are all cited as possible causes (7, p. 98). Since prostitution was condoned, a wife could not accuse her husband of adultery unless his partner was a married woman, in which case the adulterous woman's husband must divorce her while the adulterous man could remain married. A different set of laws applied to a married woman who was suspected of adultery. She had to undergo a degrading ordeal called *Sotah*, performed before the high priest in the presence of a court. She was required to drink a concoction of 'bitter water' which if she was guilty, would cause her 'belly to distend and her thighs to sag' (13, p. 185). If this occurred, she was divorced and could be flogged and cast out of her community. The children of such relationships were regarded as bastards.

Incestuous relationships are forbidden in Leviticus (2, 20.17–21) and include any sexual relations with females in an extended four-generation family except for the daughters of a man's brother or sister. According to *Halakhic* law, a man can marry his nieces; this is forbidden in Israel and in most countries today (13, p. 179). Individuals found guilty of incest were executed by stoning, burning or strangulation.

Male homosexuality and masturbation were forbidden: 'the hand that reaches below the belly button should be chopped off' (13, p. 65). There is no mention of lesbianism; women were viewed as passive and introverted (13, p. 193).

Divorce is recognized in Judaic law and could only be initiated by a man. It was relatively easy for him to obtain one for almost any reason. A wife's failure to perform any of her many duties could be grounds for divorce, in which case the husband generally had to return the marriage settlement or *Ketubah* and her dowry. Biblical law states that if a spouse fails to please him, 'because he finds something obnoxious about her, and he writes her a bill of divorcement and sends her away' (2, Deut. 24.1). All he had to do was present his wife with a bill of divorce – a *get*; her consent was not needed. The *get* was written in Aramaic and the wording had to be technically correct or the wife was not released from the marriage and was barred from remarriage. Divorce was compulsory for a man if his wife had committed adultery. A man could not remarry a woman who had been married to another man in the interval. Priests were allowed to divorce but could not marry a woman who had been divorced.

Women could not initiate a divorce. A wife could petition a court for a divorce and her husband had to grant her one if he had certain skin conditions or a discharge, or if he neglected or violated his marital obligations or if there was sexual 'incompatibility' (13, p. 84). A woman could not divorce her husband for insanity because an insane husband could not give his consent. An insane wife could not be divorced since this would deprive her of a protector (7, p. 168). Desertion by the husband was not a reason for divorce unless there was proof of his death. Missing husbands were not uncommon because of wars, *diaspora*s or evictions, and unless his death was guaranteed by the testimony of two adult male witnesses, the wife could not remarry and she became an *agunah*. This is a state peculiar to Jewish law and denotes a woman who is still bound to her husband and therefore cannot remarry. The same law applied to a woman whose husband refused her a divorce by not giving her a *get*, or if the dead husband's brother, the *levir*, refused to either marry her or free her by the ceremony of *Halitzah*. *Levirate* marriage is described in the Pentateuch (2, Deut. 25.5-10). The widow of a man who dies without a son – a *Yevameh* – is bound to her husband's brother. He is required to either marry her or renounce her formally in the *Halitzah*. A son of this union assumes the name of the dead husband. If the brother is less than 13 years of age, or mentally incompetent, or refuses to marry her, or his whereabouts are unknown, another brother can take his place and grant the woman her freedom. If no male siblings are available, the woman must remain an *agunah* and is not free to marry anyone else.

In biblical times, children were deemed the property of their fathers. This law was changed later on so that children of less than six years of age could remain with their mothers. The father assumed custody of his sons at the age of six years in order to ensure their proper education and religious instruction, a requirement imposed by Judaic law. A girl remained with her mother so she could receive appropriate instruction in the ways of modesty. Fathers were expected to provide for their children but were not required to provide for a child by a non-Jewish mother.

Jewish law regards a menstruating woman or one who has just given birth, as unclean; she is a *Niddah*. The laws governing *Niddah* refer to the body of regulations included in the *Taharoth* (Purities) order that restrict a woman's activities – sexual as well as others – at these times. The initial reason for these laws was to maintain the purity of the Temple. The law as it appears in Leviticus (2, 15.1-31) applied also to men under certain circumstances, since all bodily discharges – seminal as well as menstrual – were a source of contamination. These are similar to the laws of some other eastern cultures to prevent contamination by the unclean as well as contact between different classes and religious groups. The laws were retained despite the destruction of the Second Temple whose protection was the very purpose for their institution. By the tenth century, the purity laws were firmly in place, particularly in Ashkenazi communities. Sephardic women took them up later and observed them for a longer time (14, p. 109). By the nineteenth century, Ashkenazi women were allowed to attend synagogues and recite benedictions at all times without *Niddah* restrictions, although some women chose to continue to observe this custom (15, p. 112).

Niddah laws decree that women are impure or unclean for 7 days post-menstruation; this was later extended to 14 days by rabbinic legislation. Sex during this time was forbidden. Various household duties were permitted to the *Niddah*, but she could not wash her husband's wine glass, make his bed or wash his hands and feet (13, p. 159). The ceremonial bath or *Mikveh* taken at the end of this time, restored her purity and sex with her husband could now resume. After the birth of a son, *Niddah* was to last for 7 days (2, Lev. 12.1–8) and another 33 must elapse before she could return to the Temple. If she had a girl, the *Niddah* interval was increased to 14 days plus another 66 prior to Temple attendance. Both were to be followed by the *Mikveh*. Initially, the reason for these laws was to maintain the purity of the Temple but later their purpose was to control sexual activity (13, p. 148).

Rape was defined as any sexual act committed under compulsion and was treated as an act of passion rather than one of violence. Several categories of illegal sex are defined in Deuteronomy (2, 22.22–29); one involved sex with a virgin against her will whether she was betrothed or not. Here, the crime is against her father since he was assumed to have suffered financial loss, and compensation was required. The accused had to marry the girl and could never divorce her. Proof was required that the girl had resisted – usually a witness who had heard her cries. If proof was forthcoming, the rapist was sentenced to death by stoning. If the girl did not cry out, the rape was deemed consensual and both were stoned.

Jewish law forbade women from giving evidences or acting as judges despite evidence that there were women judges in earlier times (3, p. 36). These laws allowed all male Israelites to judge civil cases but only 'Priests, Levites and Israelites who can give their daughters in marriage into the priesthood' can judge criminal cases (7, p. 305).

Jewish inheritance laws treat men and women differently. Usually a man's inheritance went to his son and to his son's children: if he had no son, then it passed to his daughter (2, Num. 27.8). If he had neither, it passed to his brothers. First-born sons received a double share of their father's estate but not of their mother's (2, Deut. 21.17). It was assumed that daughters would be maintained out of the estate left to a son. A woman could not inherit from her children but could transmit to them as well as to her husband and his brothers by the same mother (7, p. 343).

The education of children was viewed as a major parental responsibility in Jewish scriptures, to ensure the continuity of their religious heritage. The Torah commanded parents to teach these 'diligently unto thy children' (7, p. 173), promising that 'he who rears his children in the Torah is among those who enjoy the fruit in this world while the capital remains for him in the world to come' (ibid.). Nothing here indicates any difference in the treatment of sons and daughters. But the words 'whoever has a son labouring in the Torah is as though he never dies' (ibid.) clearly identifies the son as the focus of attention.

The people of Israel were unusual for their emphasis on education. By the time the Second Temple was destroyed in 70 CE, there were said to be 394 schools in Jerusalem (16, p. 152). Teachers were appointed in every province, and children were placed in their charge at about the age of six or seven years. The Talmud recommends: 'Under the age of six we do not receive a child as a pupil; from six upwards accept him and stuff him [with Torah] like an ox' (7, p. 175). Teachers were well respected and expected to have high qualifications. Instruction was largely by rote and in Hebrew; there was no consensus concerning the teaching of Greek (7, p. 178).

There was no consensus about the education of girls. One opinion was, 'Let the words of the Torah rather be destroyed by fire than imparted to women,' but another believed the opposite: 'A man is obliged to have his daughter taught Torah' (7, p. 179). In general, the education of girls outside the home was not encouraged since it might lower their morals and distract from their intended roles as wives and mothers: this was believed to have occurred in Greece and Rome. Additional warnings came from Christian communities in which some overly devout women made vows of celibacy. This could be a disaster in a Jewish community. Better for girls to stay home and learn homemaking skills in preparation for marriage. However, these practices varied, and the education of girls depended to some extent on the beliefs and social status of their fathers. Some believed that learning Greek was an accomplishment for girls and therefore should be encouraged.

There are no words in the Talmud specifically prohibiting women from becoming priests, only the lack of precedent, their limited education, obstacles to their study of the Torah and the general belief that they were inferior and their voices were obscene. Added to this was the perception that such a role would interfere with their primary function to procreate, care for the home and children, and enable their husbands to study the Torah.

Folk Law

The Talmud addresses the question of evil spirits, susceptibility to them and the need for protection. The Lilith legend is part of Jewish folklore; Lilith was believed to be the principal female demon who threatened children (7, p. 267). Lilith was Adam's rebellious first wife, created out of earth, who believed she was his equal. This legend supports the first creation story in Genesis, and Lilith's disgrace suggests an attempt by the early sages to promote only one creation story, the second one in which Eve was created out of the body of Adam, who preceded her. Regardless, when Lilith left Adam after refusing to obey him, she was demonized. Angels were dispatched to bring her back and punish her for her independence. The legend was used to remind women to be submissive.

There was a general belief in sorcery and magic, and witches were blamed for local catastrophes such as famines, floods and plagues. Old women were particularly at risk for such accusations. The Talmud says 'women are addicted to witchcraft' (7, p. 161). These beliefs were not peculiar to Judaism.

Judaism and Women

Pre-Talmudic Period

Despite the many wars and exiles that have beset the Jewish people, their scriptures have provided a strong foundation for their cohesion and the practice of their faith, wherever they lived. The Torah spells out the requirements of a model Jewish wife as industrious, good and wise (2, Prov. 31.10–28). It told of revered models of Jewish womanhood such as Sarah, Abraham's wife; Abigail, one of the earlier wives of David; Miriam, the sister of Aaron; Deborah, a religious leader and judge; Hulda; and Hannah – all of whom were honoured as prophetesses. So was Esther, who is said to have saved the Jews from extermination in Babylon in the fifth century BCE; Bathsheba, the mother of Solomon who was influential as a queen-mother; and Ruth, as a model of loyalty.

The Torah also made examples of evil women and their fates. Jezebel, the wife of King Ahab who ruled Israel in the eighth century BCE, was accused of introducing her own polytheistic religion, the worship of Baal, into Israel. Elijah the prophet encouraged the people to rise up against her and she was thrown from a window to her death. This led later to the overthrow of Ahab's dynasty, the Omrides who had brought prosperity to the people of Israel (1, p. 175).

Despite the Judaic affirmation of monotheism and their reverence for Yahweh, a God who had masculine attributes, the people also worshipped Asherah, the goddess of fertility who was his consort, according to fourteenth-century-BCE tablets unearthed at Ugarit (16, p. 152). She was called the 'wife of El' (the Hebrew word for God) and even 'Progenitress of the God' (ibid.).

There is evidence that early in their history, Jewish women played a more prominent role in the practice of their religion. During the pre-rabbinic period, they participated in all religious festivals except for one, the Water Drawing festival (*Simhat Beit ha-Sho'evah*). Women were not segregated from men in the Temple, and they had access to the tabernacle and took part in reading the Torah (17, p. 19). There is no evidence, however, that they led prayers or that they were priests. Women were not restricted in any way inside the Second Temple, although there is mention of a woman's court. Women held administrative positions, they were included in the group of seven who were called up to read the Torah on the Sabbath and they participated in prayers and study groups (ibid.). This seems to have continued at least until the destruction of the Second Temple in 70 CE. According to the New Testament, Saul of

Tarsus – who later became the apostle Paul – expected to see women in the synagogue in Damascus (18, p. 39).

Sometime during the following centuries, the participation of Jewish women in the practice of their religion became more and more restricted. The reason for this is unknown but it seems to have been justified by two excuses: first, that women were unclean and a source of contamination for those around them and ultimately, the tabernacle, and second, that they were a sexual distraction for men when they were praying in the Temple.

Post-Talmudic Period

After the Jews were evicted from Jerusalem and for the first 600 years of the Current Era, the *Tannaim*, both in Palestine and Babylon, spent their time in the preparation of the Talmud. Their product was a set of regulations covering nearly every aspect of life: Talmudic rules were observed until the nineteenth century by observant Jews and to this day by the Orthodox. They were written exclusively by men who viewed themselves as normal and women as a deviation. Women were inferior and according to the Talmud, 'women are a separate people', and Jewish males are 'the only fully fledged partners of God' in his divine covenant (19, p. 20). This covenant was sealed by circumcision, and women were therefore excluded. Motherhood was the prime function of Jewish women and preservation of the family unit was of paramount importance. Men could indulge their sexual needs extramaritally but not women. Female sexuality was a threat to men and had to be controlled in order to maintain the cohesion of the family.

The concern about defiling the tabernacle originated in Leviticus and applied to anyone with a discharge, seminal or otherwise (2, 15. 31). Later, the Talmud singled out menstruants as impure and capable of transmitting their contamination to others. Then the *Baraita de Niddah*, a text of the sixth or seventh centuries and not part of the *Mishnah* or *Halakhah*, went even further. It included nail clippings as pollutants 'lest her husband or child accidentally step on or touch the clippings and, as a result, develop boils and die: a priest whose mother, wife, or any other female member of his household is menstruating, may not bless the people, lest his blessings become a curse: a Sage who partakes of food prepared by a menstruant will forget his learning: a menstruant's spit, breath, and speech cause impurity in others' (14, p. 108). The instructions in this text were modified later by the *Shulhan Arukh*, the 'classic code of Rabbinic Law', which permitted menstruants to hold and read a Torah Scroll. 'The only individuals legally barred from touching the Torah Scroll were men who had seminal emissions (ejaculants)' (ibid. p. 103). The concern now was not fear of contamination but control of male sexuality. But this rule was 'universally ignored' (ibid. p. 103). The *Shulhan Arukh* was written in the mid 1500s CE, about 1000 years later than the Talmud. According to

R. Moses Isserles, an Ashkenazi authority of the sixteenth century, women were not prohibited from entering the synagogue, praying, mentioning God's name or touching a Hebrew book (ibid. p. 105). Despite these words, custom seems to have been stronger than law and women applied these restrictions to themselves and only the menstruant was believed to be contaminated and impure. This addendum was generally accepted and condoned by rabbis. Besides her exclusion from the synagogue, menstruating women were barred from mentioning God's name or from approaching Hebrew books. Initially, these practices were only observed by Ashkenazi and not by Sephardic Jews. Later, this was reversed and the practice was endorsed by Sephardic but became less common among Ashkenazic women.

The practice of separating men from women in synagogues by physical barriers such as screens (*mehitzahs*) or balconies, appears to have no basis in Talmudic law. In earlier days, there was no such requirement except during one festival. The fear of distracting men at prayer and their exposure to women's sexuality seem to have been the reason for them and they remain to this day in most Orthodox and Sephardic synagogues.

One way in which Jewish women were excluded from the practice of their religion was to deny them the opportunity to read the Torah and to be counted in the *Minyan* (the quorum of ten required for prayers) and this continues to be practised in Orthodox Judaism. Admittedly this task would have been a challenge for them because of their lack of education and familiarity with the Torah. But despite improvements in their education later on, there was strong opposition to changing this practice. Women were also excluded from reciting the *Kaddish* – prayers for a dead relative lasting for 11 months – and saying grace after meals.

During the Medieval period, many Jews moved to Eastern Europe and the Ottoman empire because of their persecution in the rest of Europe and here they maintained and reorganized their lives according to their prior cultures. The Sephardim were more conservative and resisted changes in their religious practices. The Ashkenazim made some changes that benefited women: a man could no longer serve his wife with a *get* without her consent and polygyny was banned among Jews living in Western Europe (13, pp. 50, 82). By the twelfth century, the education of girls had become more general, but Jews still did not teach their daughters the Torah, except to remind them of their obligations. This practice persists today among some Orthodox Jews even in the United States.

Israel became an independent, democratic state in 1947 with an elected government but without a constitution. The state religion is Orthodox Judaism although the majority of Jews living there are secular. There are both civil and religious courts; the former include magistrate and district courts over which there is a supreme court. Religious or rabbinical courts have jurisdiction over matters of family law such as marriage and divorce. The Family Courts Law was enacted in 1995 to decide issues concerning alimony, child custody and the division of property. There are special courts for Muslims (Sharia courts) and others for Christian communities. Legislation enacted in the past 50 years protects, to some degree, the rights of women and girls. The Declaration of Independence assured equality in social and political rights, regardless of sex or religion.

Jewish Sects

Reform Judaism

Conferences for Reform rabbis were held in the 1840s and called for equality for women in all aspects of their religion and in 1892 a vote was taken to give them full membership in Reform Judaism. Despite this, change occurred slowly and it was not until 1920 that family pews replaced segregated seating in synagogues and women were called to read the Torah. Later they were admitted to rabbinical school and in 1973 Sally Priesand became the first woman to be ordained as a rabbi (20, p. 71). *Bar Mitzvahs* were reintroduced as well as *Bat Mitzvahs* for girls. Confirmation at age 15 or 16 years was retained. Women could now be counted in the *Minyan*, and recite the *Kaddish* (21, p. 98). In 1972, a committee was established to remove sexist language from the liturgy: the Benediction which offered thanks for not being a woman, was first amended and then deleted completely (22, p. 185). Despite these changes, by 1975, only about 5 per cent of Reform synagogues had appointed women to positions of authority.

Conservative Judaism

In 1955, the Committee of Jewish Laws and Standards, the official *Halakhic* body of the Conservative movement, decided to allow women to read the Torah (11, p. 171ff.). In 1973 they ruled that women could be counted in the *Minyan*, and a year later, in prayers and in offering grace after meals (ibid.). They could also testify as witnesses. After ten years of debate, women were finally admitted as candidates for the rabbinate in 1983, providing they accepted the same obligations as men. The first women rabbis graduated from the Jewish Theological Seminary in 1985. Mixed seating in synagogues was allowed in 1972 and women were accepted as cantors in 1987. They can be elected to positions of authority on synagogue committees and even to their presidencies, and have achieved leadership roles in some regional and national organizations (20, p. 63).

Orthodox Judaism

Only men can be counted in the *Minyan* in Orthodox Judaism; women cannot recite the *Kaddish*, and women cannot be called to read the Torah. Mixed seating was tried in some Orthodox congregations in 1950, but generally men and women are separated by a *mehitzah*, or they are seated in separate parts of the synagogue (23, p. 135). Women cannot be rabbis. Many Orthodox Jews observe a dress code and cover their arms and heads when they are in the synagogue. Most women observe *Niddah* rules. Outside the United States, most Jews are Orthodox.

Sephardic Judaism

Women's voices are viewed as indecent in Sephardic Judaism. They do not serve in positions of authority in the synagogue or community, or as cantors or choir members. In some communities, girls have been prohibited from studying or reading the Torah.

Changes in Israeli Laws Affecting Women

Education

The state of Israel provides 12 years of free, secular education for all children, male and female (24). There are also religious or parochial schools for Christian, Muslim and Orthodox students. Orthodox families frequently limit the education of girls to topics viewed as necessary for their perceived roles as wives and mothers. Most secondary schools segregate their students by sex. Families who moved to Israel from more primitive patriarchal communities have adapted over time to the educational and social practices in Israel. Jews who live outside Israel may follow the educational practices of their host countries, but many attend Jewish parochial schools, if they are available.

Israel has eight universities. A 1987 study found that 48 per cent of individuals aged 25 years or older had completed secondary school, and 24 per cent had obtained a higher education (25). By 2005, 57 per cent of university students were women (26, p. 119). At the present time, more girls than boys complete the twelfth grade. Literacy rates were about 95 per cent for children of 15 years or more and averaged 98 per cent for boys and 94 per cent for girls (24). In 2005 they were both 98 per cent (26, p. 119).

Employment

The Equal Work Law of 1964 gave women equal pay for equal work. Nevertheless, Central Bureau of Statistics figures indicate that women are paid on the average 23 per cent less than men (27). Thirteen per cent of C.E.O. positions were held by women in 2010, twice as many as in the United States. Both men and women serve in the military.

Inheritance and Property Rights

Talmudic oral law dictates the rights of property and inheritance. These bypass a woman in favour of her sons, daughters and her husband's father. She had the right to retain her own property, which was held in trust by her husband from the time of their marriage, but he had the right to the income it generated. Property or money acquired by a wife during her marriage, through inheritance or gifts, also belonged to her. She could not inherit from her husband but acquired back her dowry and her own property and money at his death. If she died first, he received all of her estate (28, p. 37).

Right to Vote

Men and women aged 18 years or more are eligible to vote in local and national elections. Only a few women have been elected to the Knesset, which has 120 members. Usually this number is between 7 and 9 per cent but increased to 15 per cent in the sixteenth Knesset (2003) (29). The number of women serving in municipal and local governments is also low but is increasing slowly (27). Nine women have served as cabinet officers since the state was created in 1948 and one of Israel's first prime ministers was a woman.

Dowries

A woman's family provides her with a dowry at the time of her marriage. This may consist of money, land or jewellery. It became her husband's property when she married but had to be returned to her at his death or their divorce.

Marriage

Before the Rabbinic period, a marriage was valid by intercourse, financial agreement or prior engagement. Over time and because of social disapproval reinforced by punishment, the first two were eliminated.

A wife's duties besides her three religious ones are clearly identified in the Talmud. The husband's duty is to maintain his wife and fulfil her sexual needs (*onah*), avoiding any waste of semen in the process. The Talmud is most specific in defining the frequency of, as well as the 'how' of sexual intercourse (13, p. 130). If a wife failed to live up to her husband's expectations, a list of her faults would be read aloud in the synagogue, and unless she corrected her shortcomings, she could be divorced.

Israel does not recognize civil marriages. All marriages here must follow Orthodox rites and couples wishing to avoid this must wed elsewhere. The Child Marriage act of 1951 made the minimum marriage age for girls 17 years, two years older than previously permitted (30, ch. 4).

Incest is clearly defined as a forbidden relationship in both the Bible and the Talmud. These laws have remained unchanged. While Jewish scriptures forbid incestuous relationships to men, punishment applies to both men and women.

Divorce

Jewish men have retained their biblical right to divorce their wives who have no such right. In the Middle Ages, Rabbi Gershom instituted a rule requiring a man to obtain permission from his wife before divorcing her (13, p.83). This did little to repair the inequality. In Israel today, a woman may appeal to a rabbinical court to compel a husband to grant her a *get* because of his various physical afflictions, or neglect of marital obligations or sexual incompatibility. If he persists in his refusal, she may request the intervention of a civil court and police assistance to procure a *get*. But this does not solve the problem since women still cannot initiate divorce or procure one without a *get*. Without one, women are denied the right to remarry and have to remain an *agunah*.

Outside Israel, Jews can obtain civil divorces according to the laws of the state they reside in, but recognition or approval of this by a rabbinic court is not guaranteed. To address this, the state of New York enacted legislation in 1983 to deny a civil divorce unless the seeker had removed all barriers to his former partner's remarriage or, in other words, obtained a divorce valid under Jewish law (13, p. 110). Reform Jews follow the laws of the state or country where the divorce is filed.

Levirate marriage is clearly prescribed in the Hebrew Bible and is therefore part of Jewish law (2, Deut. 25.5–10). Despite this, the state of Israel forbids this practice since the result would be polygyny. *Halitzah* provides a solution for those Jews, among them many Sephardics, who support *Levirate* marriage. A court may compel an unwilling *levir* to perform *Halitzah* by threatening imprisonment (22, p. 117). This dichotomy between Jewish biblical and civil law remains a problem in Israeli jurisprudence.

Family Courts were established in Israel in 1955 to handle many domestic matters and tend to be more generous to women. In order to limit double jurisdiction, the Knesset ruled that divorce cases that are already being handled by a rabbinic court, cannot be transferred (31).

The Agunah

Agunot (plural of *agunah*), are women whose husbands disappeared or died without valid evidence of their deaths, or are incompetent, or refuse to give them a *get*, or whose *levir*s refuse either to marry them or free them by *Halitzah*. According to Judaic law, such women are not free to remarry, and doing so would constitute adultery and their children would be bastards (13, pp. 102–13). If a woman ignores the law, she must divorce the second husband and should the first reappear, she may not remarry him. *Agunot* are peculiar to Judaic law.

Polygyny

Polygyny was banned when Israel became a state. This was a problem for Sephardic and Oriental Jews who came from countries where polygyny was still permitted by local custom. The law therefore exempts Jews who had more than one wife when they arrived in Israel. There are also other rare exceptions to monogamy, but these only apply to men in special situations as in a wife's disappearance or death without proof, her insanity or her refusal to accept a *get*. Permission for his remarriage then requires the consent of one hundred rabbis from three different regions.

Adultery

Different standards are used to judge adultery in men and women. A woman is the property of her husband and may not have sex with any other man. A man is free of this restriction, at least if the adulteress is single and available. If married, she must be divorced, but the adulterer is not punished. In addition, the adulteress is treated as an outcast in the community. The biblical punishment of death by stoning (2, Lev. 20.10) has been replaced by divorce. The ordeal of *Sotah* for married women suspected of adultery had mostly disappeared by about 70 CE (13, p. 188).

Child Custody

There are two conflicting opinions in Jewish law concerning the custody of children: one invokes Talmudic law and the other considers the best interests of the child. Talmudic law holds that all children under the age of six years must be placed in the mother's care. Boys over the age of six should go to the father, girls to the mother. The Equal Rights Law of 1951 allowed married women to be guardians of their children. While the father is obligated to support his children, the mother is not. There are variances to these rules, and here again there are two views; one follows the best interest of the child, the other modifies the Talmudic law if a parent is unfit (32).

Rape and Spousal Abuse

Rape is viewed as an act of passion in Jewish scriptures but it is now seen as one of violence and punished accordingly (13, p. 239–55). The Talmud recognizes spousal rape and a 1982 Israeli court ruling upheld this decision.

Wife beating was viewed by some as a violation of a man's duty to honour his wife, as promised in the *ketubah*. Apparently this opinion is not shared by many men, for there are reported to be 100,000 abused women living in Israel (13, p. 96).

Practice of Law

In Talmudic law a woman cannot testify as a witness but in Israel today, men and women have equal rights in the administration of civil and criminal law. The requirements to practice law in the state apply equally to men and women. Recent estimates indicate that 39 per cent of active lawyers in Israel are women and, despite Talmudic laws to the contrary, 253 or 48 per cent of their judges are women (29).

Reproductive Rights

The commandment to 'be fertile and increase' (2, Gen. 1.28) was given to both Adam and Eve, but Jewish law maintains this applies to men only, for whom procreation is a duty (13, p. 199). Jewish men may not use any method of birth control and Orthodox Jews tend to obey these laws. Israeli women must obtain prescriptions for birth control medication, diaphragms and intra-uterine-devices from physicians and these are usually restricted to married women who have had one child (33).

Jewish scriptures are opposed to abortion except to save the life of the mother. They also clearly distinguish between a woman and her foetus; the latter is not a person but an object without independent status. This interpretation was complicated by differing opinions in the twelfth century which argued about the legality of destroying a foetus before or during birth to save the life of the mother (13, ps. 227, 232). Issar Unterman – chief rabbi of Israel from 1960 to1970 – expanded the grounds for abortion to include situations causing stress to the mother. Support for more liberal abortion laws also came from Russian immigrants who were accustomed to easy access to this in their own country.

The Knesset enacted legislation in 1977 permitting abortion for many reasons including maternal health, adultery, rape, child pregnancy and foetal abnormalities, as well as pressing socio-economic factors (13, p. 237). A committee of two physicians and a social worker must authorize abortions. Opposition from *Agudat Yisrael* – an ultra-conservative political party – led to the revocation of the socio-economic reason for abortion in 1980; physical and mental health replaced it in a number of cases. Orthodox Jews remain opposed to abortion since they view it as murder, while non-Orthodox Jews interpret the law more liberally (ibid.).

Public Health Data

The birth rate in Israel was reported to be 18.67 per 1,000 live births in 2003, and there were 2.5 children born per woman; the number for Muslim women was almost double that of Jewish women (34). Infant mortality rates were 26 in Palestinian and 5.3 in Jewish infants per 1,000 live births (34). Maternal mortality was 11 per 100,000 live births in 2000; this rate included Palestinian and Jewish women (35). Life expectancy was about 82 years for women and 77 for men (34).

Summary

Jewish history extends back over several millennia during which time its people experienced repeated exiles and subjugation by foreign powers. Jews were finally evicted from Palestine in the first century CE and emigrated to Europe, the Middle East and Asia where they experienced repeated episodes of persecution. Finally, in 1947, Israel became an independent nation after which thousands of Jews returned to their homeland.

The Jewish scriptures include the Torah – dating back before the CE – and the Talmud which was assembled by rabbis in the first five centuries of the CE. It contains laws – the *Halakhah* – governing every aspect of Jewish life. In addition to the written laws, many Jews believe the Oral Torah allows for modification in these laws when appropriate to different times and places.

Prior to the Rabbinic period, Jewish women participated in Temple activities, prayers and festivals. Later they were restricted from taking part in religious rites because they were viewed as unclean: they were separated in the synagogues to avoid distracting Jewish men while they prayed and control their sexual desires. They were required to observe *Niddah* laws. Boys were valued over girls who were considered too unworthy to study the Torah. The primary focus of women was to be their husbands, families and homes. Men could be polygynous, had the right to divorce and were favoured by inheritance laws. Girls were denied an equal education, could not give evidence in court or be judges, and had to endure the indignity of the *agunah*.

Reform and Conservative Judaism began in the eighteenth century and relaxed some of the restrictions applied to Jewish women and amended their liturgies to reflect a greater respect for them. Orthodox Judaism continues the original practices and is observed in most Jewish communities outside the United States. It is the state religion of Israel. It believes the Torah is the word of God and cannot be amended or reinterpreted. Ultra-orthodox religious groups in Israel maintain an unusual degree of political power for a democratic nation.

Despite the assertions of *Halakhic* immutability, some Judaic practices have changed over time: men seeking a divorce must obtain spousal approval; the ordeal of *Sotah* is no longer used for women suspected of adultery; death by stoning is no longer the punishment for adultery, and polygyny and therefore *Levirate* marriage is illegal in Israel. This did not extend to banning the practice of *agunot*.

Israel provides equal education for girls and boys, women can vote and seek election and they serve in the military. They are still disadvantaged by divorce, inheritance and child custody laws. Women are still restricted in the practice of their religion where they cannot be called to the Torah, nor be counted in the *Minyan* and their segregation in the synagogue demeans them still further.

The basic concepts that women are inferior and that they are unclean in the eyes of the Jewish religion, have been addressed by a number of women and men who agree that these need to be changed: simply emphasizing their separate and important but unequal status is insufficient (36, 37, 38). It is difficult to see how a religion in which only men have traditionally held theological authority, can effect any meaningful progress without much more input from women.

References

1   Finkelstein, Israel. and Neil A. Silberman. *The Bible Unearthed*. New York. The Free Press. 2001.

2   *Tanakh: The Holy Scripture*. Philadelphia. Tr. Jewish Publication Society. 1995.

3   Friedman, Richard E. *Who Wrote the Bible*. New York. Summit Books. 1987.

4   Revill, T. C. *World History*. London. Longman's, Green and Co. 1953.

5   Williams, J. G. *Judaism*. Madras. Quest Theosophical Publishing House. 1980.
6   Vermes, Geza. *The Complete Dead Sea Scrolls in English*. New York. Penguin Books. 1998.
7   Cohen, Abraham. *Everyman's Talmud*. New York. Schocken Books. 1949.
8   'Biblical Literature'. *Encyclopedia Britannica* (2003). www.britannica. com/eb/article.
9   *Encyclopedia Britannica*. Ed. W. Benton. University of Chicago Press. 1968.
10   Berkovitz, Michael. 'Transcending 'Tzimmes and Sweetness': Recovering the History of Zionist Women in Central and Western Europe, 1987–1993'. In Maurie Sacks, ed. *Active Voices. Women in Jewish Culture*. Chicago. University of Illinois Press. 1995.
11   *Religion in the Holy Land*. www.ifamericansknew.org/history/religion.
12   Bariera, Julio T. *The Jewish Bible and the Christian Bible*. Grand Rapids. Brill Eerdmans. 1998.
13   Biale, Rachel. *Women in Jewish Law*. New York. Schocken Books. 1995.
14   Cohen, Shaye. J. D. 'Purity and Piety: the Segregation of Menstruants from the Sancta'. In *Daughters of the King*. Eds. Susan Grossman and Rivka Haut. Philadelphia. Jewish Publication Society. 1992.
15   Hauptman, Judith. 'Women and the Conservative Synagogue'. Ibid.
16   Picknett, Lynn. *Mary Magdalene*. New York. Carroll and Graf. 2003.
17   Grossman, Susan. 'Women and the Jerusalem Temple'. In *Daughters of the King*. Eds. Susan Grossman and Rivka Haut. Philadelphia. Jewish Publication Society. 1992.
18   Safrai, Hannah. 'Women and the Ancient Synagogue'. Ibid. 1992.
19   Baskin, Judith. R. 'Silent Partners: Women as Wives in Rabbinic Literature'. In *Active Voices in Jewish Culture*. Ed. Maurie Sacks. Urbana. University of Illinois Press. 1995.
20   Nadell, Pamela. S. and Rita J. Simon. 'Ladies of the Sisterhood: Women in the American Reform Synagogue, 1990–1930'. Ibid. 1995.
21   Haut, Rivka. Are Women Obligated to Pray? In *Daughters of the King*. Eds. Susan Grossman and Rivka Haut. Philadelphia. The Jewish Publication Society. 1992.
22   Daum, Annette. 'Language and Liturgy'. ibid.
23   Haut, Rivka. Women's Prayer Groups and the Orthodox Synagogue. ibid.
24   *Indicators on Literacy*. 2000. UNESCO. www.un.org/unsd/demographic/ social/literacy.
25   *Education: University in Israel*. Israel Science and Technology Division. 2004.
26   Seager, Joni. *The Penguin Atlas of Women in the World*. Penguin Books. New York. 2009.

27   Chazen, N. *Women in public life*. www.Jewish virtual library.org/J source and *Culture/women in public life* html.the American-Israeli Coop. Ent.- 2004.

28   Konvitz, Milton. R. *Judaism and Human Rights*. New York. W. W. Norton. 1972.

29   Globes on Line. Israel's Business Arena. www globes.co.il/serveen/globes/ print.

30   Priesand, Sally. *Judaism and the New Woman*. New York. Behrman House. 1975.

31   *Rabbinical courts versus civil courts*. Israel Yearbook and Almanac. 1999. The American-Israel Cooperative Enterprise. J. Law. com. 2004.

32   Broyde, M. J. *Child Custody in Jewish Law*. www. j.law.com/art/ childus2. 2005.

33   Shtarkshall, R. A. and M. Zemach, www. 2.hu-berlin.de/sexology/ES/ Israel. 2005.

34   *World Population Data of PRB* www.prb.org 2003.

35   Maternal Mortality Estimates by WHO, UNICEF and UNFPA. 2000.

36   Adler, Rachel. 'The Jew Who Wasn't There. Halakha and the Jewish woman'. In *Contemporary Jewish Ethics*. Ed. M. M. Kellner. New York. Sanhedrin Press. 1971.

37   Gordis, R. A. *Dynamic Halakha: Principles and Procedures in Jewish Law*. Judaism 1979.

38   Ozick, C. 'Notes Toward Finding the Right Question'. In *On Being a Jewish Feminist*. Ed. S. Heschel. New York. Schocken Books. 1980.

Additional Bibliography

Bright, J. *A History of Israel*. Philadelphia: Westminster Press. 1959.

Carmody, Denise. L. 'Jewish Women'. In *Women and World Religions*. Ed. D. L. Carmody. Upper Saddle River. Prentice Hall. 1987.

Drucker, Malka. *Women and Judaism*. Westport. Conn. Praeger. 2009.

Greenberg, B. *A Woman and Judaism: A View from Tradition*. Philadelphia: Jewish Publication Society of America. 1981.

Noth, M. *A History of Pentateuchal Traditions*. New York. Scholars Press. 1981.

Swidler, L. *Women in Judaism*. Metuchen. Scarecrow Press. 1976.

Chapter 4

Christianity

History

Jesus and the Beginning of Christianity

Christianity, the religion of nearly one third of the world's population at the present time, began with Jesus Christ, a Jew. He was born in either 3 or 4 BCE in what is now Palestine (1, p. 58). Other than his birth and infancy, the first mention of Jesus in the New Testament Gospels is his appearance at the Temple after his parents had noticed his absence (2, Lk. 2.49). The second was at his baptism by John the Baptist in about 29 CE. John was beheaded two years later (3, p. 37). A short time after, Jesus started his own ministry and this lasted only for two to three years (2, Lk. 3.12). He was then about 30 years old. He selected his 12 disciples from among John's followers and many others joined them. Jesus chose Simon (later called Peter), a married man, to lead his select group of disciples who were all Jews. The friends and followers of Jesus included many women and five of the most frequently mentioned are Mary Magdalene, Mary of Bethany, Joanna, Susanna and Salome (4, p. 54).

Jesus travelled throughout the region, teaching and performing acts perceived as miracles. He criticized and enraged the Pharisees by violating purity laws and performing miracles on the Sabbath but refused to incite rebellion against their Roman rulers. He was brought before Caiaphas, the high priest, condemned for blasphemy, then turned over to Pontius Pilate the Roman procurator and crucified, a punishment reserved for slaves and non-Roman criminals (1, p. 60). Within a short period of the death of Jesus, Stephen, the first Christian martyr died by stoning in Jerusalem, after he was accused of blasphemy (5, vol. 21, p. 29).

There are no extant accounts of the life and words of Jesus by his contemporaries. He himself wrote nothing that has survived and his followers were mostly illiterate. The information we have was passed down by word of mouth and eventually written down 40 or more years later in the Gospels and other non-canonical works, some of which were discovered very much later. The earliest account in the New Testament of the Jesus sect is by Paul and dates from about 50 CE. Paul was not one of the disciples but a devout Pharisee and a Roman citizen. Initially he persecuted the early Christians but then, after some type of event on the road to Damascus, interpreted later as a religious experience, he reversed courses and transferred all of his energies to the promotion of his new faith. Paul spent some time in Jerusalem with Peter and James the brother of Jesus, and then about ten years in Syria before embarking on his missionary journeys. It is not known whether Paul ever saw Jesus. He is credited with playing a dominant role in the spread of Christianity and its transformation into a universal religion.

The early Christians consisted of Hebrew-speaking Judaeo-Christians and a Greek-speaking group, the Hellenists (6, p. 13). They differed in their beliefs concerning the conditions of membership in their sect, and especially whether Gentiles could convert without fulfilling all the requirements of Mosaic Law, including dietary laws and circumcision. A council was held in Jerusalem to resolve these questions at which Peter and Paul had the support of James – the brother of Jesus – who headed the Jerusalem Christians called the Nazarene sect. They decided that uncircumcised non-Jews would be allowed to convert to Christianity (7, p. 24). Peter believed that Jewish dietary laws should be obeyed but festivals need not be observed. Paul argued against obedience to Mosaic Law with the exception that converts must 'abstain from what has been sacrificed to idols and from blood and from what has been strangled and from unchastity' (2, Acts 15.29). This decision to include Gentiles would convert Christianity into a universal religion, no longer a sect of Judaism. Judaeo-Christians however, maintained their opposition and this was the cause or excuse for continued opposition wherever Christians proselytized.

Paul made three well-described journeys between 45 and 54 CE before returning to Jerusalem where his preaching provoked unrest (4, p. 27). He was arrested and eventually sent to Rome where he lived under house arrest for two years, but was allowed to preach. He was eventually beheaded sometime between 62 and 64 CE during the rule of the emperor Nero (54–68 CE), some 30 years after his Christian baptism. Peter travelled to Rome where he was most likely crucified during the same period. James the head of the Jerusalem Church was seized during a Jewish riot in about 62 CE and thrown from the walls of the city (1, p. 101; 2, Gal. 1.18-19).

In 66 CE, the Jews revolted against the Romans in their homeland and four years later, Vespasian besieged and then razed Jerusalem. The Temple was destroyed and about one million Jews perished (1, p. 117). By the end of the first century of the Current Era, all the disciples were dead, new members were mostly Greek-speaking and the Church was in turmoil, beset by heresies and disputes, many of which concerned the origin of Jesus, his humanity and divinity.

The First 400 Years

The Church expanded rapidly during its first 400 years and by the end of the second century, was well established in France and North Africa and beginning to spread into Britain, Spain and Germany (6, vol. 7, p. 843). In the east, it spread through Mesopotamia to the Russian border. Opposition from Rome continued and in 202 CE Emperor Septimus Severus forbade Christian conversions and Decius (249–251) ordered all his subjects to worship Roman gods. Persecution came in waves and peaked under Valerian and again under Diocletian who reorganized the Roman Empire by dividing it into eastern and western parts, taking the former for himself (4, p. 63). Constantine eventually became the ruler of a united empire in 324. He halted further Christian persecutions and made Christianity the religion of the state, hoping this would unite his empire and bolster his own claim to divinity (3, p. 134). By then, nearly one half of his subjects were Christians. He bestowed many benefits on the Christian Church including freedom from taxation, clerical privilege and jurisdiction in civil cases. In addition, the Church was given land so that it was able to construct many churches. One of the emperor's decrees was to observe Sundays as weekly holidays (8, p. 73). In 330 – with Christian clergy presiding – the 'City of Constantine' was inaugurated at Byzantium. Constantine was baptized on his deathbed in 337 and buried in Constantinople.

The Christianization of the Roman Empire coincided with its decline and final disintegration in the early fifth century. Many blamed this on the Christians. They in turn adopted the organization and administrative hierarchy of Rome, replacing the emperor with a bishop and later, a pope. By the early second century, the Church had a three-level administration or ministry consisting of an overseer or bishop, presbyters or elders and deacons. The overseer's job was to preside over the celebration of the Eucharist, a Christian celebration similar to an old Essene rite in an otherwise Jewish service (3, p. 48). The presbyter's role was administrative but he could also preside over the Eucharist. The deacon's responsibility was mainly pastoral and he served as the main contact with the people.

After the destruction of Jerusalem, Rome became the primary *see* or jurisdiction of the Church and its bishop, the overall head. Other *sees* – each with its own bishop – were set up in Alexandria, Antioch, Constantinople and Hippo, where Augustine became bishop in 396. Alexandria grew into a major centre of Christian philosophy under Clement and then Origen, as did Carthage under Tertullian. Monasticism had its beginning at the end of the third century, starting with solitary ascetics – both male and female – who withdrew from contact with their fellow men and women to meditate, often in the desert.

Many different Christian sects appeared during the first centuries after the death of Jesus, each with its own scriptures. One of these, the Gnostics, predated Christianity but Christian Gnosticism began sometime in the second century (7, p. 21). Its followers denied the creation story and the humanity of Jesus. Valentinus (100 CE) founded a school of Gnosticism that generated great hostility in Rome and he was excommunicated. Marcion, another Gnostic, believed in two gods, one the creator and the other the one revealed by Jesus. He repudiated the scriptures particularly the Old and New Testaments, except for the Gospel of Luke and the ten Pauline Epistles. He was attacked by both Irenaeus, bishop of Lyons, and Tertullian. Monarchism started sometime in the second and third centuries and claimed God the Father was the sole deity (7, p. 40). Of its two forms, the Dynamists believed Christ was human, the Modalists that the Father and Son were the same. Montanism started in Asia Minor in the second century in response to the perceived moral laxity of the Church. It insisted that followers must be ascetics, celibate and avoid marriage. Manichaeism was a Gnostic religion originated by Mani in Babylonia (Persia) in the third century; it believed that all matter was evil. It spread to the west in the fourth century and survived in Baghdad until the tenth century. Arius, a pupil of Origen, lived in the fourth century and believed Jesus was not of one substance with the Father and was therefore separate and not divine. Arianism had a powerful effect on the early Church and influenced it for centuries (7, p. 45). Arius was exiled after the Nicaean Ecumenical Council in 435 and died a short time later, but Arianism persisted for another 300 years and for longer in certain Protestant faiths.

One group of Christians – based in Rome – eventually prevailed and became the orthodox sect, due in part to its rigidly hierarchical clergy, armed with a creed and canons (9, p. 216). It dealt with heresies initially by excommunication and banishment but later by more drastic means including execution, often by burning and eventually murdered more Christians than the Romans had done in their period of rule (10, p. 319).

The Dark Ages: 400 up to 1000 CE

The Dark Ages began in the fifth century CE. At that time, Rome still controlled most of Europe as well as the Balkans, Asia Minor, Palestine and parts of North Africa, including the cities of Carthage and Hippo, but the empire had been in decline for a number of years. The Goths occupied Northern Gaul and in 410, sacked Rome. Many of them were Arian Christians who respected the Western Church and the Bishop of Rome. They, along with many other tribes living in Europe, were under attack by the Huns, nomadic fighters who came out of the Russian steppes. They ravaged parts of Italy but according to legend, Attila, their leader, was persuaded to pull back from Rome by Pope Leo the Great (8, p. 97). The Roman Church meanwhile converted many of the barbarians and continued to expand. Patrick reached Ireland in the fifth century: the Church there was unique for a time and followed the practices of the Nazarenes without the governance of bishops and the hierarchical structure of the Roman Empire (8, p. 85). But by the end of the eighth century, almost all of Western Europe had acknowledged the leadership of the Roman Church.

Schism with the Eastern Church

Meanwhile, the Eastern Empire in Byzantium and its impregnable fortress, Constantinople remained politically strong and independent. By the end of the fifth century, Rome and Constantinople and the Western and Eastern Churches were cut off from each other (8, p. 149). The rapid spread of Islam at the beginning of the seventh century affected both Eastern and Western Churches. Muslim Arabs captured Jerusalem in 638, followed soon after by Alexandria, North Africa and nearly all of Spain. They were finally halted in 732 CE by Charles Martel at Poitiers.

By the mid-sixth century, Rome and surrounding regions were in chaos but the Christian Church provided some degree of stability. Gregory the Great was elected pope in 590 and soon after enacted major reforms in worship and church administration. 'Servile labour' on Sundays was forbidden, perjury would be punished and the right of sanctuary was established, although this had an earlier Greco-Roman origin (8, p. 300). Churches were constructed and monasteries were established and eventually became important centres of learning, literature and the arts.

Charlemagne (742–814), the grandson of Charles Martel, was crowned Holy Roman emperor in St. Peters in Rome. This apparently came as a surprise to the emperor, at the hands of a pope who had dreams of uniting the Eastern and Western Churches and restoring the Roman Empire. From now on, conversion to Christianity was by coercion or force and the alternative was death. Bishops and other clergy were usually appointed by secular leaders and often had no religious training. Most of them were men who controlled much wealth and had large landholdings. To add to this, Charlemagne instituted a tithe of 10 per cent on landowners to support the Church.

A period of civil unrest followed Charlemagne's death and by the end of the ninth century, a state of near anarchy existed in Europe (8, p. 482ff.). This together with the threat of further invasions, encouraged the spread of feudalism which had started earlier with Charles Martel. Feudalism involved the surrender of allegiance to overlords in return for protection, by freemen and peasants who worked the land (11, p. 160). These feudal lords generated the armies used for the crusades later on. This period of feudalism lasted for about 250 years during which there was practically no theological control. Meanwhile, Viking invasions were occurring in Northern Europe as well as Arab incursions into Italy, and the papacy was dishonoured and degraded.

Meanwhile, the Eastern Church was spreading through the Balkans to include Slav, Moravian and Bulgur people and much of Italy was also under its control. It spread into Russia in the eighth century following the conversion of its ruler, Prince Vladimir. Architecture and literature flourished in Constantinople where the rulers had considerable power over religious leaders.

The separation of the Eastern and Western Churches occurred over a period of time and had several causes. Barbarian invasions in the west and Arab conquests in the east were obvious causes. Differences in religious practices were another. The Eastern Church promoted mysticism and revered relics and icons. In the ninth century, Pope Leo III ordered the destruction of icons in obedience to the commandment forbidding idolatry. The Western Church promoted clerical celibacy while only bishops were celibate in the Eastern Church. In 589, the Western Church accepted the Filioque clause into the creed, thanks to the support of Charlemagne. This said that the 'Holy Ghost proceedeth from the Father and the Son' (12, pp. 152). The Eastern Church did not accept this. Neither did it believe in purgatory, the sale of indulgences, or the use of unleavened bread at the Eucharist. The Western Church objected to the requirement that the Eastern Patriarch must approve a pope before he could be elected (12, ps. 153, 154). The overall supremacy of the pope is not recognized by the Eastern Church, which has an Ecclesiastical Council rather than a single authority. For this and other reasons, three papal legates excommunicated the Patriarch and his followers in 1054. The Patriarch in return, excommunicated the legates. One additional insult to the Eastern Church was the sacking of Constantinople by crusaders in the twelfth century. This long-standing decree of excommunication was finally rescinded by Pope Paul VI in 1964.

Nestorian and Pelagian Heresies

In addition to Arianism, which persisted particularly in the Eastern Church, two important heresies occurred in this period: Nestorianism – which was influential in the east – and Pelagianism. Nestor was a monk who believed in the human nature of Christ and therefore opposed the term *Theotokos* – Mother of God – for the Virgin Mary (7, p. 63). In 431, the Ecumenical Council of Ephesus ruled that *Theotokos* was valid. The result was that Nestor was excommunicated – along with a number of others – and died in misery in the desert. Monophysites are followers of Nestor and believe in the single nature of Christ; they survive today as the Armenian, West Syrian, Jacobite and Coptic Churches of Egypt and Ethiopia. Pelagius was an English monk who was shocked by the moral laxity he witnessed at the end of the fourth century in Rome (7, p. 87). The heresy ascribed to him remains one of the most logical explanations of the nature of man and his free will. He questioned the concept of original sin – transmitted at conception – and therefore the need for infant baptism. He denied predestination and did not believe that grace was essential for the performance of good works. Rather, individuals could themselves determine to live sinless lives and achieve salvation. Pelagius was condemned as a heretic and anathematized (7, p. 91).

The Middle Ages: 1000 up to 1500 CE

The Middle Ages began in the second millennium. By this time foreign invasions of Western Europe had ceased and the region was mostly Christian (8, p. 594). Here the Western Church wielded considerable power but was disgraced by scandal and crime, in part the result of conflicts between secular and religious authorities (13, p. 205). Pope Gregory VII called for reforms, especially in clerical celibacy and simony. He confronted the Holy Roman emperor Henry IV and then excommunicated him (13, p. 212). The king retaliated and replaced the pope with a rival. This conflict over the separation of powers simmered on for centuries.

Meanwhile, Pope Urban II called for a crusade to recapture Jerusalem, which had fallen to the Seljuk Turks in the eleventh century, promising remission of sins and eternal life for all who died in the attempt (14, p. 176). Jerusalem was retaken. Six more crusades occurred over the next 200 years and during the fourth of these, Constantinople was sacked. Muslim forces led by Saladin eventually recaptured Jerusalem and treated Christians there with much more mercy than had been extended to the Arabs by Christians in the first crusade.

A crusade 'in their midst' (7, pp. 107–10) was launched by Pope Innocent III in the thirteenth century against the Albigensians, citizens of the city of Albi in the south of France. Their heresy was Dualism, which had similarities to Manichaeism of an earlier age; they believed good was a spiritual force, which proceeded from God while material things came from Satan and were therefore evil. The logical *sequitur* was the denial of Jesus' humanity since he came from God. They also denied the supremacy of Rome. These beliefs spread through Lombardy, the south of France and Northern Spain. Over 100,000 so-called heretics were slaughtered at Montsegur and this massacre remains one of the indelible crimes of the Christian Church (3, p. 222).

In the same period, Pope Gregory IX turned his attention to the Jews who were required to wear clothing identifying them as a different people and their books were burned. They were expelled from England in 1290 (13, p. 227).

Several well-known monastic orders were established in this period and provided increasingly for the social needs of the populace, including education and the care of the sick and the poor (13, p. 213). These institutions, as well as scholars like Thomas Aquinas, and mystics both men and women, helped revitalize the Western Church in the thirteenth century. Meanwhile, the feudal system was disappearing as trade and commerce developed and cities grew in importance and population. During the fifteenth century, the Bible and other books were translated into the vernacular and reading material became more generally available with the advent of the letterpress. As a result, sacred literature was no longer a monopoly of the Church and its priests.

Throughout the turmoil of the Dark and Middle Ages, the Christian Church provided some degree of stability which transcended local rulers and national boundaries. By the sixteenth century, the Church held virtually all the power, controlled nearly all the thrones of Northern and Western Europe and was its main centre of learning. But Europe was changing and the Church failed to recognize both the rise of nationalism and the need to correct its own corruption. Increasing trade brought the rise of a middle class with money to purchase books and the time to benefit from new centres of learning. The fall of Constantinople in 1453 drove the scholarship of Byzantium west and the Renaissance in Italy changed art from its focus on religious to more humanistic themes. Explorations in the New World brought additional wealth. Yet the Church continued to insist that it alone could interpret the scriptures and made little effort to correct the abuses identified by reformers like John Wycliffe and John Huss. Wycliffe, an Englishman died in 1384 but his body – or what remained of it – was exhumed and burned after the Council of Constance condemned him 31 years later (6, vol. 23, p. 830). Huss, Rector of Prague University, was burned at the stake, despite a promise of safe passage. Finally, Pope Leo X's scheme to raise funds for the repair of St. Peter's by the sale of indulgences, provided the final spark for the Reformation.

The Reformation

In 1517, the Protestant Reformation 'broke up medieval Christendom' (6, vol. 19, p. 37) and generated several new Protestant faiths. Martin Luther, a parish priest in Wittenberg (Germany) had visited Rome in 1510 and was shocked by the corruption he saw there (7, p. 126). The final straw for him was the purchase of indulgences by his parishioners, in order to shorten the time a relative's soul had to remain in purgatory. These indulgences carried the pope's signature and the larger the contribution, the greater the amount of time forgiven. Luther's objections were outlined in the 95 theses, which he nailed to the church door of Wittenberg Castle (7, p. 127). Here he argued that the pope had 'no jurisdiction over purgatory' (7, p. 127). Later he protested against 'the exclusive right of the pope to interpret the Bible' (7, p. 129). Luther was excommunicated in 1521 but saved from a heretic's death by friends in high places. He continued to attack papal power, proposed other reforms and abolished convents and many monasteries. He wrote many books and by 1522, had translated the entire New Testament into German and later did the same to the Old Testament. Lutheranism was slow to spread in Germany until the German princes' decision to determine their own state's religion. Its spread in Scandinavia, Finland and Iceland was more rapid.

Protestant Churches

Other Protestant churches appeared in the sixteenth century. John Calvin whose followers became Presbyterians, was born in France but broke with the Catholic Church in 1533 when he moved to Switzerland (7, p. 140ff.). He advocated strict adherence to the scriptures, believed in original sin and interpreted predestination to mean that only individuals pre-selected by God could achieve salvation. His goal was moral reformation and a changed form of worship. He had little tolerance for non-conformers. Calvin established a ruling church body with pastors, teachers, deacons and elders. John Knox, a disciple of Calvin, set up the Presbyterian Church in Scotland where it became the state religion. In France, Calvin's followers were the Huguenots: 20,000–50,000 of them were slaughtered in a single night in 1572 during the massacre of St. Bartholomew's Day (7, p. 145). To celebrate this, Pope Pius V ordered the singing of a Te Deum and a special medal was struck (15, p. 80). Presbyterianism also spread to Germany and to the Netherlands where it became the Dutch Reformed Church.

A more conservative Protestant church developed in England, the Church of England or Anglican Church. Here, there had been calls for church reform prior to the sixteenth century, prompted in part by papal claims to authority over the state, clerical ignorance, moral laxity and the imposition of taxes to support the bishops. The precipitating factor came out of the divorce of Henry VIII and Catherine of Aragon, who had been previously married to Henry's deceased brother, Arthur. Although illegal by Church law, the pope had given his dispensation for Henry's marriage to his sister-in-law, persuaded in large part by Catherine's powerful nephew, Charles V. Then in 1532, Parliament denied the transfer of funds to Rome. Henry was excommunicated and became the head of the English Church (7, p. 150).

Despite or perhaps because of its English rulers, Ireland's adherence to the Church of Rome grew stronger and bishops of both denominations – Anglican and Catholic – were appointed there.

Pope Paul III convened the Council of Trent in 1545, in response to Charles V who hoped for a reconciliation with the Protestants and the reunification of Germany (16, p. 274). Despite nearly eight years of effort, this failed. Conservative and orthodox views prevailed: the seven sacraments were retained as was the rule that the Church alone could interpret the scriptures. The sale of indulgences continued as did the worship of relics and images and the invocation of saints. A list of prohibited reading was issued. The Church hierarchy retained its power, the administration of the Inquisition was formalized and a new order, the Society of Jesus was founded by Ignatius Loyola. This would receive orders from and answer directly to the pope. Trade between heretical and non-heretical countries was banned, as were some other activities of a more parochial nature. For example, a doctor could not visit or minister to a sick heretic. In sum, Church rules were to be strictly enforced, deviations would not be tolerated and little effort was made to reform obvious clerical abuses of power.

By the eighteenth century Italy, Spain, France, Southern Germany, Belgium and Ireland remained predominantly Roman Catholic while England, Scotland, Scandinavia, the Netherlands and Northern Germany were largely Protestant. Most of the later religious denominations developed out of Protestant but not Catholic Churches. An exception was Jansenism, which started in the seventeenth century and spread to a community of nuns near Paris. The pope condemned it and the convent was promptly destroyed (7, p. 171).

New Protestant Churches included the Baptist Church – started in England by John Smyth in 1611 – and the Society of Friends or Quakers – led by George Fox – began at about the same time. English Congregationalists landed in Plymouth, Massachusetts in 1600 and by the end of the century, permitted Baptists and Episcopal Churches to operate in Boston. Rhode Island became a Baptist centre. Quakers were initially persecuted but eventually settled in Pennsylvania. Unitarians originated in Eastern Europe in the sixteenth century and later spread to England (7, p. 164). John Wesley started the Methodist Church in the eighteenth century after Anglicans denied him a church. Later, this church split into a number of different branches. William Miller began the Adventist movement in the eighteenth century.

The Age of Enlightenment

The period from the end of the seventeenth to the end of the eighteenth century coincided with the Age of Enlightenment, whose goal was to promote reason in contrast to religious mysticism, superstition and belief in miracles (17, p. 291). Original sin was denied in favour of man's ability to control his own destiny and hell was ridiculed (17, p. 292). This all coincided with Isaac Newton's mathematical explanation of gravity published in 1686 and the works of John Lake, Voltaire, Diderot and others. But the doubts and hostility of some of its members contributed to the Enlightenment's demise in the late eighteenth century.

Christianity in the Nineteenth Century

The nineteenth century was a period of great missionary activity among all Christian Churches. The number of British possessions overseas peaked and made it possible for the Anglican Church to promote its missionary activities under the protection of the crown. These included education, health and indigent care, and of course religion. France and Portugal brought Catholicism to their territories in Africa and Asia. Latin America had been under the control of Spain and Portugal since the sixteenth century and the indigenous people there were converted, often by force. Spain also controlled some of the Philippine Islands. The Spanish crown maintained the right to appoint bishops in these lands while the Church controlled their religion, education and ecclesiastic courts.

Several events in this period widened the separation between Catholics and Protestants. Two new dogmas were announced; one was the Definition of the Immaculate Conception of the Virgin Mary in 1854 and the other was the Decree of Papal Infallibility in 1870. Pope Pius X issued an encyclical, *Pascendi Gregis* in 1907 attacking Modernism in 'the Heresy of Americanism'; this denounced democracy unless controlled by the Church (7, p. 197). Then in 1859, Charles Darwin published the *Origin of the Species* and the *Descent of Man* in 1871. His conclusion – supported by scientific evidence and backed later by genetic data – made mankind's history incompatible with the Bible story of creation.

New Protestant Churches which began in this century include the Mormon Church or Church of Jesus Christ of Latter Day Saints, founded by Joseph Smith in 1830, the Watch Tower Bible and Tract Society or Jehovah's Witnesses, started in 1881 by C. T. Russell, the Salvation Army begun by William Booth in 1877 and the Church of Christ Scientists started by Mary Baker Eddy in 1879.

France disestablished the Catholic Church in the early twentieth century, and its property was placed under state control (16, p. 370). In 1929, the Lateran Treaty was signed between Mussolini, the fascist ruler of Italy and Pope Pius XI, establishing the Vatican as a city-state within Rome and guaranteeing its independence. Catholicism became the state religion of Italy until this part of the treaty was amended in 1984 (18, p. 368). One of the most important events within the Catholic Church in this period was the Vatican II Ecumenical Council. This was summoned by Pope John XXIII and held between 1962 and 1965. Some of the issues on the agenda included the traditions of the Church, the role of Mary, the authority of the pope and priestly celibacy.

Evangelical and Fundamental Christianity had its origin in Europe and the United States in the nineteenth century but became more of a force in the Baptist and Presbyterian Churches in the twentieth century, especially in the United States. The Pentecostal movement, which started in 1900, shares some of the Fundamentalist's beliefs and has had many schisms. The largest of these include the Assemblies of God and the Church of the Nazarene. They spread rapidly and now form the largest Protestant group in South America, particularly in Guatemala and Brazil.

The Eastern Orthodox Church headed by the Patriarch of Constantinople, developed a federation of 13 independently governed churches, which include those of Greece, Romania, Bulgaria, Yugoslavia, Cyprus and Russia; some of these achieved patriarchal status. They are administered by a bishop and clergy who are elected by priests and laity. Issues of importance have to be considered by the Ecumenical Council whose decisions are infallible (6, vol. 16, p. 1,177).

Christian Scriptures and Women

Old Testament

The scriptures of the various Christian faiths include the Bible, which is shared by all and the prayer books and religious tracts of each of them.

The Bible, the major Christian scripture, consists of an Old and a New Testament. The former differs from the Hebrew Bible in the number of books and their order; these also vary in the Catholic, Eastern Orthodox and Protestant editions. The Catholic Old Testament has 46 books and is derived from the Greek translation called the Septuagint. It includes the Apocrypha – ratified by the Council of Trent in the sixteenth century – containing some historical details of the inter-testamental period. Protestants rejected this as non-canonical. The Protestant Old Testament includes 39 books and came from the Palestinian or Hebrew canons. Some Protestant Churches use different canons in their scriptures. The Eastern Orthodox Bible has 49 books and their New Testament, 27. The Pentateuch is shared by all and includes the books of Genesis, Exodus, Leviticus, Numbers and Deuteronomy, beginning with the story of the creation and ending with the farewell of Moses to his people, followed by the historical books, then the major and minor prophets (19, p. 173).

The Pentateuch is the work of several different authors, the earliest in the seventh century BCE and the latest in the fourth century BCE, close to the end of the Babylonian exile (20. p. 46). The Greek translation of the Pentateuch was begun in about 100 BCE in Alexandria and continued in Palestine. The other books of the Old Testament were translated over the next one to two hundred years. The official text was selected in the early second century CE after it had undergone many revisions and several editions.

The Genesis story of the creation has been the cause of unending disagreement concerning the origin of Eve and her role in the so-called downfall of man. This has had a lasting influence on the status and treatment of women, particularly in Christian but also in Jewish societies. These persist despite archaeological, evolutionary and genetic evidence that the whole account is mythological and has no basis in fact. To begin with, there are discrepancies in the two accounts of creation (21, p. xxi). Gen. 1.27 reads, 'So God created man in his own image, in the image of God he created him; male and female he created them.' Gen. 2.23 has a different story which ends with 'And the rib the Lord God had taken from the man he made into a woman. Then the man said, 'This at last is bone of my bone and flesh of my flesh: she shall be called Woman because she was taken out of Man.' Pagel cites evidence that the second version may be older and dates from 1000 to 900 BCE, while the first may have been written in about 400 BCE (21, p. xxii). There is much disagreement over the sin of Adam and Eve and the apportioning of blame. Was this just disobedience and at whose instigation? We are told that Adam was ordered not to eat from the 'tree of the knowledge of good and evil' (2, Gen. 2.17). He was given this edict before the appearance of Eve and when confronted with his disobedience, Adam blamed Eve (2, Gen. 2.22-23). If Eve was created like Adam in the image of God, they were equals and equally good. If the sin was disobedience, he, Adam was the guilty one, or at most they were equally guilty.

To understand the demeaning tone used to describe women by the writers of Genesis – all of whom were men – it is well to remember that patriarchy has a long history dating back to the Bronze Age, so the custom of treating women as inferiors was well established by the seventh century BCE (22, p. 217). The human habit of blaming individuals or groups ranking below us has never changed.

The section of Judaic law containing the Ten Commandments was adopted by Christians (2, Exod. 20.3-17). Acceptable standards of behaviour for women are described very well in the Old Testament proverb *Ode to a Capable Wife* (2, Prov. 31.12-28). 'She does him good, and not harm, all the days of her life. She … works with willing hands … She girds her loins with strength and makes her arms strong … She opens her hand to the poor, and reaches out her hands to the needy … She opens her mouth with wisdom, and the teaching of kindness is on her tongue. She looks well to the ways of her household, and does not eat the bread of idleness.'

New Testament

The earliest written account of the Jesus movement is believed to have been written between about 20 and 70 CE and is known as the Gospel of 'Q', from the German word *quelle* meaning source (23, p. 47). 'It documents the history of a single group of Jesus people … from the time of Jesus in the 20s until after the Roman-Jewish war in the 70s' (23, ibid.). 'Q' was lost at some time early in the second century but was recently reconstructed, mostly from the Gospel of Luke after it was realized that the writers of both the Gospels of Matthew and Luke had used a common source for their works (23, pp. 48, 312). These two Gospels were written between the 70s and the early second century CE. The Gospel of Mark was probably the first and a source for Matthew and Luke. It was written in Greek and intended primarily for the Gentiles. The author is not known and probably not the Mark who was in Rome with Peter and Paul and then travelled to Alexandria, where he is credited with establishing Christianity (23, p. 160). His Gospel describes the ministry of John the Baptist, the baptism of Jesus, his ministry and death. Several female followers witnessed the death of Jesus (2, Mk 15.40) whose spirit first appeared to

Mary Magdalene (2, Mk 16.9). The original Gospel of Mark was amended by Bishop Clement of Alexandria and chapter 16 to the end was deleted and a new section added later on. The original was found near Jerusalem in 1958 (3, p. 58). It made no mention of the resurrection and ended with the account of the two women walking away from the empty tomb.

The official history of Christianity, as penned by Eusebius, claims there was always a single dominant, orthodox Christian faith, beginning with Jesus and continued by the disciples and many others. In 1934, Bauer published an account of his disagreement with Eusebius, indicating there was no orthodoxy during the first three centuries of Christianity and no single dominant faction (24, p. 59). The ancient documents discovered in the Egyptian desert in 1945 and others, lend support to Bauer's assertion. Instead Christianity comprised numerous distinct groups, each with its own beliefs, practices and literature and each claiming to be the true faith. This state of affairs persisted until the Roman faction won-out, due in part to its power and wealth and then declared itself to be the one orthodox church. The others were eventually denounced as heretical and their books were banned or burned. The canons selected for inclusion in the New Testament cite the orthodox view: as was the custom then, these were written anonymously and labelled with a name familiar to Christians.

The selection of texts to be included in the New Testament was made between 180–200 CE (25, p. 70), and came out of an enormous body of literature produced by many different Christian communities (23, p. 6). About 5,000 different Greek editions of the New Testament exist, many with different accounts and quotations; most reflect differences in spelling, grammar and style and rather few change the interpretation at least 'in matters of substance' (19, p. 334). There are several explanations for this; some resulted from deliberate changes in the text, some came from the translator's interpretation and some were copying errors. A well-known example of the latter occurs in Mt. 1.22 where the Aramaic word for 'girl' is changed to 'virgin' in the Greek translation (19, p. 334). In general, there was little interest in the veracity of biblical translations until the Renaissance in the sixteenth century.

The Latin translation of the Greek and Hebrew Old Testaments and parts of the New Testament were completed by Jerome in the early fifth century. The remaining text – the Epistles, Acts and Apocrypha – were probably translated by others. The final product was known as the Vulgate Bible and became the authentic version for the Western Church until the Reformation. The Roman Catholic Church adopted the Douai Bible as its final version between 1582 and 1610. The selection of New Testament passages to be read on specific dates in the Christian liturgy was made in the ninth century. The Syriac version of the Old Testament was translated from Aramaic and the New Testament from Greek in the third century but there were many later revisions. A Coptic version was prepared between 200 and 300 CE. when Coptic became a written language (19, p. 361).

William Tyndale made the first translation of the New Testament into English from the Greek Septuagint in 1525. For this, he was accused of perverting the scriptures and subsequently burned at the stake. Erasmus translated the New Testament into Latin in 1515 but the Greek original he used contained many errors and additional translations were made a short time later. Martin Luther translated the New Testament into German from both Greek and Latin texts in 1522, followed by the Old Testament in 1534. The King James Version appeared early in the seventeenth century and although praised for its prose, had serious defects and required revisions (19, p. 335).

The Matthew Gospel is the first one in the New Testament. It was written in Aramaic sometime between 80 and 90 CE, using material from 'Q' and the Gospel of Mark (23, p. 68), and translated into Greek before 100 CE. It describes the birth of Jesus, his flight to and return from Egypt, his baptism and some of his teaching, including his condemnation of adultery and lust (2, Mt. 5.27-29), divorce (except in the case of a wife's adultery) and marriage to a woman who had been 'put away' (2, Mt. 5.32). These words on adultery and divorce are repeated (ibid., 19.3-7). Women are mentioned several times including one who anointed Jesus with precious ointment (ibid., 26.9–13) and others who followed him from Galilee and witnessed his death.

Luke, who accompanied Paul on two of his journeys and was with him in Caesarea and Rome, was a physician and a Gentile. The Luke who wrote the Gospel and the Acts of the Apostles was probably someone else (23, p. 167). The Gospel was probably written just before the Acts, early in the second century CE (23, p. 45). Its sources of information were 'Q' and Mark's Gospel (23, p. 48). This Gospel contrasts pagan and Jewish womanhood and identifies some of the women who followed Jesus as Mary Magdalene, Joanna, Susanna and others (2, Lk. 8.2-4).

The last New Testament Gospel is John's and was probably written at the end of the first or early second century CE. It describes Jesus' meeting with the Samaritan woman (2, Jn 4.1-45) and another with an adulteress who was spared the usual punishment (death by stoning), through his forgiveness (ibid., 8.10–11). This Gospel also describes the death of Jesus and confirms the account of Matthew (ibid., 19.25-26).

Luke is credited with writing the Acts of the Apostles in which he relates the history of the Christian Church in its first 42 years. Much of the work is about the journeys of Paul but it begins with a meeting of about 120 followers, including Mary, the mother of Jesus and other women and presided over by Peter, to elect a replacement for Judas (2, Acts 1.24-26). It also describes the appearance of the Holy Spirit (ibid., 2.1-13), the persecution of Christians by Paul and his conversion, and Peter's cure of Tabitha, who is called a 'disciple' (ibid., 9.36-42).

The Epistles of Paul, all written in Greek, comprise the earliest extant Christian material in the New Testament and were written in the 50s CE (23, p. 99). Of the 13 credited to him, seven are thought to be genuine (21, p.

23) and include the Epistles to the Romans, I and II Corinthians, Galatians, Philippians, I Thessalonians and Philemon. There is still debate about four others: Ephesians, Colossians and II Thessalonians and general agreement that he did not write the Epistles to Timothy and Titus (21, p. 23; 23, p. 183). These later letters deemphasize Paul's pro-celibacy views in favour of marriage; blame Eve and deny women a role outside the home but rather instruct that they should be child bearers and obedient to their husbands (23, p. 24). Women are mentioned frequently in Paul's epistles; he used their homes as living and meeting places and they in turn acted as assistants and deacons. He called Phoebe a 'deacon' (2, Rom. 16.1) and thanked Prisca, Mary and other women for their help (ibid., 16.3-6). A large number of the early non-Jewish converts were women, for men faced the opposition of Judaeo-Christians who demanded their prior circumcision.

Corinth – where Paul spent two years around 50 CE – was mainly a Gentile city and – although a Roman colony – very Greek in culture. Paul's first Epistle to the Corinthians suggests sexual equality for husband and wife, 'For the wife does not rule over her own body, but the husband does; likewise the husband does not rule over his body but the wife does' (ibid., 7. 4). But in other matters he states, 'The head of a woman is her husband' (ibid., 11.3). There are instructions concerning headwear to be worn by men and women when praying (ibid., 11.4-11) and finally a directive against women preachers (ibid., 14.34-36). This letter appears to be specifically directed to the Christians in Corinth, a city steeped in Graeco-Roman cultural beliefs, where women were denied any public role in the community.

Paul stresses the equality of men and women in his letter to the Galatians, 'There is neither Jew nor Greek, there is neither slave nor free, there is neither male nor female, for you are all one in Christ Jesus' (2, Gal. 3.29). He describes Jesus as a 'Son made of a woman, made under the law' (ibid., 4.4), indicating nothing unusual occurred at his conception or birth (26, p. 88).

The Epistle to the Ephesians was probably written later, during Paul's first imprisonment in Rome and at about the same time as the Epistle to the Colossians. Both urge wives to be submissive to their husbands, 'Let wives also be subject in everything to their husbands' (2, Eph. 5.24). And 'Wives be subject to your husbands' (2, Col. 3.18). Slaves received the same directive, 'Slaves, obey in everything those who are your earthly masters' (ibid., 3.22).

Timothy was a close friend and convert of Paul. The two Epistles addressed to him were written between 63 and 67 CE while Paul was a prisoner in Rome, or by others after his death. The first includes some of the most demeaning instructions to women ever to appear in print and has been used ever since to justify their treatment as inferiors, 'Let a woman learn in silence with all submissiveness. I permit no woman to teach or have authority over men; she is to keep silent' (2, 1 Tim. 2.11-13). It is interesting that the instructions to bishops and deacons concerning marriage have occasioned less obedience in the Roman Catholic and Orthodox denominations. 'Now a bishop must be above reproach, the husband of one wife' (ibid., 3.2), and 'Let deacons be the husband of one wife' (ibid., 3.12). And once again Eve is blamed, 'For Adam was formed first, then Eve; and Adam was not deceived but the woman was deceived and became a transgressor but woman will be saved through bearing children if she continues with modesty' (ibid., 2.13-15).

The New Testament also contains epistles attributed to James, Peter, John and Jude, the twin of Jesus. James was the brother of Jesus and the first bishop of Jerusalem. His epistle was probably written in 62 CE just before his death. Peter's letters were written to Christian communities in Asia Minor probably between 63 and 64. The first includes the words 'Likewise you wives, be submissive to your husbands' (2, 1 Pet. 3.1).

Revelations, The Apocalypse in the Catholic Bible, may have been written by John or members of his school from Patmos, early in the second century. It brings a message to the angels of the seven Christian churches, warning each of the return of Jesus in the very near future. It foretells the end of the earth and a vision of heaven.

The final form of the 29 books of the New Testament had been generally accepted by the end of the fourth century, but was not finally approved until the Council of Trent (1545–63). Recognized books include the 4 Gospels, the Acts of the Apostles, the 13 Pauline Epistles and also I Paul, I John and I Clement (1, p. 424). Disputed books include the Epistles to the Hebrews, James, II Peter, II and III John, Jude and Revelations. The Gospel, Preaching, and Revelation of Peter were rejected as spurious. Also rejected were the Acts of Paul, Shepherd of Hermes, Second Epistle of Clement, the Epistle of Barnabas, the Teaching of the Apostles, the Gospels of Thomas and Matthias and Acts of Andrew and John. Despite this, many of these texts had been read publicly in both apostolic and orthodox churches in the early centuries of Christianity (18, p. 241).

Non-canonical Scriptures

Constantine ordered the building of numerous basilicas including the Church of the Holy Sepulchre in Jerusalem. He directed the Church toward a single, more uniform religion, appointed the first bishop of Rome and helped the Roman faction to achieve dominance over all other Christian sects. The literature selected for inclusion in the New Testament, conformed to the beliefs of the Roman Church. Texts which were not selected were supposed to be destroyed (26, p. 83).

But not all was lost and the many early-Christian documents retrieved much later have greatly expanded our knowledge of the Church's early history. In 1875, an important early-Christian text was found in the Patriarchal Library of Jerusalem in Constantinople. This was the Didache or Teaching of the Twelve Apostles, believed to have been written by someone who knew the apostles personally although there is no mention of them in the work (23, p. 239). It was probably written in the early second century but the writer is unknown. It lists a series of 'thou shalts' and 'thou shalt-nots' with instructions on baptisms, fasts and the Eucharist.

In 1945, a cache of 50 or more texts was discovered by chance at Nag Hammadi in Upper Egypt (21, p. 61). Some of the material was probably written in the first to third centuries and includes the Gnostic scriptures originally written in Greek and translated later into Latin, Coptic or Syrian. Most of the Greek originals have disappeared and the surviving Coptic manuscripts were copied before 350 CE (19, p. 362). These include the works of Valentinus and his followers, the Coptic Gospel of Thomas and other works. Didymus Jude Thomas was the twin of Jesus and brother of James; the New Testament Gospel of Jude is attributed to him. Thomas is credited with Christianizing Mesopotamia and India. His relic is said to be in the church of Edessa and was verified by a Spanish woman who visited the church in 384 CE (27, p. 361). Scriptures credited to Thomas include his Gospel, Book and Acts. The Gospel contains 'obscure sayings' of Jesus, 'collected and transmitted by St. Didymus Jude Thomas' (27, p. 377). Some of the material is similar to 'Q' and compiled before 200 CE and probably before 70 CE (27, p. 377). He explains that the 'kingdom of God' is not an anticipated event but rather a 'state of self-discovery' (25, p. 70). He identifies Mary Magdalene and Salome as disciples, in addition to Thomas, James, Peter and Matthew (27, p. 378). Simon Peter's comment, 'Let Mary leave us, for women are not worthy of life,' emphasizes his (Peter's) disdain for women in general and particularly for Mary Magdalene (26, p. 152). Jesus answered, 'I myself shall lead her and make her male, so that she too may become a living spirit resembling you males. For every woman who will make herself male will enter the kingdom of heaven' (26, p. 152; Gospel of Thomas 1.13ff.). This is the final saying in the Gospel and was added later. It is refuted by an earlier edition that requires 'the union of the sexes rather than preference for one over the other' (27, p. 116). The Book of Thomas may have been written slightly later and here Jesus refers to Jude Thomas as 'my double and my true companion' (28, p. 402. Book of Thomas, 11.7).

The Gospel according to Philip contains some of the collected writings of the Valentinian school, whose leader was condemned as a heretic by second-century bishops including Irenaeus, Tertullian and Clement (21, p. 61). The author of this Gospel names three women who always 'walked with the Lord: Mary, his mother and her sister and Magdalene. A Mary is his sister and his mother and his lover' (29, p. 41. Gospel of Philip v. 32). It goes on to say 'and the consort of Christ is Mary Magdalene. The [Lord loved Mary] more than all the disciples and kissed her [on the mouth many times]. The other [women/disciples] saw ... him. They said to him why do you [love her] more than all of us? The Savior answered and said to them, why do not I love you as I do her? If a blind person and one who can see are in the dark, there is no difference between them. When the light comes, then the one who sees will see the light, and the one who is blind will stay in darkness' (Gospel of Philip, vv. 55, 56; 28, p. 42). These non-canonical texts indicate that Mary Magdalene was revered as a disciple (30, v. 1, p. 81).

The Gospel of Mary Magdalene, written in the second century and discovered in Cairo in 1896, describes the words of encouragement she spoke to the dejected disciples to go out and preach, after the death of Jesus (5, p. 87). Peter then asked her, 'Sister, we know that the Savior loved you more than the rest of women. Tell us the words of the Savior which you know [but] we do not know nor have we heard them' (29, p. 36). In response, she began a long discourse but was challenged by Andrew and Peter, 'Did he really speak with a woman without our knowledge [and] not openly? Are we to turn about and all listen to her? Did he prefer her to us?' (26, p. 153). Levi answered, 'Peter, you have always been hot tempered. Now I see you are contending against the woman like the adversaries. But if the Savior made her worthy, who are you to reject her? Surely the Savior knows her very well. That is why he loved her more than us' (29, p. 37). The disciples accepted Mary's words but 'By the late second century, certain Church leaders began to denounce such teachings as heresy' (25, p. 68).

The Pistis Sophia, a Gnostic text of uncertain date, was bought by the British Museum in 1785. It describes the return of Jesus to instruct his disciples 11 years after his death. Jesus praised Mary Magdalene for her questions, 'Excellent, Mariam. Thou art blessed beyond all women upon earth ... speak openly and do not fear' (26, p.154. Pistis Sophia, v. 19). Peter responded, 'My Lord, we are not able to suffer this woman who takes the opportunity from us, and does not allow any one of us to speak, but she speaks many times' (26, pp. 154. Pistis Sophia, v. 36).

The Protoevangelium of James was probably written between 150 and 175 CE and was initially accepted and later discredited (26, pp. 83–93). It recounts the early days of Mary, the mother of Jesus, who was born to Anne and Joachim, and reared by the Temple priests from the age of 3 months to 12 years.

Another Apocryphal book, the History of Joseph the Carpenter, was probably written in the third to fourth centuries and tells how Mary was given to Joseph – a much older man who had older children – as a ward. Mary became pregnant and was 14 when Jesus was born (26, p. 94). Mary died in 40–50 CE and was more or less forgotten until the second century.

By the fourth century, the concept of the Immaculate Conception was in vogue. Augustine claimed she had always been a virgin, 'A Virgin conceiving, a Virgin bearing, a Virgin pregnant, a Virgin bringing forth, a Virgin Perpetual' (26, p. xx). But Celsius, writing in the third century CE, criticized the virgin-birth claims. He was denounced and his writings were destroyed. The dogma of Mary's Immaculate Conception was formally accepted by the Roman Catholic Church in 1854, as well as the conception of her by Anne. The dogma of her bodily assumption into heaven was ratified in 1950. Except for the Gospel of Matthew, in which the word 'girl' was mistranslated to 'virgin', there is no mention of her virginity in the New Testament. Paul describes Jesus as 'made of a woman, made under the law', indicating there was nothing unusual about his birth (2, Gal. 4.4).

The Secret Book of John depicts Eve as the source of 'spiritual awakening' (21, p. 68), rather than the cause of the 'fall' and the excuse for the subsequent subjugation of women (ibid.). In reverence to Eve, Gnostic Christians treated their women members with respect, welcomed their participation and allowed them to practice as priests, activities increasingly denied them in the 'institutionalized churches' from the second and third centuries up to the present time (21, p. 77).

Councils, Creeds and Early Theologians

The early Christian Church was preoccupied with questions concerning the divinity of Jesus, his relationship to God and the doctrine of the Trinity. The Council of Nicaea in 325 CE – the largest assembly of bishops to date – met to consider the teaching of Arius and his followers who claimed that Jesus ranked below God but above humans. 'If the son is a true son, then the father must have existed before the son: therefore there was a time when the son did not exist: therefore he was created or made.'(7, p. 46). The Council rejected this as heresy and Arius was exiled. This was not the end of Arianism, which did not disappear until the sixth century, and later reappeared in Europe and North America in the post-Reformation period and by those who rejected the Trinity. The Council declared that Jesus was 'one in essence with the Father'. (4, p. 715). The first Council of Constantinople in 381 CE defined the divinity of the Holy Spirit as equal to the Father and Son, proceeding from the Father through the Son (6, vol. 5, p. 740).

The Apostle's creed, which summarizes the essential beliefs of Christianity, was approved in the fourth century and used in the Western but not the Eastern Church (6, vol. 6, p. 717). It is essentially the same as the baptismal liturgy, which had been in use for some time. The Nicene Creed in its original form was approved by both the Western and Eastern Churches in the fourth century. The phrase 'proceeds from the Father' was expanded to 'proceeds from the Father and Son' and was used in the west from that time in the Eucharist. The Eastern Church continues to use the original in both baptismal and Eucharistic liturgies. The Athanasian Creed – a Latin document of 40 verses – deals at length with the Trinity and incarnation and is accepted as orthodox by Catholic, Anglican and leading Protestant Churches (6, v. 6, p. 720). It was probably composed in the late fifth century and has nothing to do with Athanasius.

Tertullian (160–221) was one of the most influential theologians of the early Christian era. His hostility to women was vicious, especially to those who were teaching and baptizing in the early Church. 'It is not permitted to a woman to speak in church, but neither is it permitted her to teach,' he wrote (31, p. 159). He condemned the use of make-up and jewellery and stated his opinion that women belonged in the domestic sphere. He warned his sisters in Christ, 'women you are the devil's gateway. You are she who persuaded him whom the devil did not dare attack. Because of you, the Son of God had to die' (21, p. 63). 'Do you not know that every one of you is an Eve? The sentence of God on your sex lives on in this age: the guilt, of necessity, lives on too' (21, p. 63). He defined a woman as a 'temple built over a sewer' (32, p. 140).

Augustine of Hippo (354–430), sometimes called the father of the Western Church, dominated the Christian Church, both in his own time and later. His conversion to Christianity led him to renounce sex after he had had many prostitutes and one long-time mistress (33, p. 246). He is associated particularly with the concept of original sin although he was not its originator. He reasoned that man was endowed with a higher rational sense governing a lower irrational modality involved with appetite and passion (31, p. 217). The male body was created in the image of God and represented the rational being, women only with sinful sexuality (ibid., p. 223). The first sin of Adam and Eve – original sin – was the sin of pride, leading to the loss of rational sense and the takeover of passion and lust. This is transmitted sexually 'by each generation to the next' and can be expunged through baptism (31, p. 218). Jesus was sinless because he was born of a virgin and Mary's impregnation did not involve sexual passion. A different view is provided by the Teacher in the Gospel of Mary Magdalene, who seems to address this when, in answer to Peter he says, 'There is no sin. It is you who make sin exist. It is the result of your actions' (5, p. 88).

Augustine believed sexual intercourse – even with one's own spouse – was a venial sin and permissible only in order to procreate (33, p. 58). Women in his view were nothing but 'sexual beings, limited to one dimension, one the Christian theology repudiated' (31, p. 221). Like Aristotle, he believed that sperm contributed to the form of the embryo, the egg provided only the matter. The sperm at least got credited with transmitting original sin: women were incapable of doing this (31, p. 219). Augustine's beliefs have had an enormous influence, especially on the Roman Catholic Church concerning women priests, contraceptives, sexuality and celibacy for men and women. It was not until Vatican II that the church recognized that the purpose of sex was also to 'promote bonds of affection' (31, p. 219).

Thomas Aquinas (1225–1274) was another theologian whose writings have had a lasting influence on Christian beliefs and practice, particularly after the Reformation, and became standard works for the Catholic Church (13, p. 228). His opinions continue to influence the treatment of women. Some of his views invoke those of Aristotle, especially regarding male superiority. 'For good order would have been wanting in the human family if some were not governed by others wiser than themselves. So by such a kind of subjection, woman is naturally subject to man, because naturally in man the discretion of reason predominates' (30, vol. 1, p. 254). He believed it was dangerous to have women in positions of authority such as priests: since Adam was misled by Eve, not she by him, the female must always be subject to male authority (ibid., p. 192).

Priestly celibacy was practised inconsistently until the thirteenth century when a more formal attempt was made to impose it. Since many priests were legally married by then, compliance was limited. The papacy used itinerant emissaries to denounce sexual passion and attack the wives of priests. The non-compliance of priests continued until the Reformation, but in 1563 the Council of Trent forbade marriage as well as sexual contact for all ordained priests (31, vol. 1, p. 256).

The Church believed female sexuality was the work of the devil and made some women his equivalent, witches and sorcerers (26, pp. 230–1). The Witch's Bill of 1484 attempted to control female sexuality by accusing some women of witchcraft. The Inquisition questioned them and those found guilty were burned at the stake.

The seven sacraments recognized by the Catholic Church were defined by the Council of Trent (1545–1563) and include baptism, the Eucharist, confession, confirmation, consecration of priests, marriage and the last rites. At about the same time, an index of forbidden books was established. Vatican II recommended a number of changes including the recitation of the mass in the vernacular rather than in Latin. It also recognized that salvation could be achieved through other churches, by individuals who had lived a 'religious life' (6, vol. 15, pp. 200–5).

Scriptures of Protestant Churches

The Lutheran scriptures are recorded in the Book of Concord, which is the standard text of Lutheran theology (6, vol. 6. p. 261). It comprises nine items including the Augsberg Confessions which contain articles of faith concerning the Trinity and other basic Christian beliefs: these are identical to those of the Western Church, as is most of the liturgy. There are only two sacraments, baptism and the Eucharist (communion), because they were the only ones recognized in the scriptures. Services were to be in the vernacular with greater congregation participation. Most aspects of monasticism were condemned, as was the authority of bishops, the papal claim to be the sole authority for biblical interpretation and its primacy and the power to collect taxes from German states. Luther's understanding of Gen. 1.27 differed from the Church of Rome; he interpreted this to mean both male and female are created in the image of God and therefore both are good. 'And if the body is good, then sexuality is good' (31, p. 234). He denounced celibacy since it did not comply with Gen. 1.28, which says, 'be fruitful and multiply'. But the verse referring to dominance over all living things applied only to man since woman, in his view, was inferior. Finally, the clergy could not claim to be superior to the laity, since baptism made all men equal (7, p. 129).

Calvin outlined his views of the Christian Church in the Institutes of the Christian Religion (7, p. 141). He believed in predestination, which in his view meant a chosen elect only could achieve salvation. He recognized two sacraments, baptism and the Lord's Supper (the Eucharist). The standard Presbyterian catechism contains statements concerning the nature of God and moral laws, which include inward duties (faith and repentance) and outward duties (sacraments and prayers). The Reformed Church abolished hierarchical clerics such as bishops and is controlled by elected elders and presbyters.

Anglican (Episcopalian) scriptures include the Bible, the Book of Common Prayer and Hymnal. They recognize the 39 articles (1571) as the only confessional statement: this includes the rulings of the first four councils of the Christian Church addressing the Trinity and incarnation. Purgatory, pardons, the veneration of relics and images, the invocation of saints and masses for the dead were condemned (7, p. 156). Two sacraments are celebrated, baptism and the Eucharist or Holy Communion.

The Bible is the main scripture of Congregationalists. Liturgies vary and may follow the Book of Congregational Worship (1921) or the Book of Service and Prayer (6, vol. 6, p. 321). Two sacraments are recognized and local churches usually have autonomy in selecting leaders and elders and all members are considered to be equal.

Baptists recognize the Bible as their supreme religious authority and revere it as the literal word of God. Baptism is by complete immersion. Church members all have equal status and local churches are independent and elect their own ministers.

Methodists now include a large family of churches in England and the United States. The Bible provides the rule for living and is accepted, more or less, as literal. Methodists do not believe in purgatory and the phrase, 'He descended into hell' is deleted from the Apostle's Creed (7, p. 189). Clergy are appointed by bishops and retain their positions for 12 years.

Unitarian beliefs are similar to Arians' since they do not believe in the Trinity but in a single God and in the humanity of Jesus (6, vol. 22, p. 551). In 1785, the Book of Common Prayer was revised into a Unitarian liturgy, which may be used for services. Readings may be taken from Christian or non-Christian sources.

The scriptures of the Latter Day Saints or Mormons include the Bible, the Book of Mormon, the Book of Doctrines and Covenants and the Pearl of Great Price (6, vol. 13, p. 795; 7, p. 202). Religious doctrine is believed to have two sources, the written word and direct revelation which is continuous and given by God to the president of the Church. Individual Mormons can also receive revelations but these are of a personal nature only. Polygamy was introduced in 1843, initially only for church leaders and was more or less banned when Utah joined the Union in 1896. The Church is governed by a president, vice-presidents, council, patriarchs, high priests and the 'seventy'; all are male.

The Seventh Day Adventist Church was established in 1860. Believers adhere strictly to biblical law including the Ten Commandments (7, p. 20).

Jehovah's Witnesses accept a translation of the Bible favourable to their own beliefs (7, p. 209). They promote its prophetic parts such as the book of Daniel and Revelations.

The Coptic Orthodox Church or Monophysitists began in the fifth century because of dissent concerning the human and divine natures of Jesus (7, p. 74). Most followers live in Egypt where they constitute the original inhabitants, the Copts.

The doctrine of the Eastern Orthodox Churches is based on the Bible and the rulings of the first seven ecumenical councils concerning the doctrine of the Trinity and the divinity of Christ. The dogmas of the Immaculate Conception of Mary (1854) and her bodily assumption into heaven (1950) are not accepted. Nor do they accept the concept of purgatory or the infallibility of popes. The Orthodox Church recognizes seven sacraments.

Christianity and Women

Women in the Early Church

Christianity began in a group of Jewish men and women – known as Judaeo-Christians – who resided in a homeland controlled by the Roman Empire. The new religion spread through the Eastern Mediterranean to Egypt, Asia Minor, and Southern Europe where it encountered and converted Gentiles of Graeco-Roman origin. These two cultures had some similarities, especially concerning their views and treatment of women. Judaic law regarded women as inferior, contaminated and therefore a source of pollution, reason enough to deny them permission to participate in religious rites and requiring their segregation in houses of worship. Graeco-Romans also had a long fostered belief in the inferiority of women, attributed to the myth of Pandora who was blamed for all the miseries of mankind. Although Plato argued for complete equality between the sexes, he regarded women as 'failed' males (30, vol. 1, p. 24). Aristotle (4 BCE), a student of Plato, had a great influence on Christian leaders such as Augustine of Hippo and later Thomas Aquinas. In Aristotle's view, 'The male is by nature superior and the female inferior; and the one rules and the other is ruled' (30, vol. 1, p. 27). He called women 'deformed males' (30, vol. 1, p. 29).

Greek and later Roman writers satirized women, giving rise to a 'cult of misogyny' (30, vol, 1, p. 49). The Romans believed women were the weaker sex and lacked seriousness (31, p. 43). Nevertheless, wealthy Roman women were relatively independent and the Roman wife was usually revered for her devotion and chastity. Adultery by Roman women was not tolerated. Men on the other hand could procure prostitutes and force their slaves to be their sexual partners. Prostitution was legal and subject to taxation and homosexuality was not uncommon (21, p. xviii). Both Greek and Roman societies favoured males and male children outnumbered females, mostly the result of infanticide. Divorce was readily available for men in both Graeco-Roman and Jewish societies. These were the cultures that the egalitarian early Christians encountered.

Both the New Testament and non-canonical scriptures leave no doubt that Jesus treated all people, rich and poor, men and women as equals and all of them could achieve the Kingdom of God. His many women followers including Mary of Bethany, Joanna, Susanna and Salome attest to this. His close relationship with Mary Magdalene has been noted in the non-canonical scriptures; she brought financial resources to the Jesus movement and possessed superior knowledge and intelligence. And yet the Christian Church labelled her a whore and did not correct this assessment until 1969 (4, p. 48). Many of Jesus' parables were about women and contrary to Jewish law, Jesus met and talked with a Samaritan woman (2, Jn 4.8-21). He visited Martha's house (2, Lk. 10.38-42) and acknowledged the generosity of the woman who anointed him with an expensive balm (2, Lk. 7.38). He supported a woman accused of adultery, for whom – by Jewish law – the punishment was death by stoning (2, Jn 18.10-12), and acknowledged the worth of the mite contributed by a widow (2, Mk 12.41-44; Lk 21.1-5). Apart from John, only women were in attendance at his death: his other disciples fled in fear (2, Jn 19.25). The scriptures tell us that Mary Magdalene was the first person to see the risen Christ although her account was not believed (2, Mk 16.9-11). She exhorted the discouraged disciples to go out and spread his message and she transformed them from a band of fearful followers, a role that earned her the title of Apostle to the Apostles or their leader (30, p. 10). The only woman Jesus treated with disdain was his mother; once when she came looking for him in the Temple he is reported to have said, 'How is it that you sought me? Did you not know that I must be in my father's house?' (2, Lk. 2.49), and again later at the wedding at Cana, 'Who is my mother and who are my brothers? Here are my mother and my brothers' (2, Mt. 12.46-50).

After the death of Jesus, women continued to play a major role in the Christian Church where they outnumbered men, at least in the early years. Prominent Christians, especially Paul, were dependent on their help; 16 of his 36 colleagues were women and several are identified by name including Prisca, Phoebe and Julia (29, vol. 1, p 69). He called Junia 'foremost among the apostles' (30, p. 33). Women provided their homes as early Christian meeting places and contributed financial aid and other support. Women practised as evangelists, prophetesses and deacons (ministers). Thecla, who came from an aristocratic family, chose to follow Paul rather than marry and achieved fame as a teacher and later became one of the first ascetics (29, vol. 1, p. 70). Tabitha played an important role in the early Church and was called a disciple (2, Acts

9.36). Lydia, a prosperous and independent businesswoman, founded an early church in Philippi. Meetings and services were held in her house and, true to custom, her household and slaves converted to Christianity. Paul's apparent belief in gender equality is stated in his Epistle to the Galatians, 'There is neither Jew nor Greek, there is neither slave nor free, there is neither male nor female; for you are all one in Christ Jesus' (2, Gal. 3.28). His words were repeated later by second-century Christians such as Justin and Clement of Alexandria. Despite this, he reverted to Judaic and Graeco-Roman misogyny in other epistles where women are described as inferior. Paul defines the qualifications of deacons (ministers), adding, 'Women likewise must be serious,' suggesting both sexes could play this role (2, 1 Tim: 3.11).

Women continued to play leadership roles in the early Christian Church until the fourth century by which time the male-dominated Roman faction had gained control and women were denied the roles they had held previously. Epiphanius was one of many who denounced women for their active leadership, basing this on his reading of the scriptures (30, p. 44). Another prominent Christian, Tertullian (160–221), ranted against women who taught, baptized, offered the Eucharist and prophesied, citing Aristotle as his authority. Despite the Jesus message of equality, women were once again marginalized as older cultural practices and biases prevailed.

The persecution of Christians was a prominent feature of the early years of the Church and reached a peak during the rule of the emperor Diocletian (284–305). Many women were among the 100,000 or more Christians who were martyred. Their courage came in part from faith but also from a fervent belief in the imminent return of Jesus, a belief that was almost universal among Christians of this period (30, vol. 1, p. 70). This period of martyrdom ended with the Christianization of the Roman Empire in the early fourth century. Instead of persecution, Constantine rewarded the Church with land, and money for the construction of churches. Bishops were provided with the trappings of power as well as all manner of gifts and tax exemptions.

Women from 500 CE. The First Convents

From the fifth century on, the Church restricted and then excluded women from a public role in their religion. In 441 CE, the Council of Orange forbade the ordination of deaconesses (23, p. 59). A church hierarchy was established headed by a bishop, with an all-male priesthood, which was modelled after the Roman state. Formal places of worship or basilicas replaced the house-churches presided over in earlier times by women.

The anchorite movement was another phenomenon of the early centuries of the Christian era. Men and women left their families and denied themselves marriage, food and bodily comforts, opting instead for a solitary life of prayer, often in the desert. This arose from a popular belief that salvation required chastity. Women far outnumbered men, believing that by renouncing sexuality, they could become the equals of men (31, p. 210). Thecla was a good example of this kind of woman (34, p. 25). Eventually, for the sake of safety, these hermits banded together and, over time, they evolved into the religious communities or convents described later. The early Christians viewed sex as sinful, to be confined to married couples and then only when there was intent to procreate, otherwise it was fornication. Like older religions, they believed that women could not control their sexuality and this was an ever-present threat to men. Moreover, they were inferior intellectually and emotionally and therefore belonged at home, married and procreating. This was no different to the pre-Christian practices under patriarchy except that the Church had taken over control of women's reproductive powers. Unlike Judaic and Graeco-Roman cultures, Christians believed abortion was homicide and there were penances for miscarriage and any form of contraception was condemned (30, vol. 1, p. 82).

Life in a religious community was the only alternative for a woman who refused marriage and chose to retain her virginity. Here at least she could learn to read and further her education. Wealthy women and prominent families often founded priories and convents. These places became dumping places for the aristocracy and kings to unload their excess females and escape the dowry needed to procure a suitable husband for their daughters. In the Inferno Manacle, Archangel Tarabotti, a Venetian nun, describes a family's selection of one daughter for marriage, dressing her in lustrous clothes and jewels while the other – destined for the convent – is deprived and denied the right to choose: the Church conspired with and abetted this charade (35, p. 377).

Throughout the tenth and eleventh centuries, life in convents was comfortable, at least for women whose families had donated substantial dowries; family visitation rights were liberal, living arrangements were fairly relaxed and residents could spend time away from the institution for vacations. But a second class of nuns existed; women without dowries had to serve as domestics and servants for the upper-class nuns and their lives in the convents were far less comfortable. Monasteries and convents often occupied the same or adjoining buildings and these religious centres frequently controlled large amounts of money and land. Several nuns achieved renown in scientific, musical and theological studies as well as literature. Hildegard of Bingen (1098–1179) attained lasting fame in all these areas. Convents were run by abbesses and enjoyed considerable religious and secular independence (30, vol. 1, p. 185). Nuns could hear confessions, preach and instruct novices. Nuns and monks held about equal rank in their religious houses, governed themselves and maintained independence from the hierarchy of the Church.

Women's Lives from 1100 CE. The Cult of Misogyny

This all started to change in the eleventh century when a cult of misogyny started to develop for fear of woman's power as a seductress. In the words of one Cistercian, 'It is not expedient for that sex to enjoy the freedom of having its own governance because of its natural fickleness and also because of outside temptations which womanly weakness is not strong enough to resist' (34, p. 214). Abbesses were no longer allowed to hear confessions, so that the convent community became dependent on monks who now had to live in a separate building. Then additional restrictions were added which limited the activity and freedom of nuns. Finally, the Bull of Boniface VIII was issued in 1293. This decreed that all religious women were to be strictly cloistered or 'perpetually enclosed' and their convents were to be administered by male clerics. These men were frequently appointed by a secular ruler and often had little or no education or religious knowledge (30, vol. 1, p. 193). The intent of the bill was to restrict the education and training of nuns in order to curb a spirit of disobedience. Women religious were further demeaned by the salacious story of a Dominican – Steven Bourbon – who was paraded about as Pope Joan (30, v. 1. p. 93). Despite all of this, women continued to enter convents, some to escape marriage, some to avoid marriage dowries – which cost more than those paid to the convents – some for spiritual reasons, some joined as widows and some were placed there as children, usually by a parent because they were bastards. They could take their vows at 16 years.

During this same period, 90 per cent of European women, mostly in the lower classes of society, lived off the land and worked endlessly in the fields. They had little or no education and could neither read nor write. They could recite old folk tales and usually observed Christian celebrations and holy days, which often coincided with pre-Christian festivals. They died or suffered through the numerous onslaughts of Vikings, Arabs, Huns and others. The witchcraft persecutions especially affected these illiterate peasants. These started between 1300 and 1500 CE and reached their peak in the sixteenth and seventeenth centuries during which time there were at least 500 trials (30, vol. 1, p. 161). The Church claimed the devil was abroad and coupled this with a fear of sexuality and the contaminating effect of women. Innocent VIII's Witch's Bull utilized the Inquisition in pseudo-judicial trials after which the victims were handed over to the secular power for punishment. These frenzies of persecution came in waves and mostly occurred in regions of religious conflict in Europe and America. They led to the burning or drowning of at least 100,000 and by one account, 8 million mostly illiterate women, all over Europe (ibid., p. 167; 36, p. 319). It should be noted that both Calvin and Luther supported these persecutions (30, vol. 2, p. 164). By the early eighteenth century, this insanity had mostly come to an end.

Women's Lives After the Reformation

Two major changes affected women in the mid sixteenth century and one was a direct result of the Reformation. In Protestant Europe, convents and many monasteries were closed and their immense landholdings and wealth were redistributed or sold. The women who were freed from their vows were sometimes provided with dowries to help them procure husbands (35, p. 401). Overall the closure of convents after the Reformation left fewer options for women and denied many an education. Protestant churches moved to remedy this loss, first through private and then through public means. Luther had a different interpretation of Genesis. In his opinion, both men and women were created in the image of God and therefore both were good – although women were still inferior. They should not be blamed for their sexuality but rather women should obey the command to 'be fruitful and multiply' (2, Gen. 1.28). Celibacy was out and procreation was in. Luther married a nun and they had six children.

The second change, which came at about the same time, was the invention of the printing press. Books became more readily available and reading more widespread. Luther translated the Bible into German and Tyndale's English translation was completed in the early sixteenth century. Other literature – tracts, pamphlets and engravings – also became available in the vernacular. Unfortunately for women, the early presses were filled with material derogatory to them.

Royal and aristocratic European women took an active role in the Reformation as they converted their husbands, courts and servants to the Protestant faith. Several of the new Protestant Churches including Congregationalists and Baptists allowed women to preach. George Fox, the founder of the Quaker movement, cited the scriptures to support his belief that the 'ancient assertion of women's inferiority and alleged need to keep silence was a purely arbitrary decision on the part of churchmen' (35, p. 418). Mary Fell, a leader in the same church wrote about the 'equal nature of women and their right to preach the gospel' (30, vol. 1, p. 237). But the welcome mat for the new Protestant religious women was not out for long. Male clerics soon claimed back their authority: since women were inferior, they must be subordinate to men and their proper place was in the home raising children (ibid., p. 239).

The Catholic Church reaffirmed its old rule that only men could be priests, but did allow women to teach and care for the sick outside convents: this was the beginning of its long tradition in education and health care. The Ursuline order of nuns was established in the mid sixteenth century, specifically to educate Catholic girls. These nuns were not cloistered, took no formal vows and did not wear religious habits (30, vol. 1, p. 239).

Guilds – associations of individuals practising the same crafts – began in the twelfth and thirteenth century and became more organized in the fourteenth and fifteenth centuries. Individuals belonging to a guild lived together, regulated the admission and training of its members and assisted them in times of need (30, vol. 11, p. 436). Women could become partners in a guild by marrying members and although most guilds had only male members, the textile and clothing guild members were exceptions and predominantly or only female.

By the early nineteenth century, the lives of working women had become more uniform and centralized, due in part to their migration from the countryside to the cities as a result of the Industrial Revolution. But now, as more young women were forced to work to support their families, their opportunities for education diminished (30, vol. 11, p. xviii). As yet, neither working women nor those with inherited wealth had any control of their earnings, property or children. States had laws supporting the authority of men in all these areas and there were no women in positions of power to argue for change. To back up this claim, governments and the Christian Churches had only to cite the scriptures where it was clearly stated that women should be obedient and subordinate to their fathers and husbands. Changes would depend on the intervention of women themselves and this required an education and the ability to read.

Education

Throughout history, education has been all-important to improve the lives of slaves, minorities and other subjugated people, including women. The Italian Renaissance did little for them except to encourage a select few to discover pre-Christian Greek and Roman classics. By the end of the seventeenth century, Protestants and later Catholics became more committed to female literacy (30, vol. 1, p. 264). Writers such as Olympe de Gouges wrote *A Declaration on the Rights of Women* in the eighteenth century and Mary Astell and others, emphasized the importance of education to advance women to their proper place in society. Mary Wollstonecraft (1759–1797) pleaded for reforms to improve the education of girls which was generally much inferior to boys at that time (30, vol. 11, p. 347). The Age of Enlightenment was a brief period when an attempt was made to use reason rather than superstition and religious beliefs, but it did very little for women. In fact, notables in this movement, such as Rousseau (1712–1772) denounced learned women.

During the sixteenth century, the Protestant town of Geneva required girls to receive a primary school education (30, vol. 1, p. 443). By the end of the seventeenth century, both Sweden and France had passed laws concerning female education and schools were opened for girls from middle- and upper-class homes. Public education became more general as more teachers were trained. By the nineteenth century, governments had become involved in public education and eventually many countries enacted laws to make this compulsory. Prussia was the first state to make attendance in elementary school compulsory for boys and girls and this occurred after the Franco-Prussian war of 1870. But secondary education for girls was limited until the twentieth century and acceptance at a university required the permission of a professor.

Overall, the education of girls lagged even more in Catholic compared to Protestant countries. Up until the mid-twentieth century, most girls in predominantly Catholic nations were educated by nuns who – not surprisingly – stressed traditional roles such as marriage or religious orders (30, vol. 11, p. 354). Successive nineteenth and twentieth century popes encouraged women to accept their subordinate roles and those who did not comply, found themselves isolated and outside the Church (ibid., p. 355). Despite this, France developed a state controlled and centralized educational system in the nineteenth century; primary education became compulsory, free and public for boys in 1833 and in 1881, for girls. This was extended in 1890 to include secondary schools for girls (ibid., p. 252).

In England, public education was hampered by private and voluntary organizations, both with a long history of involvement in education, resulting in some well-known private schools for boys. A commission of inquiry reported that secondary education for girls was woefully inadequate. Most girls were educated at home, although some wealthier families did send their daughters to academies or seminaries. The Education Act of 1870 concerning primary education was finally enacted ten years later, after language concerning the teaching of scriptures was amended. Early in the twentieth century, secondary schools for boys and girls became compulsory and free (6, vol. 7, p. 982; vol. 23, p. 128).

At the present time, about equal numbers of boys and girls attend primary schools in most European countries. About 50 per cent of girls attend a secondary school and 40 per cent attend college. By the mid to late twentieth century, literacy rates were 95 per cent or higher for women. In Russia, there were rapid advances in educational opportunities for girls after the Revolution and illiteracy fell from 70 per cent in 1920 to less than 2 per cent in 1960 (6, vol. 23, p. 629).

There was a surprising amount of resistance to the admission of women to universities in the United States and England into the twentieth century. So-called scientific papers claimed that 'women's abstinence from intellectual activity as part of a sexual division of labour was the highest stage of evolution' and 'intellectual work would ruin a woman's ability to reproduce and nurture' (37, p. 189). During WWI, men at English universities tried to get rid of women faculty members by conscripting them into a 'domestic service' army (ibid., p. 192) and there are numerous accounts of professors who refused to have women students in their classes.

The United States was the first country to adopt a one-track co-educational public school system. Recent population increases have led to the opening of more private including parochial and religiously sponsored schools, from primary through university levels.

Co-education was resisted in Catholic countries including Latin America. Pius XI condemned it in 1929, saying it was 'founded upon naturalism and the denial of original sin' (6, vol. 6, p. 14). Argentina has one of the best educational systems in Latin America with 99 per cent literacy for males and females (38). Improvement has been slower in other Latin American countries where literacy rates vary from about 57 per cent for females in Haiti to 96 per cent in Chile (36). These are usually about 3 per cent lower in females than males (38). Most states have enacted legislation requiring state-supported primary and secondary schooling but facilities are often sparse and inadequate, especially in rural communities.

Employment

Prior to the nineteenth century, few upper-class women worked except in a voluntary capacity and usually for charities. Poorer women, both single and married, had to work to support their families and farm work followed by domestic service were their main sources of employment. In the eighteenth century and later, the Industrial Revolution provided work in textile mills and factories for many women. Their work hours were often 14 hours a day, 7 days a week but these women had few alternatives because of their lack of education. Women continued to provide health care and teaching services through religious orders and these were mostly Catholic.

Legislation enacted in England in the mid-nineteenth century limited the hours a woman could work in a factory to ten hours a day and the Mines Act of 1842 prohibited underground work for women and boys under ten years of age (30, vol. 2, p. 288). By 1914, similar legislation had been passed in most European countries. During WWI, there was a need for munitions workers and this together with the typewriter – which had recently been invented – provided work for many women in factories and offices. Here, her wages were higher than in competing occupations but a woman's salary was usually one half to two thirds that of a man in the same position: this was based on the belief that they needed less because they ate less than men! (34, p. 283).

After hostilities ended in 1918, several different schemes were used to force women back into their traditional roles at home, so that their jobs could be freed up for men. Britain denied women unemployment benefits and prevented married women from obtaining certain jobs, including teaching positions. France used bribery, offering bonuses to women who would relinquish their jobs and Germany enacted legislation ordering the dismissal first of women whose husbands worked, and a few years later, of married women who were employed by the government (30, vol. 2, p. 207). France offered medals to women who had five or more children (ibid., p. 209) and, to add some additional pressure, contraceptives were banned in 1920 and abortions were criminalized. Fascist countries – Germany, Italy and later Spain – followed suit. In 1931, Pius XI called for an end to the employment of married women (ibid., p. 208).

Some progressive legislation was enacted and in Britain, the Sex Disqualification Act of 1919 allowed women to be lawyers, judges, jurors and Members of Parliament, but these positions were scarce (6, vol. 23, p. 624). Almost 20 years later, WWII led to the remobilization of women for the armed forces and munitions factories.

The United States enacted a series of laws in the mid-nineteenth century, allowing women to practice law and providing them with equal employment opportunities and the Civil Rights Act of 1964 prohibited discrimination in hiring and employment. Although women now make up more than 50 per cent of the labour force in North America and most European countries, only 12 Fortune 500 companies and 25 Fortune 1,000 companies, had women chief executive officers or presidents in 2009 (39). These numbers demonstrate progress during the past 50 years but also show how much remains to be achieved. Girls are still greatly under-represented in science although more are being attracted into this area, thanks to improvements in education.

Inheritance and Property Rights

Women were classed as minors and subordinate to their husbands in Europe and North America until the later part of the nineteenth century. They could inherit money and property, but control of both passed to their husbands when they married. This had not always been so; Danish women could own land until the law there was changed at the end of the seventeenth century; so could Prussian women until the end of the eighteenth century (30, vol. 2, p. 149). The Code Napoléon classed women with 'children, the insane and criminals, as legal incompetents' (ibid., p. 149). French law was not changed until 1938 and again in 1942. Until then, French women could not buy, sell or receive property and financial assets owned by them prior to marriage, or money earned after this, belonged to their husbands (ibid., p. 150). Unless she already had a legacy, a French widow's share of her husband's estate was less than that of a twelfth degree relative. This was eventually changed to one quarter and one half if there were no children.

There was no such legal code in English law and yet, a husband had the right to control his wife's property, inheritance and earned income. In 1856, a group of women petitioned Parliament after collecting 26,000 signatures from supporters (30, vol. 2, p. 360). Their request was denied. After several more attempts, they were successful and in 1878, women were finally allowed to control their own earnings and in 1882, their own property. This coincided with the beginning of the Women's Movement in England.

The Women's Property Act of New York was passed in 1849 and gave women control of any property they owned before marriage or acquired later. Scandinavian countries and Germany gave women control of their own property in 1957 and assets were equally divided at the time of divorce or the death of her partner.

Right to Vote

Most European countries did not enfranchise women until well into the twentieth century. Since legislatures were entirely masculine, denial was a simple matter. In the United States, it took intense effort by Susan B. Anthony, Elizabeth Cady Stanton and others and several attempts in the House and Senate to finally change this in 1920. Until then, a small number of women had sided with nearly all men to block this change. Meanwhile, New Zealand had allowed women to vote in 1893, Finland in 1906 and a few European countries did the same during or shortly after WWI, sometimes in recognition of their war efforts. Restrictions were often attached to the legislation; England allowed women who were over 30 to vote in 1918 but did not extend this privilege to 21 year-olds until 1928. Other countries required women to have a number of children or earn school diplomas first. Some disenfranchised women again later; Fascist states like Germany did so in 1933 and Spain followed in 1939 (30, vol. 1, p. 211). Greece copied them in 1936 and so did Poland in 1933. France, Italy, Switzerland, Portugal, Belgium and Bulgaria did not allow women to vote until after the end of WWII in 1945. A male-only referendum in Switzerland rejected women's suffrage in 1959. Catholic countries were usually a generation behind in the women's suffrage movement despite support from Pope Benedict XV in 1919 (30, vol. 2, p. 366). Latin American countries were also slow to enfranchise women; Brazil and Uruguay were the first and did this in 1932, Argentina in 1947, Chile in 1949, Mexico in 1953, Colombia in 1954 and Peru in 1955 (40).

Relatively few women have been elected to legislative offices in local or national elections, although there are some well-known examples of women prime ministers in India, Sri Lanka, Europe, Argentina and Chile. Very few women have achieved offices of importance in their governments. In 1960, only 6.4 per cent of the United States House of Representatives were women, but their number in both the 111th Congress and Senate is 17 per cent. This compares with 20 per cent in the British, 22 per cent in the Canadian, 18 per cent in the French and 47 per cent in the Swedish Parliament (41).

Marriage

The Roman Catholic Church elevated marriage to a sacrament in the twelfth century. This was confirmed again at the Council of Trent when it was decreed 'If anyone shall say that matrimony is not truly and properly one of the seven sacraments of the Evangelical Law instituted by Christ our Lord, but was invented by men, and does not confer grace, let him be anathema' (42). Marriages required the assent of both parties but were often arranged for political and financial reasons, particularly among the upper classes and frequently involved the exchange of money and or property.

Starting in the early nineteenth century, civil law usually replaced church law for family matters, except in Catholic countries such as Spain, Portugal and Italy. France accorded some degree of equality to women during the Revolution of 1789. But Napoleon, who became emperor in 1804, believed women should be subordinate to men and these laws were rescinded. There were other sweeping changes in French law, which became known as the Code Napoléon. At the time of her marriage, a girl passed from her father's to her husband's control. He was now the head of the household with full legal control and had the right to decide where they should live and work. A wife could not work or make a charitable donation without her husband's permission. He owed his wife protection and she owed him obedience (30, vol. 2, p. 149). She could not plead in court or sign a contract without his authority. The law allowed a husband to use physical means to enforce his will although this was supposed to be moderate. He also had complete control of their children. These Napoleonic laws were adopted by most European countries except England, where there were different but equally misogynistic practices. Similar laws were adopted in French Canada, Louisiana and most Latin American states and were not revised until the twentieth century.

Christian marriage ceremonies still retain the word 'obey' in the vows made by the wife, but this is voluntary and generally most churches recognize the equality of the partners in a marriage. There are exceptions and these include the Southern Baptist Convention, a fundamentalist division of the Baptist Church. They adhere to a literal translation of the scriptures, interpreted by them to mean women are subordinate to men; further, the wife should accept this situation 'graciously'.

Divorce

Divorce was not an option in most Christian countries until the eighteenth century (6, vol. 7, p. 513). Protestant and Catholic Churches view this differently; since marriage is a sacrament in the Catholic Church, it is indissoluble. This ruling is inconsistent with Old Testament and New Testament scriptures, which state a man, should divorce his wife if she commits adultery (2, Mt.

19.9). The Catholic Church has always permitted the annulment of marriage – and subsequent remarriage – for special reasons, depending on the wealth and power of the supplicants.

Neither Luther nor Calvin viewed marriage as a sacrament but rather as a civil contract. Divorce was permitted on specific grounds such as adultery and 'malicious desertion', and the innocent party was allowed to remarry. Puritans in England were advocates of divorce but this was generally denied to them and required a private Act of Parliament. During the second part of the nineteenth century, the jurisdiction of family law cases was transferred from ecclesiastic to civil courts in England and a man could then seek to divorce his wife for adultery but she had to cite a second cause in addition to his adultery. This was equalized in 1923 and additional grounds for divorce were added in 1950. The same practice was followed in the United States until the Revolution, after which divorce was adjudicated according to the statutes of each state. Residency requirements varied but have since been standardized.

Civil courts grant divorces now in most Protestant European countries. In France, divorce was freely available in 1792 after the Revolution, but denied again when the monarchy returned. Then it became legal again in 1884 but an addendum stated that thereafter a woman could no longer use her husband's name. Scandinavia, Belgium and the Netherlands allow divorce by mutual consent. Divorce was legalized in Italy in 1970 but for a limited number of reasons. The Catholic Church's campaign for the repeal of this law backfired and it was reaffirmed by a majority of the electorate (30, vol. 2, p. 418). Spain and Portugal have limited grounds for divorce except for non-Catholics in Portugal. Ireland does not recognize divorce unless the parties have lived apart for four of the preceding five years. In 2000, admission to the European Union equalized divorce proceedings in all member states but this covered civil and not religious partnerships. The Orthodox Church usually accepts the civil divorce code of each state, but Greece requires an attempt at reconciliation.

Divorce was not permitted in any Latin American countries until the mid-twentieth century and this continued in five countries until the 1960s. Chile retained its old law until 2004 when divorce was finally allowed but for a very limited number of reasons. All marriages here require a civil ceremony and divorce can be obtained through civil courts.

Child Custody

Until the twentieth century, the father as head of the family had complete control of all the children of a marriage and the mother had no rights in the event of a divorce (6, vol. 5, p. 511). This changed in England in 1925 when both parents were awarded equal rights and financial support was provided for the mother. Her rights were expanded later so that she now has a greater claim to custody than the father. These changes coincided with legislation giving greater consideration to the welfare of the child. Similar laws were passed in the United States and most other European countries.

Reproductive Rights

Christianity opposed the killing of female infants from its earliest days. In contrast to some older cultures, it has a long history of opposition to birth control. Jerome called it murder of 'a man not yet born' (30, vol. 1, p. 82). Calvin echoed Jerome's earlier views and described *coitus interruptus* as 'monstrous' (ibid., p. 260). The Christian Church took no position on abortion for its first six centuries, in accordance with the teaching of Aristotle, upheld by Augustine, that the foetus had no soul until 40 days after conception for a male and 90 days for a female (43, p. 87). Abortion was not viewed as murder and was therefore punished no more severely than theft but nevertheless, it was a crime because it concealed 'adultery and fornication' which were of far more concern to the Church (ibid.). The reason the Reformation leaders – Luther and Calvin – opposed abortion was because they viewed childbirth as the way for a woman to achieve salvation (30, vol. 1, p. 260). Women were expected to do penance after a miscarriage and Puritan women were taught that failure to breastfeed was a sin (ibid., p. 82).

In 1588, Pope Sixtus V issued his decree that abortion and contraception were murder, only to be annulled by Gregory XIV in 1591. Innocent XI again declared abortion to be murder in 1679 as did Pius IX in 1864, who ordered excommunication for abortion at any stage of pregnancy (43, p. 88). In 1965, contraception and abortion were both forbidden by Paul V1.

Condoms became more readily available for men as rubber became cheaper and more plentiful and women – who could afford them – were fitted with diaphragms. In 1882, Aletta Jacobs opened the world's first birth control clinic in Holland (30, vol. 2, p. 445). Marie Stopes did the same in England in 1921 and contraception became more generally available in Germany and Scandinavia. The Church of England approved its use in 1931 (ibid., p. 203). The Catholic Church opposes any artificial method of birth control and permits only the rhythm method. In 1965, Paul VI reaffirmed that every act of sexual intercourse must be open to the transmission of life (44). In the United States, birth control became available in the 1950s.

Russia was the first European country to legalize abortion in 1920 (30, vol. 2, p. 210), and Stalin banned it in 1936, in an attempt to increase the birth rate. Abortion has remained the most common method of birth control in Russia. It was illegal in Western Europe until the mid-twentieth century but was legal and generally easy to obtain in Eastern Europe from the 1950s, except in Romania from 1966 to 1989 under Ceaucescu (43, p. 102). France enacted laws to punish abortionists and the women who had them and executed a practitioner in 1943. Women who had many children were rewarded with medals (30, vol. 2, p. 209). Then in 1968, the sale of contraceptive devices was permitted and despite the opposition of the medical profession and the Catholic Church, abortion was legalized in 1975 (ibid., p. 418). Demonstrations led by women clearly made a difference here. Many other European nations enacted similar laws. Fascist governments under Mussolini in Italy, Hitler in Germany and Franco in Spain denied the sale of contraceptives and abortion services; Jews and gypsies were exempted (ibid., p. 210). Spain legalized birth control clinics in 1978 and abortions in 1985. Italy did the same in the 1980s. Irish law has permitted the sale of contraceptives since 1980 but does not allow sterilizations or abortions. Irish women needing these services must travel to England.

Abortion within the first two trimesters of pregnancy was legalized in the United States in 1973. Latin American countries do not permit abortion and there are no well-organized women's movements to promote changes in the laws, as in France and Italy. The Catholic Church as well as Fundamentalist and Evangelical Christians oppose it. Reports from Latin America estimate that 30–50 per cent of their maternal deaths result from attempted abortions. Ten to 15 per cent of women in Peru's prisons are there because of illegal abortions (43, p. 90). Despite this opposition, birth control clinics are being organized, some with government support. In 1986, the Peruvian Institute for Responsible Parenthood established clinics for youths aged 10 to 25 years in five cities. Nicaragua started to do the same in 1986 and Ecuador in 1998. This has become more critical in light of the AIDS epidemic and some countries in Latin America such as Guatemala, have established clinics to dispense condoms, sometimes with the support of the local priests (45). A leftist government was elected in Nicaragua in 2008 because of support from the Roman Catholic Church and subsequently banned abortions for any reason.

Except for Catholic and Evangelical Christians, most Christian religions permit abortion, usually with some restrictions. The latter have taken over the leadership of the Southern Baptist Convention and oppose abortion for any reason including rape and incest (43, p. 65).

The European Union enacted laws through its Parliament to promote equal rights including reproductive rights for women; these must be addressed before a country seeks admission. However, states like Malta and Ireland can claim religion as an excuse for denying these.

Rape and Violence Against Women

Rape and acts of violence against women are common and are governed by secular laws in most Christian states. Many now have improved services for rape victims and do not require a woman's prior sexual experiences to be cited as evidence. Nevertheless, many cases of rape are not reported because of individual or family reticence, out of fear for the future prospects of the victim. Marital rape is now viewed as a crime in many countries.

In Catholic countries, the care of prostitutes was generally left to nuns who established houses of refuge to care for them. Protestant countries had no such provision. From the early nineteenth century, many European countries followed the example of France and legalized prostitution. They were required to register and had to be 16 years or older. Brothels were inspected and the women they employed were required to have regular medical examinations to detect venereal disease, mainly to protect their male patrons. Those who resisted or disobeyed were imprisoned and there were repeated complaints of abuse by the police. Most prostitutes were poor women and at least 25 per cent had been domestic workers who lost their jobs once their pregnancies were discovered (30, vol. 2, p. 258).

Both men and women have worked to reform laws governing prostitution and especially to ban police inspections. One of the best-known reformers of the late nineteenth century was Josephine Butler. Her efforts were met with the retort 'there is no comparison to be made between prostitutes and those men who consort with them. With the one it is a matter of gain and with the other, an irregular indulgence of a natural impulse.' (ibid., p. 265). The campaign for the abolition of state regulations succeeded in England and Norway but was unsuccessful elsewhere in Europe (ibid., p. 421).

Women in Religion

Many arguments have been used to prevent women from becoming priests and these include the claim that they are inferior, or could cause pollution or contamination because of their natural bodily functions, or because their female bodies lack resemblance to Jesus, or because none of the disciples were women. The first two of these excuses are incorrect and as for the third, there is no extant description of Jesus and for the fourth, Mary Magdalene and certain other women were disciples (30, vol. 1, p. 69). The Gospel of Thomas identifies Mary Magdalene and Salome as such, in addition to Thomas, James, Peter and Matthew (28, p. 378). Paul called Junia 'foremost among the apostles' (31, p. 33) and Tabitha was also identified as a disciple (2, Acts 9.36).

A review of the history of the Christian Church reveals the presence of women in the priesthood during the first millennium (31, p. 2). A woman founded the Philippi church at the time of Paul. Until the third century, there were women deacons, presbyters, priests and even bishops. Bishop Theodora is a good example (31, p. 10). By the fourth century, Christians were beginning to worship in churches and basilicas rather than private homes and other meeting places and with this change to a more formal place of worship there was pressure particularly from the hierarchy, to subordinate women. This was endorsed by the bishop's courts, which had almost unchallenged authority after the Christian Church became the official religion of the Roman Empire. By the thirteenth century, its priesthood was closed to women, a policy endorsed by the influential Thomas Aquinas who argued that women were inferior, a belief he gleaned from Graeco-Roman culture and one of its best-known philosophers, Aristotle. The Reformation leaders, Luther and Calvin concurred (30, vol. 1, p. 246), as did the Catholic Counter-Reformation at the Council of Trent in 1560.

Differing views concerning the ordination of women are held by the various Protestant denominations that began after the Reformation. Those that practise sacramental rites argue that a priest must resemble Jesus in order to effect the transubstantiation of wine and bread at the Eucharist. These include the Roman Catholic, Episcopalian and Eastern Orthodox Churches (46, p. 86). Others – mostly non-hierarchical and non-sacramental – believe men and women are equal, and from their inception approved the ordination of women. These include the Friends (Quakers), Salvation Army, and Church of the Nazarene. Congregationalists ordained women first in 1853 but rarely allowed them to serve as pastors until later (46, p. 6).

Today, about one half of all Christian denominations in the United States grant full equality to women priests. The Roman Catholic, Eastern Orthodox, Southern Baptist Convention and Church of Latter Day Saints (Mormons) do not. The African Methodist Episcopalians ordained women in 1898, Methodists and Presbyterians in the United States in 1956, American Lutherans in 1970 (Scandinavia where Lutheranism is the state religion, did so earlier), Episcopalians in 1976 and the Church of England – by a margin of three votes – in 1992. The Methodist Church elected its first woman bishop in 1980; the Episcopalian and Lutheran Churches did so at a later date. A 1970 United States census report, found that 3 per cent of the clergy were women and this had increased to 10 per cent in 1990 (46, p. 15). These numbers are well below those in the medical and legal professions, both of which respect statutes concerning gender equality.

The Vatican continues to deny ordination to women nor will it allow them to hear confessions or officiate at mass. Nevertheless, women are ministering a large number of parishes because of the acute shortage of priests (46, p. 5). In 1930, Pius XI stated, 'Women's efforts for equality are debasing and unnatural' (46, p. 203). Two papal statements in 1994 and 1995 toned this down but the basic denial remains. The Southern Baptist Convention issued its revised statement of faith in 1984; this denied the right of women to become priests, citing 1 Cor. 14.34 that states women should be silent and subordinate and explains that this is because Adam was created first and Eve was the first to fall (46, p. 89). This occurred despite its earlier post-Reformation acceptance of women in this role. According to its scriptures, all male Mormons are allowed to preach and there is no distinction between the clergy and laypersons. Women are however excluded (47).

Public Health Data

Mortality figures are not strictly a religious issue but rather the result of the practical application of public health measures depending for implementation on the economic conditions of a state. Nevertheless, maternal and infant mortality rates as well as the reproductive practices of women are influenced by the way a state upholds the rules of its state or dominant religion.

Improvements in public health allowed more children to survive to adulthood and with this came an initial increase in family size followed by a steady fall, with the exception of post-war periods. In Britain in 1890 there were 5.11 children in a working-class family and 2.8 in a professional-class family. By the 1920s, this had decreased to 3.05 in the former and 1.69 in the latter and the difference between the two has continued to decrease (30, vol. 2. p. 285). Birth rates in most countries in Europe have steadily declined from over 20 per 1,000 population in 1920 to 10 in 2003 and fertility is less than 2.0 in most European countries (48). In North America, the estimated birth rate for 2009 was 14 per 1,000, and the fertility rate was 2.0 (48). This compares to 20 per 1,000 for the same period in Latin America and an average of 2.3 children per woman (48).

Maternal mortality rates measure deaths from pregnancy complications per 100,000 live-births; these have generally fallen and estimates for 2005 show they were less than 12 in most European and North American countries and on average, rates were 10 times higher in Latin-America (49). Maternal mortality is closely related to the number of pregnancies a woman has and their spacing, as well as the availability and standard of prenatal care. Lack of family planning facilities as well as the denial of safe abortions result in more pregnancies and complications and therefore adversely affect the general health of women and maternal mortality rates. Some method of birth control was used by 74 per cent of women in Western Europe, 64 per cent in Eastern Europe, 73 per cent in North America and 71 per cent in Latin America and the Caribbean (48). Infant mortality estimates for 2009 showed a decline to 4 per 1,000 live-births in Western Europe, 8 in Eastern Europe, 6 in North America and 23 in Latin-America and the Caribbean (48).

Summary

Christianity began in about 30 CE, in what is now Palestine. Its leader was Jesus whose message was a promise of eternal life to those who obeyed the commandments to love God and their fellow men. He attracted a number of followers, all of them Jews. His ministry lasted only for two to three years until he was condemned to death. He left no written record of his teaching and his closest associates were illiterate. After his death, Christianity continued to spread throughout the region.

Jerusalem, the Jewish capital, was destroyed in 70 CE and most of its inhabitants fled. Although the first group of converts had been Jews, the second group were mainly Gentiles from Asia Minor, the Near East and Southern Europe, for whom some of the strict Judaic laws were relaxed. Women outnumbered men among these early converts; some supplied money and meeting places while others became disciples, priests and prophets in the new faith.

There was a plethora of Christian sects in the first few centuries of Christianity, with different beliefs concerning the humanity or divinity of Jesus, his relationship to God, his second coming and his message of eternal life. These early Christians experienced nearly 400 years of persecution at the hands of their Roman rulers. Many – including a large number of women – died as martyrs. Then, in a move to bolster his failing empire, the Roman emperor Constantine halted further persecutions and made Christianity the state religion and granted the early Church many favours. He supported their claim that Jesus was divine in order to bolster his own claim to divinity.

Over time, the Roman faction gained control of the early Church and installed a hierarchical administration modelled on the Roman Empire and headed by a bishop who eventually became the Pope. Despite the original message of gender equality, women were marginalized more and more, denied any role in the priesthood and made subordinate to men in all things. In this, Christianity was conforming to the beliefs and practices of society and older religions but disobeying the message of its founder.

The Christian scriptures include the Jewish Bible, which became the Old Testament, together with its own story recounted in the New Testament. The official doctrines of the Church were decided at several councils of bishops and by about 400 CE, the Gospels and Epistles for the New Testament had been selected. Tracts containing dissenting accounts together with other early literature deemed unworthy of inclusion were destroyed. Some of these survived, to be discovered about 1,800 years later and provide additional and sometimes differing accounts of its leader and his message.

Rome was defeated in about 400 CE, and during the ensuing Dark Ages the Christian Church provided an anchor of stability. It continued to grow until virtually all of Europe, with the exception of Moorish Spain, had converted to its faith.

The first major schism occurred in the eleventh century and resulted in the separation of the Eastern Church with its capital in Constantinople, over disputes concerning papal authority, the creed and religious practices. The second was the Protestant Reformation in the sixteenth century, precipitated by Martin Luther and others over the misuse of papal authority, the sale of indulgences and the Church's claim to the sole right to interpret the scriptures. The Reformation gave rise to several Protestant Churches, which in time led to others. The response of the Roman Church was the Counter-Reformation, which simply restated its old beliefs but did little to correct abuses. Eventually, most of Northern Europe except for Ireland became Protestant while Southern Europe remained Roman Catholic: Eastern Europe and Russia followed the Eastern Orthodox religion. Spanish invasions of Central and Southern America and the Philippines in the fifteenth and sixteenth centuries ensured the conversion of their native people to the Roman Catholic faith, often under threats of force.

After its first few centuries, the Christian Church demoted women and treated them as inferiors, blaming them for the initial sin at Creation. Despite their founder's teaching that men and women are equal, women were denied any religious authority.

Until the nineteenth century, most women living in Christian countries could neither read nor write, had no control of their own earned or unearned incomes or any right to the custody of their children: they could not vote, be ordained as priests, initiate a divorce or control their own reproductive functions. It was not until the mid to late nineteenth and early twentieth centuries that any remedial action was taken, primarily by secular authorities. With some exceptions, the Protestant Churches have been more supportive of women's rights with regard to property and finances, family law, suffrage and ordination. Many of their reforms occurred only through the concerted efforts of women themselves. In predominantly Catholic countries, the Church has had a strongly deterrent influence on any legislation which affects family law particularly divorce and reproductive choices, which were long delayed or are still denied to women in Latin America, the Philippines, Ireland and Malta.

Women have made rapid progress within a short period of time toward equality in education and employment, especially in Europe and North America. They remain markedly under-represented in national legislatures and government which are the most promising avenues to correct inequalities and thwart the efforts of fundamentalists whose goal is to return women to their previous subjugation in the name of Christianity.

References

1   Eusebius. *The History of the Church from Christ to Constantine*. Tr. G. A. Williamson. New York. Barnes and Noble. 1965.
2   *Holy Bible* Revised Standard Version. New York. Oxford University Press. 2000.
3   Gardner, Laren. *Blood Line of the Holy Grail*. Gloucester. Fairwinds Press. 2002.
4   Picknett, Lynn. *Mary Magdalene*. New York. Carroll and Graf. 2003.
5   *Encyclopedia Britannica*. Ed. W. Benton. University of Chicago Press. 1968.
6   Christie-Murray, David. *A History of Heresy*. Oxford University Press. 1976.

7   Chadwick, Henry. 'The Early Christian Community'. In *The Oxford History of Christianity*. Ed. John McManners. Oxford University Press. 1990.

8   Ehrman, Bart D. *Jesus Interrupted*. Harper One. 2009.

9   Daniel-Rops, H. *The Church in the Dark Ages*. Tr. Andrew Butler. London. Phoenix Press. 1959.

10   Whalen, John P. 'The Forging of Christendom'. In *Great Religions of the World*. Ed. Merle Severy. National Geographic Society. 1971.

11   Revill, J. C. *World History*. London. Longmans, Green & Company. 1953.

12   Ware, Kallista. 'Eastern Christendom'. In *The Oxford History of Christianity*. Ed. John McManners. Oxford University Press. 1990.

13   Morris, Colin. 'Christian Civilization'. Ibid.

14   Johns, Jeremy, J. 'Christianity and Islam'. Ibid.

15   Wilson, Derek. *Sir Francis Walsingham*. New York. Carol and Graf. 2007.

16   Collinson, Patrick. 'The Late Medieval Church'. In *The Oxford History of Christianity*. Ed. John McManners. Oxford University Press. 1990.

17   McManners, John. 'Enlightenment: Secular and Christian (1600–1800)'. Ibid.

18   Chadwick, Owen. 'Great Britain and Europe'. Ibid.

19   Barrera, Julic T. *The Jewish and the Christian Bibles*. Tr. W. G. E. Watson, Brill Eerdmans. 1998.

20   Finkelstein, Israel, and Neil A. Silberman, *The Bible Unearthed*. New York. The Free Press. 2001.

21   Pagels, Elaine. *Adam, Eve, and the Serpent*. New York. Vintage Books. 1998.

22   Lerner, Gerda. *The Creation of Patriarchy*. Oxford University Press. 1986.

23   Mack, Barton. L. *Who Wrote the New Testament?* New York. Harper Collins. 1995.

24   Baum, Walter. *Orthodoxy and Heresy in Earliest Christianity*. Tr. Philadelphia Team in Christian Origin. Philadelphia. Forrester Press. 1970.

25   Pagels, Elaine. *The Origin of Satan*. New York. Random House. 1995.

26   Jordan, Michael. *The Historical Mary*. Berkeley. Seastone. 1988.

27   Davies, Stevan. *The Gospel of Thomas*. Boston. Shambhala. 2004.

28   Layton, Bentley. *The Gnostic Scriptures*. New York. Doubleday. 1987.

29   Ehrman, Bart D. *Lost Scriptures: Books That Did Not Make It Into The New Testament*. Oxford University Press. 2003.

30   Anderson, Bonnie. S. and Judith. P. Zissner. *A History of Their Own*. Vols 1 & 2. New York. Harper and Row. 1988.

31   Torjesen, Karen J. *When Women Were Priests*. San Francisco. Harper Collins. 1993.

32   Wilson, A. N. *Paul*. New York. Norton and Co. 1997.
33   Clark, Elizabeth A. *Women in the Early Church*. 1983. Michael Glazier Inc. Wilmington DE.
34   McNamara, J. A. *Sisters in Arms*. Harvard University Press. 1996.
35   Hufton, Olwen. *The Prospect Before Her*. New York. Vintage Books. 1998.
36   Gimbutas, Marija. *The Language of the Goddess*. New York. Thames and Hudson. 1989.
37   Bonnie, G. Smith. *The Gender of History*. Harvard University Press. 1998.
38   *Indicators of Literacy*. www. Index Mundi. 2009.
39   www. infopleaase.com/spot/womenceol.html
40   www. newworldencyclopedis.org/entry/Women suffrage.html
41   www. Ipu.org/wmn-e/speakers.htm
42   www. godweb. org/marriagesanaments.html.
43   French, Marilyn. *The War against Women*. New York. Ballantine Books. 1992.
44   Templeton, C. *Farewell to God: My Reasons for Rejecting the Christian Faith*. www. submission.org.christians.
45   Repogle, J. *Sex and the Catholic Church in Guatemala*. Lancet. 366. 622. 2005.
46   Chaves, Mark. *Ordaining Women*. Harvard University Press. 1997.
47   Longaker, J. *The Role of Women in Mormonism*. www. exmormon.org/mormwomn.htm 1995.
48   www. *World population data*. Population Reference Bureau. Washington. 2003. www.prb.org.
49   Hill, Kenneth *et al*. *Estimates of Maternal Mortality Worldwide between 1990 and 2005*. Lancet, v. 370, 1311, 2007.

Additional Bibliography

Brooke, Rosalind and Christopher Brooke. *Popular Religion in the Middle Ages*. Barnes and Noble. 1984.
Evangelistii, Silvia. *Nuns: A History of Convent Life*. Oxford University Press. 2007.
Franzmann, Majella. *Jesus in the Nag Hammadi Writings*. Edinburgh. T and T Clark. 1996.
Sigmund, P. E. *Religious Human Rights in Latin America*. www. law.emory.edu/EIRL/volumes/spring96
Stark, Rodney. *The Rise of Christianity*. San Francisco. Harper. 1997.

Chapter 5

Islam

History

Arabia Before the Prophet

Arabia, at the time of the Prophet's birth, was situated between two strong neighbours who had been in conflict for several centuries, the Byzantine Empire in the north-west and the Sasanian or Persian Empire in the north-east. The influence of Rome had declined and Constantinople – or Byzantium by its old name – had become the centre of power and the capital of the empire. The city was more Greek than Roman and the majority of its population was Christian and comprised several different sects. The Sasanians were multi-ethnic and their religion was Zoroastrianism, a monotheistic faith of about the same age as Vedism. Arabia's southern neighbours included the kingdom of Axum (Ethiopia) across the Red Sea in the Horn of Africa – where Coptic Christians predominated – and Hinyar (Yemen), a polytheistic society. There were prominent Jewish centres of learning, particularly in Hijaz and a centre of Christianity in the Hiraz (1, vol. 2, p. 177).

The land here was mostly desert, dotted with oases and scattered mountainous regions. Society was tribal, each tribe claiming descent from a single ancestor whose unwritten laws – including ones to maintain tribal purity – had evolved over generations (2, p. 10). Disputes within a tribe were usually settled by arbitration, those between tribes by force, whose degree depended on the assessed value of the loss, which was often exaggerated by the aggrieved tribe. Retribution was important, because it was believed the soul of the victim could not rest in peace until this had been exacted. Most of the people were nomads who tended herds of camel, sheep and goats. Others raised crops and Medina was the centre of the agricultural region. Mecca was a commercial centre and the hub of trade routes to and from China by the silk roads, and the East Indies for the spice trade. Its main attraction was the Kaaba, a well-known shrine attracting many worshippers and pilgrims as well as merchants trading religious objects. Religion was mostly polytheistic and some of the shrines were dedicated to female gods (3, p. 77).

Life of the Prophet ~570–632CE

Muhammad was born in Mecca in the sixth century CE – around 570 – into a family of traders who were members of the Banu Hashim clan, of the Quraysh tribe. His mother died when he was quite young and he was raised first by his grandfather and then by his uncle Abu Talib, for whom he worked as a camel driver. When he was about 25 years of age, he married Khadijah, a widow who was his senior by 15 years. They had two sons who died as children and four daughters.

When he was about 40, Muhammad had some kind of religious experience during which he believed he communicated with God through the Angel Gabriel. After an interval of two years, these visions continued over the next 22 years. Muhammad could neither read nor write but the revelations he witnessed were communicated orally to his companions and eventually recorded to become the Quran. They included the injunction to 'obey God and his Prophet'. Polytheism was a sin: there was only one God who created the world, man and all else, and it was man's duty to obey and worship him (2, p. 9). Eventually this command would unite believers and transfer power to a higher authority, diminishing the control of tribal leaders.

During the next decade, the Prophet attracted a loyal group of followers in Mecca, but he also raised opposition, especially from members of his own tribe who served as guardians to the pagan shrine of the Kaaba. Some plotted to kill him and his situation became critical. He left for Yathrib – later called Medina – a town 222 miles north of Mecca and is believed to have arrived there on July 16, 622 CE. The Muslim calendar begins with this day and it marks the Muslim New Year called the Hejira (4, p. 17). The Islamic lunar calendar is 11 to 12 days shorter than the solar year, so this date changes annually. Muhammad was then about 40 years old. He continued to teach in and around Medina and this became his capital from where he controlled much of Arabia. Despite its initial hostility, his following in Mecca continued to grow and in 629 CE, the city surrendered to him without a fight.

Muhammad's wife – Khadijah – died before he left Mecca, followed shortly after by his uncle Abu Talib. The Prophet had at least ten more wives and many were the widows or daughters of his followers. His favourite was Aisha, daughter of Abu Bakr, one of his earliest supporters; she accompanied him on many campaigns and is remembered for her intellect and leadership. Their daughter Fatima married Muhammad's first cousin Ali, who would eventually become caliph. Muhammad returned to Mecca in 632 where he died in the same year. His tomb is in Medina.

The First Four Caliphs: Sunni and Shiite Sects

Abu Bakr (r. 632–643), Muhammad's father-in-law, followed him and became the first caliph (5, p. 11). This was opposed by tribal groups and led to the Apostasy wars, but within a period of two years, all of Arabia had come under the caliph's control. Umar, the brother-in-law of Abu Bakr followed as second caliph and appointed a council of six elders to name his successor. He was murdered in 644 and the council then selected Uthman (r. 644–656), son-in-law of the Prophet, as the third caliph. Uthman continued the campaign against the Sasanians whose army suffered a major defeat in 637 at modern-day Kadisiya in Southern Iraq (5. p. 12).

Christianity was the dominant religion along the Mediterranean coast of Africa at that time, but this changed during Uthman's caliphate. Islam spread into the Byzantine and Sasanian empires, which included Syria, Iraq and parts of Persia as well as Egypt, Jerusalem and North Africa. Followers of other monotheistic religions who lived in these regions were not forced to convert to Islam but adult males – called *dhimmi*s – were protected and allowed to practise their religion in private and govern themselves, but had to pay a poll tax (6, p. 307). Initially Muslims were in a minority here, but over time more and more of the inhabitants converted to avoid paying the tax, and for other reasons including force.

Uthman was murdered in 656 and this led to the first civil war over accusations of nepotism, misappropriation of money and lands and unfair practices by the caliph (5, p. 15). Muawiyah, a nephew of Uthman, was a contender for the caliphate and had the support of the Prophet's clan including Aisha, but Ali, son-in-law of the Prophet, opposed him and was backed by the Medinans (2, p. 103). Ali was victorious over Aisha, who led the opposing forces, in the famous Battle of the Camel. He became the fourth caliph. Ali's next major battle was against Muawiyah who belonged to a different clan although the same tribe as the Prophet. The outcome was eventually decided by arbitration and Muawiyah was selected as the next caliph – the first of the Umayyad dynasty (661–750). This was an important period in the history of Islam because it caused the first major division of Islam into the Sunni and Shiite sects. The Shiites (Shiat Ali or party of Ali) believed the caliph should be a member of the Prophet's family whose leadership was a 'divine right' (2, p. 104).

Ali was murdered in 661 by a member of an ultra-pious, militant sect of Islam – a Kharijite – who believed their leaders should be selected because of ability and like qualities, rather than by descent from the Prophet or membership in the Quraysh tribe.

Muawiyah's death in 1680 ended the period of the first four caliphs, called the *Rashidan* or Rightly Guided (4, p. 25). A second civil war erupted after this, Umayyad forces were victorious and al-Husayn – Ali's younger son – was killed at Karbala in 680 CE. He is revered as a martyr by Shiites and his death is remembered each year at Muharran in the first month of the Islamic calendar. A pilgrimage to Husayn's shrine in Karbala continues to earn great merit for Shiites.

Al-Husayn was succeeded by a series of Shiite imams, until the ninth century when his descendants died out with the Twelfth Imam who disappeared when he was nine years old. His followers believe he will reappear at some appointed time. The majority of Shiites – and nearly all of the ones in Iran – are Ithna-Ashariya or Twelvers who believe the Twelfth Imam is hidden and guides his people through a living imam or ayatollah (7, p. 95). This sect and two other much smaller ones form the three main groups of Shia. One, the Zaydites believe the imam is elected by the community and the other, the Ismailis or Seveners accept the first seven imams but believe succeeding ones were named by the preceding imam. The Ismailis later split into several groups and the Aga Khan is the imam of one of these. The Druzes are another sect of Shia and a later one, the Assassins, became the radical terrorists of the Islamic world (5, p. 49).

Sufism, another sect of Islam, probably started in the eighth century during the Umayyad caliphate but was not formally organized until the twelfth century (4, p. 74). Sufis are Muslim mystics who stress introspection and a personal relationship with God, achieved by prayer, fasting, self-denial and discipline. Sufis were involved in structured social programmes by the twelfth century, and later, of education and health care. In some regions, they were politically active and incited protests and rebellion. Their religious leaders are *Shaykhs*.

Umayyad and Abbasid Caliphates

The Umayyad caliphate lasted from 661–750 and included 14 caliphs. They were Sunni as are 90 per cent of Muslims today and their capital was Damascus. During this period, Islam expanded rapidly to reach Lahore, India in the east and into Turkistan in the north-east – then part of China – and across North Africa to Morocco. An army of Arabs and Berbers – the indigenous people of North Africa – crossed the Straits of Gibraltar into Spain, overthrew the Visigoth king in 711 and eventually occupied the whole Iberian peninsula (7, p. 25). From Spain they crossed the Pyrenees into France and into Sicily from Tunisia. Two of the holiest places in Islam were erected in this period, one, the Dome of the Rock in Jerusalem and the other the Great Mosque in Damascus.

Militant Arabs carried Islam into North Africa but stopped at the edge of the Sahara. They spread into the interior of Africa along established trade routes, south of the Sahara along the Atlantic coast and inland to Lake Chad; south into mostly Christian Nubia from Egypt; across the Red Sea to the Horn of Africa into Somalia and into mostly Christian Ethiopia and further south along the east coast of Africa (8, p. 475). By the thirteenth century, there were large Muslim populations in Kenya, Madagascar and Tanzania, so that when the Europeans arrived in the sixteenth century, Islam was well established in the coastal regions of East Africa.

Several factors contributed to the rapid expansion of Islam in the Umayyad caliphate; Muslims were imbued with *jihad* or spirit of 'militancy in extending the interests of Islam' (7, p. 313), opposing forces were weak and disorganized, the Byzantine and Sasanian empires were in decline, Europe was in the Dark Ages, Christianity was beset by schisms and there was no single power capable of opposing them in North Africa.

In 750 CE, the Abbasids – another branch of the Prophet's family – overthrew and slaughtered the Umayyads and their capital was moved from Damascus to Baghdad. One Umayyad survivor – Prince Abd al-Rahman – escaped from Syria and captured Cordoba, Spain where he united Moorish Spain. He developed Cordoba into a centre of culture. A period of peace followed between Islam, Jews and Christians and lasted until the mid-eleventh century when the Almoravids invaded Spain and fanaticism replaced tolerance. Then after the union of Castile and Leon in the thirteenth century, Christian forces recaptured Cordoba and Seville. Granada remained under Moorish control until 1492. The large Moorish and Jewish communities in Spain were given the choice of conversion to Christianity or expulsion: those that converted were known as Moriscos. The period from the eighth to the thirteenth centuries is remembered as the Golden Age of Islamic Culture. Art and architecture flourished, technical achievements including the astrolabe and pendulum clock and Arabic numerals were devised (zero was borrowed from India) and libraries and centres of learning were established (7, p. 30).

Islam Fourteenth to Twentieth Centuries

The spread of Islam and territorial conquests appear to have been a priority for the Umayyads, but their successors, the Abbasids were more concerned with Islamic religious beliefs and practices and they established several different schools to interpret Islamic law. Their product was the Sharia, the Islamic sacred law that prescribes and proscribes behaviour for all Muslims. No changes were made in the Sharia after the tenth century and over time it became increasingly remote from the daily lives of Muslims. The power of the caliphs declined after the tenth century, and local rulers in independent states replaced their centralized rule. Buyid-Shiites – who came from Northwest Iran – captured Baghdad (5, p. 32). Further north, Turkic-speaking people occupied Afghanistan and the Middle East. They had converted to Islam by the eighth century. Fatimid caliphs, claiming descent from the Prophet through his daughter, ruled Egypt (5, p. 49). The great mosque-university of al-Azhar was built in Cairo and became a centre of Sunni theology. Cairo replaced Baghdad as the centre of Islamic power.

Jerusalem had been occupied by Muslims in 658 CE but Christian pilgrims continued to visit the Holy Land in increasing numbers (6, p. 335). Pope Urban II called for a crusade to recapture Jerusalem because of reports of the desecration of Christian holy places in Jerusalem by Seljuk Turks, as well as his own commercial interests in trade centres. The first crusade – consisting mostly of men from France and Italy – set out in 1096. Antioch was captured and Jerusalem was sacked in 1099 and untold numbers of Muslims were massacred in the process. Nearly 50 years elapsed before Saladin defeated the Crusaders in 1187 at the battle of Hattin: Jerusalem was recaptured and became once more a Muslim city. The Church of the Holy Sepulchre was turned over to the Greek Orthodox faith but most of the other churches were converted into mosques. Six more crusades followed in the next 200 years until the Christians were finally driven out.

Islam's spread to South-east Asia followed trade routes between India and China through the Straits of Malacca. By the end of the thirteenth century, Islam was well established in Indonesia, particularly in the kingdom of Aceh on the island of Sumatra. It spread to Java in the fourteenth century and then to other South-east Asian islands and the Malay peninsula. Generally these settlements were in coastal regions while tribal religions persisted in other areas. Hinduism and Buddhism were already well established here by the time of Islam's arrival.

Arab merchants and soldiers brought Islam to China and Central Asia in the seventh century (9, p. 442). There are now more than 30 million Muslims in China belonging to ten different minorities of whom the Hui – the only Chinese speaking Muslims – are the most numerous. Second to them are the Uygers who live mainly in Xinjiang province.

Mughal, Safarid and Ottoman Empires

Three Islamic empires controlled the Middle East from the fourteenth to the twentieth centuries: the Shiite Safavids ruled the region between the Caspian and Arabian seas; the Ottomans who were predominantly Sunni, controlled parts of the Balkans, Southern Russia, Greece, Asia Minor and eventually lands along the Eastern and Southern Mediterranean, including the two holy cities of Mecca and Medina (10, p. 374); the Mughals ruled Afghanistan and most of Northern India including the Deccan (11, pp. 397ff.).

Two major changes affected Islam in the eighteenth century: the encroachment of European powers and the decline of the three great Muslim empires. The British and French expanded their spheres of interest and control in Africa and then Asia, the Dutch in Indonesia and, to a lesser degree, the Portuguese in all three regions.

The Safavid or Persian Empire was in decline by the early eighteenth century, and its ruler was deposed (12, p. 514). After a period of turmoil, the Qajai dynasty ruled the country until 1924 and was followed by the Pahlavi shahs – father and son – whose goal was to modernize and secularize Iran, using the model of Mustafa Kemal in Turkey. Shiism was established as the official religion. No law adverse to Islam could be considered by the state Assembly. Reza Shah began a process of secularization including educational reforms ensuring 12 years of education, and the Family Protection Law – granting women more rights – was enacted. Increasing opposition led to his exile in 1978 and Iran became a theocracy. The country has seen a great deal of unrest especially in the last five years, culminating in a series of riots over false election claims in 2009. So far the repressive regime – run by the mullahs – has managed to maintain its control.

The Indian mutiny or revolt of 1857 ended the rule of the last puppet Mughal emperor and the British crown then assumed control of India from the East India Company. The Indian penal code became law and eventually applied Western law to both civil and criminal proceedings. The Muslim League was formed in 1906 and played a major role in future negotiations. India achieved independence in 1947 but as two states divided by religion. In 1971, after armed conflict, East Pakistan became the independent state of Bangladesh. Here, 88 per cent of the population is Muslim – mostly Sunni although Sufism has been quite influential – and about 10 per cent is Hindu (13). Pakistan became an Islamic republic in 1956 and re-introduced Sharia law in 1977. About 90 per cent of its population is Muslim; the majority is Sunni but there is a sizeable Shiite population.

The Ottomans – who had adopted the Hanafi School of Islamic law – were forced to make changes in their laws because of increasing contact and trade with European countries by the end of the eighteenth century. Initially this affected commercial practices and then spread to criminal law, with little change in personal or family law. The European powers insisted that their citizens who lived and worked in the Ottoman Empire, had to be treated in accordance with the laws of their own governments. Familiarity with these led to the *Tanzimat* reforms of 1839–1876 (2, p. 149–50). Most of the changes were based on French law and new courts or *Nizamiyya*s were set up to administer them. Other parts of the Empire in the Arabian peninsular states – Saudi Arabia, Yemen, and the gulf principalities – continued to practise fundamental Islamic law. By the mid-twentieth century, most Muslim countries had adopted Western codes of law except for those in Arabia where the Sharia remains the standard.

The Empire underwent a continuous contraction of its borders in this same period. First, the Serbs revolted and then the Greeks gained independence, and by 1913 the Ottomans had lost virtually all of their European lands (4, p. 279). Then a group of Turkish army officers called the 'young Turks' seized power: their goal was bureaucratic and military reforms. Turkey entered

WWI on the side of Germany and after its defeat in 1918 lost all of its former empire. The Caliph was banished and in 1923, Turkey was declared a republic. Mustafa Kemal (1881–1938) who had led the resistance to the allies at Gallipoli in WWI, became president and a parliamentary democracy was established. Sharia and religious courts were abolished and Turkey became a secular state. A civil code based on Swiss law was adopted, as was a penal code based on Italian law. Roman script replaced Arabic and the fez was banned in government and public offices, as was the veil. Islam would no longer be the state religion and religion was to be a private matter. The President's view was that reform of Islam was a waste of time and 'as useless as a graft on dead wood' (14, p. 535). About 98 per cent of Turks are Muslims and most are Sunni.

Islamic States Today

Egypt became a British protectorate in 1918, independent in 1922 and a parliamentary democracy with a monarchy a short time later, and then a republic in 1953. It was the first Arab state to abolish Sharia courts. An independent judiciary was established and civil and penal codes based on French law were adopted.

Hasan al-Banna created the Muslim Brotherhood in 1928. His goal was to reapply Islamic doctrine in a modern society. He was critical of both the West and its secular society and the extreme conservatism of the *ulama* or religious scholars (15, p. 652). He believed Islam was a comprehensive way of life and there should be no separation of religion and government and the Sharia should be the law of the state. The Brotherhood appeared to threaten the peace of the state and many of its members were imprisoned.

The Sudan – the largest nation in Africa – became a theocracy from 1881–1898, independent in 1962 and an Islamic republic 21 years later. The population of its northern part is mostly Muslim while a large number of Christians live in the south. A recent election will decide whether the south is to become a separate state.

Syria and Lebanon became mandates of France after WWI and independent countries after WWII. Most Syrians are Sunni Muslims but there are sizeable Shiite (Alawite) and Druze populations living there. Religious courts continue to handle family law but other legal issues are under the jurisdiction of civil courts. About one half of the population of Lebanon is Muslim and mostly Sunni, and the other half is Christian. Jewish, Christian and Muslim courts deal with issues relating to family law but an independent judiciary handles all other matters, based on French law.

Palestine was a protectorate of Britain until 1948 when its administration was handed over to the United Nations. Jerusalem and Palestine proper are included in the state of Israel and no agreement has been reached about a future Palestinian state. The majority of its people are Muslim and mostly Sunni.

Iraq was a British mandate until 1932 and Feisal I was king. The monarchy ended in 1958 when the king was assassinated in a military coup. Five years later, a secular government was established until another coup brought the Baath party into power. The rule of its dictator was terminated after war with the United States, assisted by other powers. It is now an independent democracy. The majority of its population is Arab but 18 per cent are Kurds who are racially more akin to the Iranians. Ninety-seven per cent of Iraqis are Muslims of whom 60 per cent are Shiites (7, p. 176).

Ninety-two per cent of the population of Jordan is Muslim and Sunni, and about 10 per cent are Christian.

Saudi Arabia became a state in 1932 after Sheikh Ibn-Saud invaded the Hijaz and captured the two holy cities of Mecca and Medina. The country has remained an absolute monarchy ruled by the al-Saud family and without any form of representation for its people. The king is advised by the ministers he has appointed, a consultative council and the *ulama*. He established a council – the Majlis al-Shura – in 1991, consisting of 150 members appointed by him. No woman has ever been appointed to serve (16, p. 267). Municipal elections were held in 2005 but only men could vote.

Sheikh Ibn-Saud's financial resources were initially dependent on pilgrims, but oil – which was discovered in the Persian gulf shortly before and developed by the United States after WWII – has provided him and his family with enormous revenues and brought a large influx of foreign workers into the country. Oil revenues have financed Wahhabi *madrasa*s in Europe and other countries where they teach their extreme views of Islam (17, p. 20). The restrictive practices of the Wahhabi sect of Islam are strictly enforced, with the help of the fortunes and power of the Saud family. Muhammad al-Wahhab was an eighteenth century religious scholar who called for a return to orthodox Islam, as prescribed by the Hanbali School of law. The constitution is the Quran and the Sharia is the law of the land and dictates civil and penal codes, public and personal law. Vice guards called the Muttawa enforce the rules. A majority of the population is Muslim, mostly Sunni. Slavery was not abolished in Saudi Arabia until 1962.

Yemen became a republic in 1962 after an armistice was signed with Saudi Arabia and Egypt. Islamic law applies to civil, penal and family law and the population is mostly Zaydi Shiite.

Libya and Tunisia achieved independence after WWII. The people are nearly all Muslims and Sunni. Libyan civil courts follow Italian law but religious courts handle items of family law. Habib Bourguiba was Tunisia's president until he was deposed in 1987. He modernized the country and improved women's rights. The country is in a state of turmoil at present following the ousting of its second president, Zine el-Abidine ben Ali.

Algeria and Morocco were French possessions until 1962 and 1961 respectively. *Qadi* courts may be the first to hear cases in Algeria but appeals are referred to ordinary civil courts where the system is organized as in France. The Fundamentalist Muslim movement had its start here in 1964 and since then has continued its often violent attempts to establish orthodox Islam as the state religion. Morocco is a constitutional monarchy and its present ruler, Mohammed IV, claims descent from the Prophet. The judicial system is modelled after French law but family law is based on the Maliki School of Law.

Nigeria has the largest population of any African country. The north is 80–90 per cent Muslim, the south Christian and traditional tribal religions exist in both. The judicial system and civil and penal codes follow the Sharia but like other strict Islamic countries, it now has a system of appeals from the decision of the *qadi*.

More than 84 per cent of the population of Mali, Senegal, Gambia, Guinea, Niger and Somalia are Muslim (18). The number in other African states varied from less than 12 per cent in Kenya and Uganda and between 15 per cent and 56 per cent in Tanzania, Ethiopia, Chad and the Ivory Coast.

Indonesia has a population of about 238 million and is the largest Muslim population in the world. The majority are Sunni. The country became a republic and secular state after the Japanese defeat in 1945 when Dutch colonial rule ended. Sukarno – its first president – introduced the *Pancasila* or five-pillar ideology in 1967; this includes nationalism, democracy, internationalism, social justice and belief in one God (7, p. 195).

Malaysia includes Peninsular and Eastern Malaysia. It became independent in 1957 and Islam is the state religion but the constitution promises freedom to practise religion. Sixty per cent of the population is Muslim, 19 per cent Buddhist, 9 per cent Christian and 6 per cent Hindu (18). Sharia law applies only to the Muslim population. Appeals for an Islamic revival threaten the future of the secular government as well as the freedom of other religious groups (7, p. 197). In 2007, the government announced it would raise the status of Sharia courts to that of civil courts but this met with strong opposition and has not been enacted.

Muslims are the largest religious minority in India where they number over a 100 million or 11 per cent of the population, except in Kashmir and Lakshadweep where they outnumber Hindus. India is a secular state with religious freedom for its 22 per cent non-Hindu subjects (7, p. 198).

Six Muslim countries (Azerbaijan, Kazakhstan, Kyrgyzstan, Tajikistan, Turkmenistan and Uzbekistan) became independent of Russia in 1991. Its people are mostly Sunni Muslims. Russia has several other states with large Muslim populations (7, p. 201).

The majority of Albanians were Muslim until the communist takeover in 1944, after which religion was suppressed. Large populations of Muslims remain in Yugoslavia where most lived in Bosnia-Herzegovina.

Muslims now form the largest ethnic minority in the United Kingdom where they number about 1.6 million (19). They are well organized and are making demands that schools meet Islamic requirements, including separation of the sexes and instruction in the Quran.

The Muslim population in the United States derives from two sources; immigrants seeking better job opportunities and their children and converts who are United States citizens and mostly African-Americans and their children. Their number is unknown but is believed to be about 2.6 million (20). They have established schools, mosques and Islamic centres. The Nation of Islam originated in Chicago in 1925 and called for the separation of whites and blacks, a separate state, release of all blacks from prison and tax exemptions. There has been dissension and internal conflict among its leaders. Islamic authorities view the Nation of Islam as a heretical sect (7, p. 238).

Today, there are over 50 Muslim states and although some have become wealthy from oil revenues, most are underdeveloped and have poor standards of living. A few have become secular states while others like Iran and Saudi Arabia, are theocracies.

Islamic fundamentalism appeared as a form of protest during the colonial period and then subsided until the beginning of the twentieth century. It emerged again after WWII when most Muslim countries achieved independence and the State of Israel was established. Fundamentalism is described as a 'return to the roots and a recapture of both the purity and the vitality of Islam as it was at its inception' (21, p. 198). Mernissi describes fundamentalists as high achievers coming from middle class parents and stable families who experienced upheavals in their moves from rural backgrounds to large metropolitan areas (22, p. xxi). She identifies two requirements for its establishment: 'unplanned rural migration coupled with a mushrooming state-funded university'. Forty-three per cent are students, 13 per cent professionals, 15 per cent workers and 11 per cent are unemployed. Most of its members were recruited in Iran and Egypt but more recent members came from families who moved to the United States and England (ibid.).

No single authority speaks for Islam or appears willing to condone or condemn the conduct or behaviour of its followers. The Organization of Islamic Conference (O.I.C.) is based in Saudi Arabia and has a membership of 57 Muslim states. It meets every three years to consider new issues including political developments and could provide a forum for unity under Islam (23, p. 150). It has not as yet concerned itself with human rights' abuses or with civil wars involving Muslim states (17, p. 15). The Muslim World League is another Islamic organization, also based in Saudi Arabia, which distributes funds to propagate its beliefs. Their degree of interaction with other religions and states is not known.

Islamic Scriptures and Women

Quran

Islamic scriptures consist of the Quran and Hadith. Muslims believe the Quran is the infallible Word of God, 'a transcript of a tablet preserved in heaven', transmitted to the Prophet Muhammad through the Angel Gabriel (24, p. 1). Muhammad could neither read nor write but the messages he received were repeated verbally to his Companions who recorded them in various ways. The initial transcriptions were in *Kufic* script, later translated into Arabic and interpreters added their own variations during this process. The texts were prepared during Umar's caliphate (*r.* 634–644), between two and 12 years after the Prophet's death, but the authorized version was completed in Caliph Uthman's time (*r.* 644–656). The Quran contains 114 chapters and 350 verses of which 140 concern prayer, alms, fasting and pilgrimage; 70 cover family law; 70 concern commercial transactions, 30 cover crime and punishment; 30 concern justice and 10 cover economic affairs as well as parables and history. They are not classified by subject, nor are they arranged in any particular order.

Hell and the punishments prescribed for unbelievers and those that commit evil are mentioned several times in the Quran (24, sura 3: v. 197; sura 2: vv. 23, 81; sura 18: v. 29) as is paradise (ibid., sura 18: v. 30; sura 43: v. 72), warnings about false gods (ibid, sura 14: v. 30) and judgement day (ibid., sura 2: v. 62). There are admonitions to 'show kindness to your parents, to your kinsfolk, to orphans and to the destitute' (ibid., sura 2: v. 83). Rules for prayer and prior purification are clearly explained (ibid., sura 4: v. 43; sura 5: v. 6; sura 2: v. 150).

The Quran mentions other scriptured religions such as Zoroastrianism, Judaism and Christianity, as well as some of their literature, including the Gospel of Jesus, the Torah and the Psalms of David, but to Muslims, the most sacred parts are the words of the Prophet (7, p. 47). There is frequent mention of Job, Lot and other Old Testament figures. Earlier prophets are also recognized including Abraham, the father of both Islam and Judaism through Ismail and Jacob, as well as Noah, Adam, Moses and Jesus, whose name appears more than 90 times (7, p. 49). No one, including Muhammad is divine, he performed no miracles, is the last prophet and will have no successors: anyone claiming to be a prophet at a later date is an imposter.

Hadith

The Hadith records the Sunna or customs and practices of the Prophet and is therefore a model for Muslim behaviour. Initially many versions existed whose authenticity was determined by religious scholars – the *ulama*. The best known – but not the only edition of the Hadith – is the one prepared in the ninth century and attributed to al-Bukhari. This is the primary source of Islamic law for Sunni Muslims (25, p. 75). The Hadith was completed in the second half of the ninth century, about 250 years after the death of the Prophet, and contains six major collections called the al-Kitub al Sittah or Six Books (ibid.). These clarify some of the statements in the Quran but never contradict them. Both the Hadith and Quran are divine revelations and therefore unchanging and immutable. They include the Hadith of Gabriel which identifies the Five Pillars or Tenets of Islam, to: proclaim out loud that there is no god but Allah and Muhammad is his messenger: pray five times daily at dawn, noon, mid-afternoon, sunset and evening facing toward Mecca, after ritual ablution with water or sand: pay a yearly tithe (estimated to be 2.5 per cent of each believer's income-generating property or assets), to be used to feed the poor, ransom prisoners and encourage conversions: observe the fast of Ramadan: make a pilgrimage to Mecca at least once in a lifetime. Shiites pay an extra tithe amounting to 20 per cent of new income (25, p. 83). Additionally, each Muslim must actively work toward the spread of Islam or *jihad*. The Six Articles of Faith for all Muslims are to believe in: Allah; Allah's angels; Allah's revealed books (the Quran, New Testament, Psalms of David, Torah and the Pages of Abraham); Allah's messengers and previous prophets; Judgement Day; Allah's control of all things good and bad (25, p. 88). Shiite Muslims take their traditions from their imams since they believe they are the descendants of the Prophet. These traditions were compiled in the tenth century (25, p. 75).

Al-Bukhari accepted over 7,000 Hadiths as authentic out of many times that number reviewed by him (26, p. 44). Aisha, the Prophet's favourite wife is said to have been the source of 1,210 of these (26, p. 77). Forty-three are about women (27). Aisha is said to have objected when women were blamed, along with 'dogs and asses', for interrupting men's prayers (26, p. 70). Two Hadiths say that women should 'not be prevented from attending mosques but praying at home is better'. Umar – the second caliph – objected to his wife's prayers in the mosque. The topic of women's travel is mentioned in several; another Hadith says a woman should not be married against her will; another, that she should not seek a divorce without reason – men could divorce for any or no reason at all; they are reminded it is their duty to obey their husband's demands for sex – even if they are busy – for instance 'while on a camel'; that most of the individuals the Prophet observed at 'hell-fire' were women because they were 'ungrateful'. Many Hadiths concern women's dress, her make-up, her jewellery and her hair colour. Another Hadith says 'those who entrust their affairs to a woman will never know prosperity' (26, p. 50). These words are said to have been spoken by the Prophet after he learned that the Persians had named a woman to rule them; she happened to be the daughter of their assassinated king (ibid.).

Sharia

The Sharia or Sacred Law of Islam, started to take shape within 100 years of the Prophet's death and was influenced by existing practices in the region including Roman, Byzantine, Sasanian and Jewish laws. It consists of four parts, the Quran, the Hadith, Ijma and Qiyas. The laws and acceptable behaviour described in the Quran are included but items of history and parables are omitted. Both of these are revealed or divine parts of the law and therefore unchanging and unchangeable. However, they do not cover all aspects of human conduct, which were provided by the *ulama*. They are divided into five categories and may be commanded, recommended, neutral, not recommended and forbidden by God. The last category includes murder, illicit sex, cheating, gambling, alcohol consumption and usury. Ijma is the consensus of the *ulama* concerning situations not covered in the Quran and Hadith. If the *ulama* gave their universal consensus on a point under discussion, that decision became binding for all Muslims, as Sacred Law. Most proposed laws did not achieve universal consensus and are therefore not binding. Qiyas covers additional interpretations decided by analogy to a previous law or situation included in the Quran, Hadith or Ijma. Analogical reasoning is based on human logic and is therefore not divine or binding.

Shiite law rejects Qiyas and makes the interpretation of Sacred Law the responsibility of the imam who is their supreme authority (2, p. 107). The Kharijites and Zaydites follow the Sunnis but base interpretations on the opinions of their own schools of law.

The Sharia is the product of the Sunni and Shiite Schools of Law. The four surviving Sunni Schools are the Hanafi, Maliki, Shafi and Hanbali, each named after a leading religious scholar. The Hanafi School was based in Kufa, Iraq and is the most liberal of the four. It utilizes analogical reasoning. For example, since adult women are permitted to arrange their own financial contracts, they can by analogy, arrange their own marriage contracts, without the consent of a guardian. Hanafi Law has the largest number of followers since the Ottoman Turks adopted it in the sixteenth century. The Maliki School was founded in Medina at the end of the eighth century and is more traditional, basing interpretations mainly on the Quran and Hadith. It predominates in Northern and Western Africa, the Sudan, Bahrain and Kuwait. Over time it has become more liberal, as practised in the Muslim west. The Shafi School adopted an intermediate position and is similar to the Maliki in its adherence to the Quran and Hadith but includes analogical reasoning and prioritizes the sources from the Quran, Hadith, Ijma and Qiyas. It predominates in Eastern Africa and in South-east Asia. The Hanbali School dates from the ninth century and is the most restrictive of the four; the Wahhabis of Saudi Arabia, Qatar and Oman adopted it much later.

The dominant Shiite school of law, the Jafari School, is similar to the Hanbali but includes the traditions of the twelve Shiite imams (25, p. 95). The

Schools of Law do not differ to any major degree in devotional matters but do so in their interpretation of civil law pertaining to the exchange of values, equity and trust, matrimonial law, civil litigation and the administration of estates. Crime and punishment are considered separately.

Fiqh

Muslims view the Sharia as the command of God, while *fiqh* is the study of Islamic jurisprudence and is covered in its entirety in the 30 volumes of the Kitab al-Mabsut (23, p. 110). Kamali identifies six stages in the development of *fiqh* starting with the first stage which occurred during the Prophet's life time, followed by a period of supplementation by the Prophet's Companions (23, p. 107). Next, came the period of the Umayyads when two schools emerged, the Traditionalists and the Rationalists, the latter being the more liberal (23, p. 112). The fourth period (750–900), the one of 'independent reasoning', occurred during the emergence of the Schools of Law. The fifth period was one of rigidity and isolation and lasted for 900 years. The sixth period began with the twentieth century when there were attempts to make *fiqh* more relevant to modern society, either by state laws, judicial or scholarly opinions. The results have varied from almost complete separation of political and religious control, as seen in Turkey, to theocracies where no action can be taken without the approval of the mullahs, as in Iran. Saudi Arabia provides another example of a Muslim state where a monarchy enforces the Wahhabi interpretation of the Hanbali School of Islamic law: no change is permitted if it occurred later than the Prophet's Companions' lifetimes or the time period just after this. Some states selected positions between these two extremes, replacing civil and penal codes but retaining the Sharia for matters of family law. These are adjudicated according to *fiqh* by a single *qadi* or judge. There are no ordained clergy and religious leaders – imams, mullahs or ayatollahs – are all male. These men teach, preach in mosques and lead discussion groups.

Quran and Women

The Quran makes it clear that women will be judged by the same standards as men (24, sura 4: v. 32) and they can also attain paradise (ibid., sura 9: v. 72). And 'Men shall be rewarded according to their deeds, and women shall be rewarded according to their deeds (ibid., sura 4: v. 32). But, 'Men have a status above women' (ibid., sura 2: v. 228). 'Men have authority over women because God has made the one superior to the other, and because they spend their wealth to maintain them. Good women are obedient. As for those from whom you fear disobedience, admonish them and send them to their beds apart and beat them. Then if they obey you, take no further action against them' (ibid., sura 4: v. 34). Men have rights over women: 'Women are your fields: go, then, into your fields whence you please' (ibid., sura 2: v. 224) and the testimony of women is worth one half that of men; '… but if two men cannot be found, then one man and two women whom you judge fit to act as witnesses; so that if either of them make an error, the other will remind her' (ibid, sura 2: v. 282). Behaviour and dress receive considerable attention but these instructions applied to the 'believers' wives'. Women are not to 'display their adornments' and they are 'to draw their veils over their bosoms and not to display their finery except to their husbands, their fathers, their step-sons' (ibid., sura 24: v. 31). But, 'It shall be no offence for old spinsters who have no hope of marriage to discard their cloaks without revealing their adornments. Better if they do not discard them' (ibid., sura 24: v. 60). And 'Prophet, enjoin your wives, your daughters, and the wives of true believers to draw their veils close round them' (ibid., sura 33: v. 59).

In contrast to the tribal customs existing in Arabia before the Prophet, the family is the central unit of Islamic society and therefore marriage and its preservation receive considerable attention in the Quran. Forbidden marriages are clearly identified: 'the women whom your fathers married: all previous such marriages excepted … Forbidden to you are your mothers, your daughters, your sisters, your paternal and maternal aunts … the mothers of your wives … (it is no offence for you to marry your step-daughters if you have not consummated your marriage with their mothers)' (24, sura 4 vv. 22, 23), 'two sisters at one and the same time; all previous such marriages excepted' (ibid, sura 4: v. 24). Marriage to a slave was allowed even if she was already married (ibid, sura 4: v. 24). But, 'You shall not wed pagan women, unless they embrace the Faith' (ibid, sura 2: v. 221).

Dowries

The marriage contract includes the dowry or *mahr* which is to be paid by the groom; this is to be given to women 'as a free gift; but if they choose to make over to you a part of it, you may regard it as lawfully yours' (24, sura 4: v. 4). Concerning the dowry, 'If you wish to replace one wife with another, do not take from her the dowry you have given her even if it be a talent of gold' (ibid., sura 4: v. 20). However, 'It shall be no offence for you to divorce your wives before the marriage is consummated or the dowry settled. Provide for them with fairness … but after their dowry has been settled, give them one half of their dowry, unless they or the husband agree to waive it' (ibid., sura 2: vv. 236, 237).

Marriage

As for the duties of women, 'Good women are obedient ... As for those from whom you fear disobedience, admonish them and send them to their beds apart and beat them. Then if they obey you, take no further action against them' (24, sura 4: v. 34). Polygamy – or rather polygyny – was allowed, 'then you may marry other women who seem good to you: two, three or four of them. But if you fear that you cannot maintain equality among them, marry one only or any slave-girls you may own' (ibid., sura 4: v. 3). This law did not apply to the Prophet who could wed 'any believing woman who gives herself to the Prophet and whom the Prophet wishes to take in marriage. This privilege is yours alone being granted to no other believer' (ibid., sura 33: v. 50).

Divorce

The Quran encourages intervention when a marriage is threatened: 'If you fear a breach between a man and his wife, appoint an arbiter from his people and another from hers' (24, sura 4: v. 35). However, this was not always successful and one whole chapter and more than twenty verses are devoted to the subject of divorce. Divorce was up to a time revocable, 'Those that renounce their wives on oath must wait for four months. If they change their minds, God is forgiving and merciful' (ibid., sura 2: v. 226). In order to ascertain paternity, the Quran adds, 'Divorced women must wait, keeping themselves from men, three menstrual courses. It is unlawful for them to hide what God has created in their wombs' (ibid., sura 2: v. 227), and, 'When you have renounced your wives and they have reached the end of their waiting period, either retain them in honour or let them go with kindness' (ibid., sura 2: v. 231). 'Prophet (and you believers), if you divorce your wives, divorce them at the end of their waiting period' (ibid, sura 65: v. 1). 'As for pregnant women, their term shall end with their confinement' (ibid, sura 65: 4). 'Mothers shall give suck to their children for two whole years if the father wishes the suckling to be completed. They must be maintained in a reasonable manner and clothed in a reasonable manner by the child's father' (ibid., sura 2: v. 233). 'If a man divorce his wife, he cannot remarry her until she has wedded another man and been divorced by him' (ibid., sura 2: v. 230), and 'Reasonable provision shall also be made for divorced women' (ibid., sura 2: v. 241).

Widows

The Quran tells widows, that they 'shall wait, keeping themselves apart from men, for four months and ten days after their husband's death. When they have reached the end of their waiting period, it shall be no offence for you to

let them do whatever they choose for themselves, provided that it is decent'
(24, sura 2: v. 234), and 'You shall bequeath your widows a year's maintenance without causing them to leave their homes; but if they leave of their
own accord, no blame shall be attached to you for any course they may deem
reasonable to pursue' (ibid., sura 2: v. 240).

Adoption

Concerning adoption, the Quran says, 'He (God) does not regard... your
adopted sons as your own sons' (24, sura 33: v. 3), and 'Name your adopted
sons after their fathers; that is more just in the sight of God' (ibid., sura 33:
v. 5).

Inheritance

Islamic law changed the pre-existing custom of agnate inheritance to 'Men
shall have a share in what their parents and kinsmen leave and women shall
have a share in what their parents and kinsmen leave; whether it be little or
much, they shall be legally entitled to a share' (24, sura 4: v. 8). But, 'A male
shall inherit twice as much as a female' (ibid., sura 4: v. 11). 'You shall inherit
the half of your wife's estates if they die childless. If they leave children, one
quarter of their estate shall be yours after payment of any legacy ...' (ibid.,
sura 4: v. 12). 'Your wives shall inherit one quarter of your estate if you die
childless. If you leave children, they shall inherit one eighth' (ibid., sura 4: v.
13). 'If a man die childless and without living parents and he has a sister, she
shall inherit the half of his estate. If a woman die childless, her brother shall
be her sole heir' (ibid., sura 4: v. 176).

Orphans

'Give orphans the property which belongs to them' (24, sura 4: v. 3). And,
'Let not the rich guardian touch the property of his orphan ward' (ibid., sura
4: v. 7), but 'Do not give the feeble-minded the property with which God
has entrusted you for their support; but maintain and clothe them with its
proceeds and speak kind words to them' (ibid., sura 4: v. 5).

Crimes

The Quran identifies theft, suicide, unlawful intercourse, usury, consumption
of wine and gambling as crimes against religion and therefore against God and

'those that make war against God and his apostle and spread disorder in the land shall be slain, or be banished from the land' (24, sura 5: v. 34). 'As for the man or woman who is guilty of theft, cut off their hands to punish them for their crimes' (ibid., sura 5: v. 38).

About usury, 'Believers, do not live on usury, doubling your wealth many times over' (24, sura 3: v. 130) and 'Those that live on usury shall rise up before God like men who Satan has demented by his touch' (ibid., sura 2: v. 275).

Concerning gambling and drinking, 'Believers, wine and games of chance, idols and divining arrows, are abominations devised by Satan.' (24, sura 5: v. 90) and to those that ask you about drinking and gambling, say 'There is great harm in both, although they have some benefit for men; but their harm is far greater than their benefit' (ibid., sura 2: v. 219).

Suicide is not allowed, 'Do not kill yourselves ... he that does shall be burned in fire' (24, sura 4: v. 29).

As to adultery, the Quran says 'You shall not commit adultery, for it is lewd and evil' (24, sura 17: v. 32) and, 'Do not commit adultery, he that does shall meet with evil; his punishment will be doubled on the Day of Resurrection' (ibid., sura 25: v. 68). And 'The adulterer and the adulteress shall each be given 100 lashes' (ibid., sura 24: v. 2). And, 'The adulterer may marry only an adulteress or an idolater; and the adulteress may marry only an adulterer or idolater' (ibid., sura 24: v. 4).

False accusations of adultery are dealt with sternly, 'Those that defame honourable women and cannot produce four witnesses shall be given 80 lashes' (24, sura 24: v. 5), but 'If a man accuses his wife but has no witnesses except himself, he shall swear four times by God that his charge is true' but 'If his wife swears four times by God that his charge is false ... she shall receive no punishment' (ibid, sura 24: v. 6). In general, 'He that commits an offence or a crime and charges an innocent man, shall bear the guilt of calumny and gross injustice' (ibid., sura 4: v. 112).

'If any of your women commit a lewd act, call in four witnesses from among yourselves against them; if they testify to their guilt, confine them to their houses till death overtake them or till God finds another way for them' (24, sura 4: v. 15). 'If two men among you commit a lewd act, punish them both. If they repent and mend their ways, let them be' (ibid., sura 4: v. 16). 'Wives of the Prophet! Those of you who clearly commit a lewd act shall be doubly punished' (ibid., sura 33: v. 30).

Homicide, bodily injury and property damage are identified as crimes of private vengeance and the next of kin or injured party has the right of retaliation rather than the tribe, as in Beduin law. 'It is unlawful for a believer to kill another believer, accidents excepted. He that accidentally kills ... must free one Muslim slave and pay blood money. He that lacks the means, must fast for two consecutive months' (24, sura 4: v. 92). 'He that kills a believer by design shall burn in hell for ever' (ibid., sura 4: v. 93) and, 'You shall not kill ... except for a just cause' (ibid., sura 6: v. 151).

In the 1,350 years that have elapsed since the authorized version of the Quran was prepared, it has been translated into many languages. However, many Muslims contend that the true meaning of the text can only be fully comprehended if it is read in the original Arabic form.

Islam and Women

Women's Lives in Arabia Before the Prophet

Before an assessment can be made of the impact of Islam on women's lives in Arabia, we need to know more about the customs and practices there before the Prophet's arrival. The information available suggests a few women here were relatively independent and managed their own businesses and finances; a good example is Khadijah, Muhammad's first wife. She was a wealthy widow who ran her own business and employed Muhammad as her agent.

This was a tribal society and some families were matriarchal and men – often a number of them – behaved as visitors in a woman's home. Children remained with their mothers and there was not much concern about their paternity (3, p. 78). They received support and protection from members of their tribe. Others were patriarchal and wives were often bought and the proceeds pocketed by their fathers or male relatives. Divorces were relatively easily arranged and women remarried promptly without a waiting period (3, pp. 76–8). Veils preceded the Prophet and were commonly worn by urban and some tribal women but more rarely by village or nomad women who usually worked in the fields or cared for their flocks. Inheritance was patrilinear, probably to retain property within a tribe and assets were passed down only to male heirs.

By the time of Muhammad's birth, Mecca had become an important trade centre because of its strategic location on routes to and from Asia. Opportunities for work there attracted men and women from the countryside and this served to weaken already frail tribal loyalties.

Women's Losses Under Islam

Islam brought an end to matri-linear customs and society became strictly patri-archal. From now on, a man owed his wife food and maintenance and in return, she became his property and sexually available only to him. To ensure this, he had the right to restrict her movements when she left the home (28, p. 54). This was her space and every place else was his space. She owed him obedience in mind and body and if she failed in this, he had a right to punish her. The Quran decreed that in temporal matters she was inferior to him, her testimony had one half of the value of his and she counted for half his worth as a witness. She could have one husband only until his death or their divorce, while he was allowed four wives at the same time and unlimited relations with other women, so long as they were unmarried. He could divorce her simply by verbal repudiation, at any time and without a reason. She had no right to divorce unless she could prove before a judge – a *qadi* – that he was either impotent or insane or that he had some chronic disease. Children belonged to their father. This rule did not change until later when different Islamic Schools of Law gave the mother limited rights, usually to keep daughters until age nine and sons until age seven years (3, p. 75). Her husband maintained the right of guardianship but if she remarried, custody of the children automatically reverted to him.

Women's Gains Under Islam

Islam improved the lives of women in some respects. Spiritually and morally they were the equals of men and subject to the same religious laws. They would be punished for their sins and achieve paradise or hell by the same criteria as men.

At the time of her marriage a girl received a dowry or *marh* consisting of money, property or both, agreed on by her husband or his family in the marriage contract. This was a gift to her and her personal property. There were ways of course of deferring this payment and the bride could agree to its use by her husband. Property, money or jewels owned by her before marriage, would remain in her possession during marriage and after their divorce or his death, as did gifts to her from her family.

Her husband owed her maintenance, in the style to which she had been accustomed previously – including lodging, food and clothing – throughout their marriage.

The major change – placing Muslim women ahead of their sisters in the Western world – was an end to the old agnatic laws of inheritance in her favour: she could now inherit, although not to equality with males.

Lastly, the practice of killing female infants was outlawed.

Muslim Societies

By the tenth century, Islam had spread into Iran, the region beyond the Oxus river and part of Iraq with Baghdad as its centre. Persians retained their old cultural traditions both in language (Pahlavi pronounced Farsi by Arabs) and in literature, but over time they changed their religion and laws to Islam. A new literature appeared in the tenth century, written in Persian with the addition of a few Arabic words but transcribed in Arabic script (4, p. 87). Persian continued to be used for secular literature but Arabic replaced it for legal and religious matters (ibid.).

The lives of most women were little changed. They were often part of multi-generational families and village women continued to care for their homes and children, helped in the fields and tended their flocks. Urban women had more limited roles: they helped their husbands especially if they were craftsmen or traders: some worked as domestic servants, or entertained as dancers and singers (4, pp. 119ff.). Harems – sections of homes reserved for women only, except for the eunuchs who guarded them – became more common, especially among wealthy families. These preceded the Prophet and achieved greater prominence in Turkey, lasting well into the twentieth century. On the rare occasions when they left their homes, women were usually veiled. A fourteenth-century Egyptian jurist, Ibn al-Hajj wrote a 'Woman should leave her house on three occasions only: when she is conducted to the house of her bridegroom, on the deaths of her parents and when she goes to her own grave' (4, p. 120). The custom of segregating and shrouding women suggests that Islam viewed women as dangerous and threatening and in need of constraint (22, p. 19).

Arabian society was made up of free men and women and slaves who were non-Muslims bought or captured in war or the children of slaves. Muslim women could not marry non-Muslims nor could non-Muslims inherit from Muslims. Muslims could not convert to another religion and apostasy was punished by death (4. p, 116). The Sharia, as interpreted by the *ulama*, was accepted and obeyed by both rulers and people, but had little relevance to commercial and constitutional issues. The ruler dictated criminal justice, but the *qadi* controlled the rest of the law and there was no appeal to his decision.

Over time, Islamic countries used different ways of adapting to its religious laws: the Ottoman Empire eventually became a secular state, Iran and for a while Afghanistan, became theocracies and Saudi Arabia remained an absolute monarchy and obeyed the dictates of Wahhabism.

Turkey

Turkey became a republic in 1923 and Mustafa Kemal was elected its first president. New laws were passed placing public education under state control and religious instruction was forbidden in schools. Later on, there was some relaxation in this policy and by 1948 a few Muslim schools were allowed to train religious personnel. Education – from 7 to 17 years – was free and compulsory, but initially there were too few trained teachers or schools to fulfil this requirement (1, vol. 22, p. 394). The 1926 new civil code of personal status became an important step in the emancipation of Turkish women for which the President was justly praised (14, p. 437). Women achieved equal inheritance rights with men and in 1930, the right to vote and to stand for election. Polygyny was banned and a minimum age for marriage was established (29, p. 64). Women were awarded equal rights in divorce and child custody. Threats against the country's secular status in later years were zealously guarded by the Turkish military. Recently there has been some relaxation in the law banning the fez and *hijab* in public places.

Iran

The Family Protection Law had been passed in 1967 in Iran, resulting in improved conditions for women: polygyny was restricted, divorce was made easier and they were no longer required to wear the *hijab* (7, p. 174). But the Shah's despotic rule met with increasing opposition, especially from religious leaders and the younger members of the population. Women were persuaded by the promises of an influential teacher – Ah Shariati – that only Islam could provide them with equality. He criticized Muslim women for accepting their traditional roles without question and for aping the West by becoming 'mindless consumers' (30, p. 288).

The revolution of 1978–9 ended the Shah's rule and Ayatollah Khomeini returned from France to the acclaim of 100,000 women who gathered at Tehran University. This despite the Ayatollah's plans – made clear to all before he returned – to restrict women's rights.

The Islamic Republic, a theocracy, began its rule in 1979. Soon after, the Family Protection law was annulled and segregation of the sexes was ordered in schools, buses and other public areas, and, despite Khomeini's previously stated position that women 'dress modestly', full Islamic dress (the chador) became mandatory (29, p. 233). Religious police were hired to enforce these orders. Women were no longer allowed to practise law and all women judges were fired. Article 163 of the Islamic Constitution states 'Because of their delicate and emotional nature, women are incapable of correct judgement' (30, p. 302). The old rule that the evidence of two women equalled that of one man was reinstated, with a new addendum that her evidence would not be accepted unless it was corroborated by a man; further, women faced prosecution for slander if they insisted on 'giving uncorroborated evidence' (21, p. 202). Women required the permission of their husbands in order to work, and after divorce, men had automatic custody of children. *Hudud* punishments were applied according to Sharia law, for drinking alcohol, theft, adultery and bearing false witness. Murder remained a crime of retribution although it could be settled by payment of blood money; a woman's murder counted as a lesser crime than a man's.

The *ulama* consolidated its power and instead of returning to the mosques, continued to rule the country. There was democracy to a degree since parliament was elected but no law could be enacted without the mullahs' approval (15, p. 664). The Council of Guardians decides who is eligible to run for election and makes the ultimate decision concerning acceptable and unacceptable behaviour.

Despite a long history of educational reform in Iran, women suffered acutely in the early years of the Islamic Republic and their university enrolment fell to 10 per cent of the total student body. This improved later. Certain academic areas of study such as engineering remain closed to women. They are still barred from serving as judges but can act as legal advisors, particularly in family courts (21, p. 206). They have been quite successful commercially and now operate a variety of businesses (21, p. 204).

Afghanistan

The people of Afghanistan are predominantly Sunni Muslims. After domination by Persia, the Mughals and then England, the state became an absolute monarchy and then a democracy in 1931. After war with Russia, the Taliban took control and established a theocracy in 1979. They imposed an extreme form of Islamic rule with severe restrictions on women who were not allowed to work. Girls were forbidden from attending school. They could not leave their homes without a male relative and unless completely shrouded in a *burkha*; they could not vote or hold public office. Religious police enforced Sharia laws in public places. Their medical care became extremely limited since only female physicians could provide this, and there were very few left in the country. Eventually the Taliban was driven out in 2001 but continues its aggressive tactics to regain control.

Saudi Arabia

Women are marginalized in Saudi society. Secular schools for boys had existed from the early part of the twentieth century, but girls were still taught at home in the 1930s, and their education consisted mostly of memorizing the Quran. A secular school for girls opened in Jeddah in the 1960s. Earlier, wealthy families often sent their children abroad for their education, but more Saudi girls have been educated in their own country since the 1970s, and now attend one of the Saudi universities accepting women (16, p. 270). There is strict segregation of the sexes in the work place. Women are not allowed to drive or walk in the streets without a male relative and must be completely covered. Women cannot travel outside the country without the written consent of a male guardian. Women rarely appear in courts of law where they are represented instead by male relatives. These rules are enforced by the *Muttawa* (religious police). Sharia courts handle all family law cases.

Strict Muslims view secular government as incompatible with a religion they believe applies to every aspect of life, religious as well as political. In their view, the western model for separation of mosque and state is an artifice. Others – including several notable Islamic authorities – have called for a modification of

Sharia law as approved in the tenth century. Muhammad Abdur writing at the end of the nineteenth century, called for a reinterpretation of these laws by a process called *ijtihad* or independent judgement but others view this as heresy (15, p. 648).

Women's Lives in Present-day Islamic Countries

An increasing number of young women have started to wear headscarves and interest in religious books and classes has increased. Loyalty to Islam explains some of this, together with disapproval of Western feminism – which many associate with colonialism – and a general fear of women's emancipation.

The status of women in many Islamic countries has improved in the past half century, and many now receive better educations and employment opportunities (15, p. 687). In 1957, the Tunisian President Habib Bourgiba enacted the Code of Personal Statute, requiring the consent of both the man and woman for marriage, setting a minimum age for this and ensuring equality in child custody, divorce and education. He used the Quran to justify these changes. In time women became judges and enjoyed equal political and reproductive rights and abortion was free in the first three months of pregnancy (29, p. 68). Egypt too had its share of strong advocates for women's emancipation, and in 1956 it was the first country – other than Turkey – to abolish Sharia courts. Many Islamic states have now adopted the civil and penal codes of western states but continue to observe Sharia Family Law with or without religious courts. Laws may be modified by judges who select the jurisprudence of another Islamic school of law with a more liberal attitude. Traditionally, Muslim courts depend on the decision of a single *qadi* but now all have systems of appeal.

Education

Islam recognized the importance of education for women, because it believed it allowed them to become better wives and mothers. Colonial governments or missionaries established a number of schools and universities (31, p. 578). Between WWI and WWII and later, the education of girls was encouraged in the spirit of Arab nationalism and the number of female students increased dramatically in Egypt and Lebanon and a few other Muslim states (4, p. 389). Large revenues generated by oil wealth in the 1970s and later, were shared – to a degree – between developing countries in the region, allowing many to improve their educational facilities. Despite this, many Muslim states have poor records with regard to the education of their female citizens.

Several factors influence the education of girls in Islamic countries and include poverty, lack of facilities and teachers – especially female teachers, since they are required for girls, isolation in remote villages, social customs prescribing early marriage, and an insistence on isolating girls from society in order to control their sexuality. Economic pressures affect both boys and girls, but families tend to maintain the schooling of their males for a longer period: in 1975, there were 22 per cent more boys than girls in secondary school (29, p. 78). Some Islamic states require the separation of girls and boys in primary and secondary schools and even in universities, although the Quran makes no such stipulation. Segregation has further compromised the education of girls, especially if resources are limited. On the other hand, improved job opportunities have provided an incentive to change. An example is Bahrain where labour needs resulted in major increases in the enrolment of girls in both primary and secondary schools (32, p. 79).

Primary school attendance by girls has improved and many Muslim countries report this is now nearly 100 per cent. About 87 per cent of girls in Turkey attended primary school in 2003–8, 75 per cent of girls in Pakistan and 64 per cent in Yemen (33). Far fewer girls attended secondary school in the same period: 43 per cent in Turkey, 33 per cent in Pakistan and 27 per cent in Yemen (34). In all countries, school attendance was poorer in rural areas. Once admitted, girls generally do well in school and they are less likely to repeat a grade than boys.

There were no women university students in Kuwait in 1960 but by 2005 they accounted for 66 per cent of the student body (29, p. 127). In the same year, women accounted for 65 per cent of university students in Saudi Arabia, 46 per cent in Pakistan and 43 per cent in Turkey (35, p. 121–3).

Illiteracy in women has steadily declined: for example, 94 per cent of Egyptian women were illiterate in 1937, 83 per cent in 1960, 56 per cent in 2000 and 41 per cent in 2007 (4, p. 390: 34). Afghanistan, Chad and Niger have the worst records with over 85 per cent female illiteracy (35, p. 79). By 2007, illiteracy in females aged 15 and over, was less than 20 per cent in Bahrain, Indonesia and Turkey: 20–40 per cent in Algeria, Tunisia and Saudi Arabia and over 50 per cent in Morocco, Pakistan and Yemen (34). The literacy gap between the sexes is a measure of the repression experienced by women and averages two to three times higher than in males (35, p. 79).

Employment

Segregation of the sexes – which may be enforced – as in Saudi Arabia, or customary – as seen to some degree in Turkey – has both restricted the employment of women in general and limited them to certain types of work. This varies in different Muslim states (3, p. 71). Statistics compiled in the late 1980s show that women comprised a very small part of the total labour force (29, p. 207). Less than 1 per cent of wage earners were women in Saudi Arabia despite an acute shortage of labour, necessitating the import of foreign workers. In regions where unemployment is high as in Algeria and Egypt, women are discouraged from seeking jobs and are often shunted into more menial positions. Nevertheless, this practice is changing and in Oman for instance, female employment has increased rapidly over the last decade and women now hold administrative positions in the government and work as pilots and police officers (36, p. 258).

Customs or laws may determine which jobs or professions are open to women. In Saudi Arabia for instance, women cannot obtain degrees or work in geology, engineering, oil or law. They are encouraged to become professionals such as physicians and teachers for female children, rather than health care workers such as nurses (16, p. 277). A number of businesses such as women's boutiques and banks are now run by and serve only women. Besides the practice of law, science and medicine attract Turkish women as do politics and banking, which is now regarded as an almost feminine occupation (29, p. 212). Professional fields also attract women in Syria, Egypt and Libya. In Lebanon, women are found in nearly every occupation but their numbers are sparse in politics, government and public administration (37, p. 231). There are no restrictions on women lawyers but women are poorly represented in academia. In contrast to most Islamic states, Tunisia allows women to be judges (29, p. 214). Uneducated and poor women tend to work as paid and unpaid agricultural labourers and in urban areas they are more often employed as domestic servants in homes and offices. It is likely that economic needs will continue to increase the number of working women in Muslim countries.

Inheritance and Property Rights

Islam changed inheritance laws for women, allowing them the right to inherit but only to one half the share received by men with similar relationships. Before this, only males could inherit. The Sharia permits a man to leave a third of his assets to whomsoever he pleases or those not in line to inherit (4, p. 121). The remaining two thirds must be distributed according to a specific formula: his wife (or wives) receives not more than one third of his estate and his daughters one half of the amount left to his sons. If there are no sons, his daughters may inherit a share but the remainder is left to male relatives. Shia law differs in this respect and if there are no sons, daughters receive the entire amount.

The Muslim system of bequests called *waqf* dates back to the Sharia or earlier times. This is an arrangement of charitable trusts whereby property and other assets can escape legal distribution at death. This was a way of bypassing individuals who would have had the right to inherit. Virtually anything could be identified as a charity and assets could then be used to support the family of the trust's owner. Syrian law abolished *waqf* in 1949 as did Egypt in 1952. Tunisian succession laws were revised in 1959 and improved the daughter's and later the son's daughter's shares of inheritances. Any lineal descendants, male or female, can exclude collateral relatives from an inheritance (2, p. 220). About one half of the Muslim population in Morocco follows the old (pre-Islamic) Berber custom of denying inheritance rights to women. Tribes in Yemen, Indonesia and Nigeria have similar practices (2, p. 136). Muslims in Lebanon follow Sharia inheritance laws but non-Muslim women usually inherit equally with men although individual families may elect to exclude daughters (38, p. 327). Saudi Arabia and the Gulf states continue to follow Sharia law in this respect, as do most Islamic states (2, p. 154). A few have retained pre-Islamic agnatic laws and very few countries, such as Turkey and Tunisia, have given women equal inheritance rights.

Right to Vote

A pamphlet produced by the Institute of Islamic Information and Education in Chicago states 'A right given to Muslim women by God 1,400 years ago is the right to vote'(6, p. 155). Despite these words and assurances made during the recent Gulf War, women were not allowed to vote in Kuwait until 2005. In 1985, the Ministry of Islamic Affairs issued a ruling that 'The nature of the electoral process befits men, who are endowed with ability and expertise: it is not permissible that women recommend or nominate other men or women' (36, p. 257). Neither men nor women have the right to vote in Saudi Arabia where there is no parliament. Lebanese women have been allowed to vote since 1952 but have rarely been elected to positions in the government. In the election of 1992, 3 of 128 elected members were women, all of whom were related to men who were well known in Lebanese politics (37, p. 231). This increased to six (4.7 per cent) in 2009 elections. A few women have been elected to the Iranian Majlis but none have served in the cabinet. Their constitution states that the leader and president of Iran must be a man. Egyptian women won both the right to vote and to stand for elective office in 1956 (36, p. 74). Lack of education, ignorance and segregation rules have contributed to the low turn-out of female voters: legislators attempted to remedy this in 1979 by reserving 30 of 392 seats in the Egyptian People's Assembly for women. More recently, Pakistan has adopted a similar measure (36, p. 78).

Marriage

Islamic Family Law includes marriage, divorce, polygamy, child custody, adultery, crimes-of-honour, segregation and dress for women.

Because of the importance of the family in Islamic society, considerable attention has been given to marriage and related issues. A marriage involves a legal contract between two individuals who are usually selected by their families, based on specific criteria and without the requirement of mutual love (28, p. 51). A girl's father or male guardian(s) usually selects a husband for his daughter and she may or may not have met him prior to her wedding, or had any say in choosing him. This practice continues in rural areas but has changed to varying degrees elsewhere. Hanafi law allows an adult Muslim woman to make her own contracts, including marriage, but this may be declared invalid if deficient under the Laws of Kafa (suitability or equality) (28, p. 53).

The marriage contract is a verbal agreement between the man and the woman's guardian and does not become valid until the marriage is consummated. The marriage occurs in the presence of two witnesses (two men or one man and two women). A girl who is a minor at the time of her marriage – which usually means she is pre-pubertal – can reject the contract when she attains her majority, but this is a questionable right if the guardian was her father. The girl is expected to be a virgin and can be divorced if the groom finds this is not so; this would bring discredit to her family and could even lead to her death at their hands (see crimes of honour). The marriage contract may stipulate that the wife has the right to initiate a divorce in specific circumstances including polygyny or when her husband's work requires her to live outside her hometown. This kind of contract is more commonly obtained by a well-informed Muslim woman and her family but is less likely to be utilized by women lacking this degree of sophistication. The groom's commitment is to provide the girl with a *mahr* (dowry), which remains her property, and also with food, shelter and clothing. The amount of her dowry is agreed on before the marriage and can include property whose value is determined earlier. This substitutes for her alimony in the event of divorce. If this occurs before the marriage is consummated, she is entitled to only one half of the dowry (28, p. 54). The girl's obligation is to be obedient and sexually available to her husband. This can limit her ability to travel or even spend time outside her home. Disobedience can result in forfeiture of her maintenance allowance. A girl is not required to perform household chores if they are inconsistent with her previous lifestyle.

A man may marry a non-Muslim but a woman can only marry a Muslim whose family is of equal or superior status to hers, at least at the time of the marriage: paternal, not maternal lineage is of importance to children. This is illustrated by Lebanese law which stipulates that a woman's nationality cannot be passed on to her husband and children, while the opposite is true for a Lebanese man (38, p. 322).

Some aspects of Family Law have been amended by statute in different Islamic countries. Kuwaiti law was changed in 1984 so that women who were less than 25 years had to have the approval of male guardians. Sharia law continued to be observed by Muslims in India, although parts of it were modified by Anglo-Muhammadan jurisprudence (39, pp. 94–6). Tunisian law since 1957 required the consent of both man and woman to a marriage (39, p. 108). Algerian law was amended in 1959 so that the consent of both parties was required for both marriage and divorce and a minimum age for marriage was established. Most Gulf States continue to observe Sharia family laws (39, p. 98).

Islamic law makes no stipulation concerning a girl's age at the time of her marriage. The Prophet is said to have married Aisha when she was six years old. The 1917 Ottoman law of Family Rights states that no child can be contracted in marriage before the age of puberty. Although this was later changed to an older age in Turkey, the same law continued to be valid in Syria, Lebanon, Palestine and Jordan. The interpretation of puberty varies in different countries; it is 12 for boys and 9 for girls in Jordan, Syria, Tunisia and Morocco, while in Iraq puberty is at age 16 for both sexes. Fifteen years is the minimum age for marriage in Kuwait, but the Gulf States leave the decision to male relatives. The 1991 census in Qatar reported that about a third of all married women were between 15 and 19 years of age (36, p. 258). Seventeen per cent of all married women in Bahrain were 15 or younger. A 2007 report found that 48 per cent of women in Yemen married before they were 18 as did 23 per cent of Turkish women and 10 per cent of Tunisians. In India, child marriage was ruled invalid and a criminal offence under British rule but continued nevertheless. In 1931, Egypt passed a law stating that marriage certificates would not be issued unless the bride was 16 and the groom 18 years or more (2, pp. 178, 179). Qadis in Algeria were ordered not to issue a marriage certificate if the bride was under the age of fifteen.

Shiite but not Sunni law recognizes temporary marriage or *muta*; this is a form of contract allowing a woman to live with a man for a specific period of time up to 99 years and receive some remuneration. She has no inheritance rights from her partner but their mutual children can inherit (23, p. 130).

Polygamy

Both polygyny and polyandry occurred in pre-Islamic days but only polygyny survived and is approved in the Quran. It allowed a maximum of four wives at one time and on the condition that a man was financially able to provide for them all. Turkey and Tunisia banned polygyny, the former after it became a secular state and the latter in 1957 (36, p. 252). Other Middle East countries also restricted a man's right to additional wives; Syria's Personal Status Law (1953) required a man to seek court permission before he took a second wife. Morocco, Iran and Iraq adopted similar laws and Egyptian law (1979), allowed a wife to obtain a divorce if she disapproves of his choice (29, pp. 172, 173). Women can include clauses requiring their permission or other stipulations in their marriage contracts. This tends to protect well-informed and educated women but not the illiterate and naive. Polygyny has become less common with changing socio-economic and housing conditions. Nevertheless, by 1985, more than 50 per cent of men in Kuwait had more than one wife: by 1991 the figure was about 5 per cent in Bahrain and Qatar (36, p. 259).

Adultery

For a woman, adultery means sex outside of marriage, and if she is married to anyone other than her husband. For a man, adultery does not exist in Islamic law, unless it occurs with another man's wife. A married man has a perfect right to have sex with prostitutes or unmarried women. The penalty for adultery used to be death by stoning but this was changed to 100 lashes early on in Islam's history. Northern Nigeria has retained this form of punishment. Most Muslim countries had enacted new codes of criminal procedure by 1960, but traditional lashings or worse can still occur for crimes of fornication or false accusations (39, p. 179; 2, p. 159). In 1977, a Saudi princess was shot for committing adultery and her lover was beheaded. Under Lebanese law, adultery for a woman must fulfill three requirements; intercourse with someone other than her husband, an existing marriage and criminal intent. It is not a crime for a married man to have sex with someone other than his wife outside his home, unless it is done repeatedly and becomes public knowledge (38, p. 326). The penalty for the woman is imprisonment for 1 to 12 months. Adultery by an unmarried man incurs a lesser penalty if his partner is a married woman, but the punishment is the same whether she is married or not for the woman. Kuwait, in contrast, treats men and women as equals with regard to adultery.

Divorce

Islam encourages couples to obtain the assistance of two arbitrators before they seek a divorce. Nevertheless, its inevitability is recognized and there are very specific rules concerning divorce. Here men have all the power and women practically none. He can repudiate his wife at any time and with no reason, simply by triple renunciation (39, p. 164). She has no escape from a marriage without his consent, unless she can prove one of several very specific deficiencies such as chronic illness, insanity or impotence, a process called *khul*. In some countries such as Northern Nigeria, women can obtain a divorce by an exchange of assets, a procedure that usually involves the return of her dowry, with his consent (2, p. 137). After her repudiation, a wife must wait 3 to 12 months to ensure she is not pregnant, during which time her prior husband can revoke his repudiation. The wife usually receives financial support during the waiting period. If she is pregnant, her waiting period lasts until delivery. After this, she has the right to her dowry and any money, jewels and property that belonged to her at the time of the marriage. Women without these assets are left penniless and must depend on the largesse of her family who may have their own dependants to provide for (29, p. 175). A few women insert clauses in their marriage contracts to cover this eventuality, but they are of questionable value, for 'there is no condition that can restrict a husband's right to repudiate his wife at any time, for any reason or for no reason at all' (36, p. 177).

Turkey made changes in the divorce section of its Family Law during the past century. The first, in 1917, called the Ottoman Law of Family Rights, allowed wives whose husbands had some serious disease or had deserted them, to seek a divorce. Later, reforms made divorce subject to civil courts (2, p. 186). Tunisian law has in effect made men and women equals and divorce is handled by civil courts of law. Syria requires a man to justify his divorce in court and in addition, he must provide his wife with maintenance for up to one year (39, p. 108; 2, p. 209). In most other Islamic countries, divorce remains unilateral and under the jurisdiction of Sharia courts: Islamic fundamentalist groups and the *ulama* have resisted attempts to change this.

In Shia communities, there is almost no way a wife can be freed from an unwilling husband (40, p. 334). Divorce rates are relatively high in Muslim countries, particularly in Morocco and the Gulf states: 18 per cent in Bahrain in 1992 and 29 per cent in Qatar (36, p. 259).

Child Custody

The custody of children goes to the mother in the event of her divorce or widowhood, but only for a limited period of time and this varies according to the different Islamic Schools of Law. According to Hanafi Law, this is nine years for girls and seven for boys (36, p. 259). The father retains the rights of guardianship during this time and the children are returned to him if the mother remarries during this period. If the mother dies, custody is transferred to the nearest female relative, first on the mother's and then on the father's side (39, p. 167).

A man must provide support for his children: this includes children born between six and twenty-four months from the time the parents separated (39, p. 166).

Social Issues and Reproductive Rights

Social issues include dress, reproductive rights, contraception and abortion. The Quran says that the wives of the Prophet and true believers shall wear veils. In some Islamic countries, nearly all women wear veils. They were banned in government offices and schools in Turkey and Tunisia and were worn less frequently in Egypt and Indonesia (41, p. 224). More and more Islamic women have started to wear them again and they vary from a head covering only, to complete envelopment of the body as is customary in the Gulf States. Women wear these only when they are outside their homes.

Islam has no specific laws concerning birth control, but the Prophet is said to have advised his followers not to have more children than they could feed and Islamic jurists did not change this (29, p. 64). Several Islamic countries have state-sponsored family planning clinics. Egypt and Tunisia provide free services at these clinics. Turkey, Morocco and Pakistan made similar commitments although their availability may be limited for economic reasons. Iran withdrew its support for family planning services shortly after the Islamic revolution, but restored it later but with certain restrictions (29, p. 165). Estimates for 2001 show that fewer than 35 per cent of women in Pakistan, Yemen, and Saudi Arabia used any method of birth control but the number was 37–57 per cent in Iran, Turkey, Lebanon and Egypt. These compare to 72 per cent in Northern Europe (35, pp. 111–15).

Abortion is not mentioned in the Quran and is therefore controversial. Some jurists disapprove of any practice that destroys human life, while others believe abortion is permissible within the first 120 days of pregnancy, before the foetus is believed to have a soul and in certain situations where the mother's health is in jeopardy (29, p. 166). Tunisia provides free abortions in the first three months of pregnancy. Costs are often a determining factor and may limit services to women who have the financial resources.

Female genital mutilation is an ancient practice dating back to the pharaohs. Its goal was to control female sexuality and parents promote it to make their daughters acceptable as wives. It is not confined to Islamic countries but is more common there (29, p. 163). It is not mentioned in the Quran. Efforts by the United Nations and human rights groups have decreased its frequency but the practice continues (29, p. 97). Its most mild form involves removing the tip of the clitoris. The more extreme and mutilating form is called infibulation, and is practised in Somalia, Ethiopia, Djibouti and parts of the Sudan, Kenya, Egypt, Nigeria, Mali and the Arabian peninsula (ibid). Clitoridectomy (complete removal of the clitoris) is more common and practised in 26 countries in Africa and the Middle East. Estimates suggest that 2 million girls undergo this procedure each year (35, p. 54).

Crimes-of-Honour and Violence Against Women

A crime-of-honour is defined as the killing or maiming of a woman because she has engaged in or is suspected of any type of social encounter with a male before marriage that could compromise her virginity. It can include just being seen with or talking to a man, as well as more overt behaviour. It is usually a primitive, premeditated act committed by a girl's father, brother or other male relative, often with the support and connivance of females in the family. It includes attacks on women found not to be virgins on their wedding nights or pregnant. She must be returned to her family whose shame may lead to violence. Local custom may hold that a man who does not act against his daughter or sister in such a situation is no longer a man (42, p. 152). In the Arab world, a woman's virginity is the 'index of masculine reputation' (42, p. 153).

Crimes-of-honour are peculiar to the Arab world and nearby countries such as Pakistan and Afghanistan. They arose from a concept of preserving tribal or family honour, or of a belief in the ownership of women or because society demanded their virginity before marriage, or for all three reasons. Rather a woman should die than raise any suspicion that could reflect on either the tribe or her family. These crimes are often unreported and undiscovered but are not exempt from punishment. In Kuwait, they are treated as misdemeanors: Jordan reduces the sentences if the act was provoked: Lebanon also reduces the sentence if the woman's behaviour is shown to be 'socially unacceptable' (34, p. 31).

Crimes-of-honour have increased since 2004 (35, p. 31). Three women each day are murdered for this reason in Pakistan and 10 per cent of murders in the Punjab and Haryana in 2006 were honour killings (ibid.). Twenty to 30 women die for this reason each year in Jordan (ibid.). Fifty occurred in Afghanistan in 2006 and over 1,800 occurred in Turkey between 2001 and 2006 (ibid.).

Crimes of passion differ from crimes-of-honour because they are immediate, sometimes irrational acts of violence committed by a husband or fiancé when confronted with apparent adultery or infidelity. They also occurred in some European countries, including France, Spain, Portugal and Italy until 1975 and 1979 where they were punished with lighter or no penalties (42, p. 144). The penal codes of countries excusing them state that a man who 'beats, injures or kills his wife or female *unlawfuls* (women he cannot marry) when she is committing adultery or is found in the same bed with a man, shall be excused from punishment' (42, p. 143). Although the statutes are similar, their interpretations vary. Egypt, Tunisia, Libya and Kuwait allow this excuse for adultery only and reduce the penalty. The Iraqi code requires the presence of both in the same bed but reduces the penalty to three years (ibid.). Others prescribe exemption for adultery and otherwise, a reduction in the penalty. Syrian law includes adultery or suspicion of it. Some limit the exemption to the husband and others extend it to sons, father and brothers. Egyptian law requires the husband to catch his wife in the act and his response must be immediate. The Algerian code treats husbands and wives as equals (42, p. 145).

Domestic violence appears to be common in Arab families: 77 per cent of females aged 12 to 55 years who were seen in a Tunisian women's centre in 1993 had been victims of domestic violence (3, p. 71). In Iran, a woman must show proof of 'extreme physical violence' to obtain compensation or a divorce, according to a report of 1994 (30, p. 310). The deliberating judges are males and many of them believe a man has a right to beat his wife.

Women in Religion

Islam has no ordained clerics but instead mullahs and ayatollahs serve as religious teachers and leaders. No women have served in this capacity although Islamic scriptures have no law to prevent them. Within the past year, some women have been trained as mullahs in Morocco but they may not preach in a mosque. Women are segregated in the mosque: this custom is said to have originated with Umar, the second caliph. Most mosques allow women to enter the building but by a separate door which is reserved for them. They cannot sit with men but usually occupy an area at the back of the mosque or an upstairs room.

Public Health Data

The relationship between women's literacy and birth rates is well documented. A Turkish study of the 1960s reported that women with university degrees had on the average 1.4 children, high school graduates 2.0, and primary school graduates 3.8. Illiterate women had 4.2 children (29, p. 166).

Birth rates (births per 1,000 population) in the Arab states are high: >6 in Yemen, 4–6 in Sudan, and 2–4 in Pakistan, Iraq, Jordan and Saudi Arabia. Infant Mortality rates (infant deaths per 1,000 live births) were high and highest in Iraq (103) and lowest in Bahrain, Kuwait and Qatar (8). These compare to 4.0 in Western Europe and 6.9 in the United States (43).

Maternal mortality figures relate directly to the number of children a woman has, their spacing and the kind of prenatal care she receives. Although usually under-reported, maternal deaths numbered more than 300 in Pakistan, Djibouti, Yemen and Sudan in 2007, compared to 9 per 100,000 live births in Western Europe (43).

Summary

Arabia in the sixth century was a polytheistic, idol-worshipping society whose primary loyalty was to family and tribe. Muhammad changed this, and replaced tribal loyalty with obedience to one God, Allah. The message of the Prophet was passed on orally by his Companions and recorded in the Quran a number of years after his death. The Sharia, the sacred law of Islam was assembled later and dictates the rules of behaviour for all Muslims. Islam spread rapidly throughout Africa, the Middle East and Asia. Its main schism into the Sunni and Shia sects occurred in the eighth century.

Before Islam, some but not all segments of Arabian society were matri-archal and children, sometimes fathered by different men, lived with their mother. Polygamy and concubinage were universal and divorce was relatively easy for either sex to obtain. Women were able to own and run their own businesses but they could not inherit or own property. Veiling which preceded the Prophet, was relatively common among tribal and urban women, but rare among their village and nomadic sisters.

Islam had a major impact on the lives of women. From now on, they were regarded as the equals of men but only in their spirituality and ability to attain eternal life. In all other matters, men were superior and their testimony was worth twice as much. Islam gave women the right to own property and inherit, albeit one half as much as men. A woman's marriage contract gave her a dowry or gift of money and/or property from her husband and this and the jewels and property she owned before her marriage were regarded as her personal property. Her husband was expected to provide for her, while her primary duty was to obey and be sexually available to him. He could obtain a divorce for any reason by verbal repudiation only, while she had no such right except in very special situations. She had very limited rights to the custody of their children. Polygyny was allowed and he could take up to four wives and have unlimited access to concubines and unmarried women. She could not have a relationship with any man other than her husband and adultery was punished severely.

With the exception of polygyny and her inheritance rights, the situation of Muslim women differed little from that endured by women in other societies, up until the nineteenth century and sometimes later. While Europe was still enduring the Dark Ages, some Islamic centres developed advanced cultures with notable achievements in mathematics, science and literature. But starting in about the sixteenth century, Islamic culture stagnated and their women lagged further and further behind their sisters in Western and some Asian cultures. Since women constitute one half of the population, this has affected the prosperity of the entire state. On average, Islamic countries rank among the world's poorest with high illiteracy and birth rates and lower life expectancies. Their survival has depended on their one major resource, oil.

Devout Muslims believe that Islamic law is sacred and immutable and applies to all aspects of life including government: the Sharia, which has not changed since the tenth century, should be the law of the land and there is no place for the separation of politics and religion, as practised in a secular state. Despite this, Islamic laws have changed, including ones concerning slavery and punishments for theft and adultery, and the right to polygyny is now exercised much less frequently and is illegal in some Islamic states.

No statement in Islamic scriptures says that women may not have equality in education, employment, religion and political rights but this has clearly not been practised. Crimes-of-honour are remnants of tribal society but continue to be perpetrated against women and are not condemned by religious leaders. They are unworthy of Islam.

Some Islamic theologians have called for a reinterpretation of Sharia Law by an extension of Ijtihad, either by qualified jurists or by scholars and experts in different fields of religion. For others, the goal of reform should be a return to the original Medinan society they view as a perfect egalitarian culture that was marred by later laws (44, p. 266). The potential of Muslim women has been stifled and their voices are largely ignored by the male-dominated religious authorities who dictate the policies and practices of Islamic countries.

No single authority speaks for Islam and women do not participate in the Organization of Islamic Conference (OIC) that includes most Islamic states and meets every three years. As yet, human rights issues, which directly affect the lives of women, have not even appeared on their agendas.

References

1   *Encyclopedia Britannica*. Ed. W. Benton. University of Chicago Press. 1968.
2   Coulson, Noel. J. *A History of Islamic Law*. Edinburgh University Press. 1964.
3   Karmi, Ghada. 'Women, Islam and Patriarchalism'. In *Feminism and Islam*. Ed. Mai Yamani. NewYork University Press. 1996.
4   Hourami, A. *A History of the Arab People*. Belknap Press of Harvard University. 1991.
5   Donner, Fred. M. 'Muhammad and the Caliphate'. In *The Oxford History of Islam*. Ed. John, L. Esposito, Oxford University Press. 1999.
6   Smith, Jane, I. 'Islam and Christendom'. In *The Oxford History of Islam*. Ed. John L. Esposito, Oxford University Press. 1999.
7   Braswell, George W., Jr. *Islam: Its Prophets, People, Politics and Power*. Nashville. Broadman and Holman. 1996.
8   Levtzion, 'Nehemia. Islam in Africa to 1800'. In *The Oxford History of Islam*. Ed. John L. Esposito. Oxford University Press. 1999.
9   Gladney, Dru. C. 'Central Asia and China'. Ibid.
10 Lapidus, Ira. M. 'Sultanate and Gunpowder Empires'. Ibid.
11 Lawrence, Bruce. B. 'The Eastward Journey of Muslim Kingship'. Ibid.
12 Voll, John, O. 'Foundations of Renewal and Reform'. Ibid.
13 www. discoverybangladesh.com/meetbangladesh/people.html
14 Mango, Andrew. *Ataturk*. Woodstock. Overlook Press. 1999.
15 Esposito, John, L. 'Contempory Islam'. In *The Oxford History of Islam*. Ed. John L. Esposito. Oxford University Press. 1999.
16 Yamani, Mai. 'Some Observations on Women in Saudi Arabia'. In *Feminism and Islam*. Ed. Mai Yamani. New York University Press. 1996.
17 Lewis, Bernard. *The Crisis of Islam*. New York. Modern Library. 2003.
18 www. en.wikipedia.org
19 www. News, bbc.co.uk
20 www. Pewresearch.org
21 Afshar, Haleh. 'Islam and Feminism: An Analysis of Political Stratagies'. In *Feminism and Islam*. Ed. Mai Yamani New York University Press. 1996.

22   Mernissi, Fatima. *Beyond the Veil*. Bloomington. Indiana University Press. 1987.

23   Kamali, Mohammad. H. K. 'Law and Society'. In The *Oxford History of Islam*. Ed. John L. Esposito Oxford University Press. 1999.

24   *The Koran*. Tr. N. J. Dawood. New York. Penguin Books. 1994.

25   Cornell, Vincent, J. 'Fruit of the Tree of Knowledge'. In *The Oxford History of Islam*. Ed. John L. Esposito. Oxford University Press. 1999.

26   Mernissi, Fatima. *Women and Islam: An Historical and Theological Enquiry*. Oxford. Blackwell. 1987.

27   www.rasonlalleh.net/subject_en.asp/hit=1&parent_id=82&sub_id=1389

28   Siddiqui, Mona. 'Law and Desire for Social Control: An Insight Into the Hanafi Concept of Kafa'a with Reference to the Fatwa Alamgiri' (1664-1672). In *Feminism and Islam*. Ed. Mai Yamani. New York University Press. 1996.

29   Minai, Naila. *Women in Islam: Tradition and Transition in the Middle East*. New York. Seaview Books. 1981.

30   Mir-Hosseini, Ziba, M-H. 'Stretching the Limits: A Feminist Reading of the Sharia in Post-Khomeini Iran'. In *Feminism and Islam*. Ed. Mai Yamani. New York University Press. 1996.

31   Nasr, S. V. R. 'European Colonialism and the Emergence of Modern Muslim States'. In *The Oxford History of Islam*. Ed. John L. Esposito. Oxford University Press. 1999.

32   Alia, Kecia. 'Progressive Muslims and Islamic Jurisprudence'. In *Progressive Muslims*. Ed. G. Safi. Oxford. One World. 2003.

33   www. childinfo.org/education_primary.php

34   www. photius.com/rankings/ ... literacy-female-2007-ohtml

35   Seager, Joni. *The Penguin Atlas of Women in the World*. Penguin Books. 2009.

36   Fakhro, Munira. 'Gulf Women and Islamic Law'. In *Feminism and Islam*. Ed. Mai Yamani. New York University Press. 1996.

37   Makdisi, Jean S. 'The Mythology of Modernity: Women and Democracy in Lebanon'. Ibid.

38   Mokbel-Wensley, Souad. 'Statutary Discrimination in Lebanon: A Lawyer's View'. Ibid.

39   Schacht, Joseph. *Introduction to Islamic Law*. Oxford. Clarendon Press. 1964.

40   Hamadeh, Najla. *Islamic Family Legislation: the Authoritarian 'Discourse of Silence'*. Ed. Mai, Yamani. New York University Press. 1996.

41   Azzam, Maha. *Gender and the Politics of Religion in the Middle East*. Ed. Yamani, Mai. New York University Press. 1966.

42   Abu-Odeh, Lama. *Crimes of Honour and the Construction of Gender*. Ibid.

43   World Population Data Sheet.

44   Aslan, Reza. *No God but God*. New York. Random House. 2005.

Additional Bibliography

Connor, Jane. 'The Women's Convention in the Muslim World'. In *Feminism and Islam*. Ed. Mai, Yamani. New York University Press. 1996.

Dallal, Ahmad. 'Science, Medicine and Technology'. In *The Oxford History of Islam*. Ed. John L. Esposito. Oxford University Press. 1999.

Jurji, Edward J. (ed.). *Great Religions of the World. Muhammed is His Prophet*. National Geographic Society. 1971.

Lester, T. *What is the Koran?* The Atlantic Monthly, p. 43. Jan. 1999.

Lewis, Bernard. *What Went Wrong?* Oxford University Press. 2002.

Missailidis, K. and M. Gebre-Medhin. 'Female Genital Mutilation in Eastern Ethiopia'. Lancet. 356: 137. 2000.

Nasr, S .V. R. 'European Colonialism and the Emergence of Modern Muslim States'. In *The Oxford History of Islam*. Ed. John L. Esposito. Oxford University Press. 1999.

Robertson-Smith, William. *Kinship and Marriage in Early Arabia*. London. Adam and Charles Black. 1907.

Simmons, G. Z. 'Are We Up to the Challenge?' In *Progressive Muslims*. Ed. O. Safi. Oxford. One World. 2003.

Stern, Gertrude H. *Marriage in Early Islam*. London. Royal Asiatic Society. 1939.

Chapter 6

Ancient Cultures and Tribal Religions

Zoroastrianism

The two oldest organized religions are Vedism (early Hinduism) and Zoroastrianism. Both shared Sanskrit, the earliest written language. Zoroastrianism was the religion of the ancient Persians, founded by the prophet Zarathustra, who lived about 3,500 years ago. The religion was monotheistic but dualistic because of a belief in two opposing spirits, good and evil. Its one God had seven Attributes, each one shared with humans (1, vol. 15, p. 11).

Its sacred texts are the Avestas, of which the central part is the Gathas, five songs composed by Zarathushtra (2). Zoroastrians do not believe in a heaven or hell or in reincarnation but they do believe in a future saviour, born of a virgin who was impregnated by the seed of Zarathushtra. Fire was regarded as a sacred symbol as was the juice of a plant similar to Soma, also revered by the Vedic people.

Their religious texts treat men and women as equals and like the early Hindus, they allowed women to participate in their initiation ceremony. They believed in the existence of six immortal beings of whom three were female. According to their scriptures, women are prone to temptation and should be kept under regular supervision. They are told to show reverence to their husbands and obey them. They were polluted by menstruation and childbirth, and had to be isolated and purified before they could rejoin society.

Many Zoroastrians converted to Islam after their country was overrun by its followers. Some continue to live in Iran and nearby countries and others, the Parsees, moved to India.

Taoism

Taoism, attributed to Lao Tzu, is the native religion of China and dates back to the sixth century BCE, although its roots are probably older (3, vol. 21, p. 677). It is a flexible, gentle religion providing peace of mind, and teaches that the focus of life should be nature and not man. This contrasts with Confucianism, which was more concerned with education, duty and order in the state. Taoism rivalled Confucianism between 200 BCE and 200 CE after which Confucianism became dominant until the twentieth century. Nevertheless, Taoism continued to influence Chinese thought and behaviour until the Communist takeover in the twentieth century. Ancestor worship is a prominent part of both Taoism and Confucianism.

Confucianism

Confucius was born in about 551 BCE and was therefore a contemporary of the Buddha (4, pp. 18ff.). His father died when he was young and he was poor and self-educated. His goal was to improve the lives of people and he is remembered as one of the world's great philosophers. He was an outstanding teacher and his students attained positions of authority in China, where they had an enormous influence until the Communist Revolution.

Confucianism is not a religion but a philosophy or sociopolitical way of life. There is no creed, church or clergy and each person's primary responsibility is to his family and next to the state and last, to the world. Rulers, parents, husbands and older siblings hold superior positions. Women are inferior to their fathers, husbands and sons. This differs from Buddhism where individuals are equal – except among monastics – and responsible for themselves. Confucius believed in the innate goodness of human beings and promoted the three universal virtues of wisdom, humanity and courage. Learning and scholarship were highly respected, as were moral correctness and duty to society.

Mencius (371–289 BCE), a pupil of Confucius, continued his master's work and taught that the four virtues or essentials of a moral life are humanity, righteousness, propriety and wisdom (3, vol. 15, p. 145). Faithfulness was added later and these became known as the Five Constant Virtues. Filial piety was basic to all of these and therefore children should obey, serve and support their parents and honour them in death. Parents, usually the father, made decisions concerning the choice of spouses and other family and business matters.

Mencius described the five human relationships and their goals: between father and son there should be affection: between ruler and minister there should be righteousness: between husband and wife there should be attention to separate functions: between older and younger brothers there should be order: between good friends, good faith (5, p. 138).

Confucianism was declared the state doctrine of China in 136 BCE and continued to control education until 2000 CE when it was discarded as too esoteric, impractical and restrictive. It also controlled some aspects of government since state employment depended on the results of a competitive civil service exam, which although open to all, required knowledge of the Confucian classics. This practice lasted until the twentieth century.

The Egyptians

The Egyptian civilization lasted from about 4000 BCE until 700 CE when North Africa was overrun by Islamic Arabs. Initially there were two Egyptian kingdoms, a Northern and a Southern, which united in about 3000 BCE, when Heliopolis became the religious capital. Each town or village had its own protective god (6, p. 132). Some were male, others female, and many had animal forms such as Sekhmet, the lioness protector goddess of Memphis. Some goddesses became the wives of gods; for example, Isis, who with her husband-brother Osiris and their son Horus, constituted the 'triad or holy family' (6, p. 137). She was one of several goddesses belonging to Greek and Middle East religions. All claimed parthenogenic or virgin births, so this was not unique to Christianity.

The cult of Isis was known to the Greeks by the fifth century BCE, then grew in the following centuries and spread to Rome (7, p. 27). Her reputation was enhanced by her search for her brother-husband who, according to legend, had been murdered. She was known as the goddess of life and fertility and became one of the most revered deities in Egypt. She represented the ideal wife and mother, the 'divine patroness of family life' (ibid.). She was the mistress of the heavens, earth, sea and the under-world. She was the goddess of women and 'gave them equal power with men' (7, p. 28).

Ancient papyri suggest that Egyptian women were 'the freest in the known world, and were seen as separate entities, both legally and morally, from the men folk in their lives'. They were permitted to own property and obtain divorces (8, p. 163). But they could not hold positions in government (3, vol. 8, p. 42). Some were priestesses who served the cults of Hathor and Neith, and at least two were Pharaohs: Hatshepsut (1504–1482 BCE), after she usurped the throne of her young nephew Thutmose III, and Cleopatra, the last of the Ptolemaic rulers of Egypt, who died in 30 BCE. However, most women who achieved high rank in Egyptian society were the wives of nobles. The women who served in temples were of lower rank.

The Greeks

The Greeks were a polytheistic society who absorbed most of their deities from civilizations in Asia, Egypt and Crete. For example, Zeus the father or leader of their gods was imported from Asia Minor. Isis was imported from Egypt in about the fifth century and identified with women, treating them as the equals of men (7, p. 27). Cybele – the Earth Mother – was an oriental deity.

She was widely accepted among Greeks who knew her as the Mother of Gods. Her cult was open to all but membership required fasting and purification: the reward was security and a hope of salvation. Isis and Cybele were adopted later by the Romans, like many other deities, often with different names. The Greeks regarded their gods as human in mind and body and treated them with respect but not servility. They appear to have had no expectation of a life after death, at least not initially.

During the fifth and fourth centuries BCE, women had important roles in the state, especially as prophetic priests, but were otherwise excluded from most civic events. Greek society was strongly patriarchal and Athenian women rarely ventured out of their homes except to attend funerals and religious festivals (9, p. 290). They were regarded as inferior and were treated as the equals of children and slaves (10, p. 202).

Greeks became less provincial but more cosmopolitan and insecure, after Alexander's conquests in Asia in 300 BCE. They began to lose trust in their many gods and turned instead to mystery cults and religious philosophies, seeking a closer personal relationship with a deity as well as security and eternal life. The cult of Demeter was one of these, as was that of Dionysius.

Several well-known religious philosophies developed in the last centuries BCE and early CE. The goal of most was to provide their followers with self-sufficiency and security. The Stoics for example, believed that the world was controlled by an organizing authority, a Divine Reason or God, who oversaw a recurring cycle of worlds. They believed each individual contained some of this reason, and men and women were equal. Stoics encouraged brotherhood and public service.

The Romans

Roman religions passed through several periods, beginning as a primitive village culture and then absorbed some of the Etruscan beliefs and many of the Greek gods and later, Oriental ones (3, vol. 19, p. 555). They developed an intricate and hierarchical priesthood with a series of underlings, all male. The chief priest was the Pontiff Maximus. The only women who could participate in religious rites were the six vestal virgins who mostly came from patrician families. They served for 30 years and tended the state hearth in the forum. Except for this, women were much less involved in religious rites than in Greece (9, p. 3).

Rome had a strongly patriarchal culture although women seem to have been able to voice their opinions in Forum gatherings and attend dinners and festivals. They were regarded as inferior to men but some wealthy or aristocratic women owned or managed businesses. They married at 12 years or younger and had as many children as possible, often dying when they were quite young. They had no rights to their children and were entirely subservient to men – their fathers and then their husbands. They were not allowed to drink wine – an offence punishable by death – because it was believed to lead to adultery (11). Roman men engaged in prostitution and used their slaves for sex.

The Palaeo-Indians

The Palaeo-Indians are believed to have travelled across the Bering land bridge from Northern Russia and Siberia into North America. The first immigrants probably arrived 40,000 years ago, to be followed by others in about 13000 and 10000 BCE (12, p. 169). In time they spread all over the Americas. Few written records exist of their cultures and religions.

In the very north were the Inuit who inhabit the arctic regions of Canada and Greenland. They live in small family groups in which men and women have separate and clearly defined roles, but are regarded as equals (13). They have great respect for the old, many of whom are camp leaders. The Inuit believe in Sila, an ever-present spirit, and in Sedra, a goddess who lives at the bottom of the sea and controls sea creatures. The spirits of their dead are believed to inhabit animals and other objects of nature.

More than 450 native tribes occupied North America and spoke over 300 languages and dialects (14, p. 9). Estimates suggest that there were about 10 million Native Americans before the arrival of the Europeans. They were decimated by imported diseases, especially measles and smallpox, for which they had no immunity. Additional losses followed attacks by settlers and military forces, as well as direct and indirect attrition of their food supplies, especially the bison.

These tribes differed in their religious beliefs, but many identified with sacred places such as mountains or lakes. They revered spirits who resided in natural objects like the sun, moon and stars. Many believed their Indian culture was derived from woman, and in some form, she was both the source of life and the provider of sustenance (14, p. 21). Each tribe had its own creation story to explain its origin (14, p. 22).

Men and women had separate and complementary roles. Men hunted and cleared the fields, defended their lands and families and participated in tribal meetings and festivals. Women tended the crops, gathered berries and other foods, made hide-skin clothes and tepees, ceramics, quilts and sometimes jewellery. Childcare was usually communal and involved the extended family. Many tribes were matrilinear in both descent and property rights, and women had a voice in selecting leaders. North-eastern and South-eastern Native Americans often had female rulers. Women selected the leaders and clan mothers who headed each of the three clans of the Iroquois tribes and could also remove them. Other tribes like the Oneala, were patrilinear and patrilocal (15, p. 292).

Women could be traders, farmers, artisans and healers. Village councils, in which women participated, usually made important decisions affecting the tribes. Voting was done by directing smoke up or down from the peace pipe which was passed around the circle of members. Many tribes had vision seekers, both male and female, whose role was to obtain spiritual guidance; preparation for this role required four days of fasting, prayer and a sweat bath. Some tribes like the Iroquois practised human sacrifice: the Pawnee sacrificed a virgin each year, preferably one captured from another tribe but if not, one of their own.

Most tribes celebrated a girl's puberty: the Apaches did this in their sunrise dance. Marriages were usually arranged by a male relative, but interest in a particular boy or girl could influence his decision. Many native girls maintained their virginity until marriage, but pre-marital sex was not treated as a serious crime. In some tribes, such as the Arapaho and Cheyenne, men were faithful to their wives (12, p. 159). Others practised polygamy or encouraged their women to enhance business arrangements by providing sex for traders or visitors (16, p. 179). In some cases, women learned sexual skills from older men and taught them to their younger husbands (16, p. 63). Native American women retained control of themselves and their property; it was said that an 'Indian woman never submits entirely to her husband'. A white woman who was freed many years after her capture commented, 'as an Indian woman, I was free. I owned my home, my person, the work of my hands, and my children could never forget me. I was better as an Indian woman than under white law' (14, p. 77).

The women of the same family group or clan usually shared childcare duties. A mother's brother had priority over the children's father in their care. Divorce was common and easily arranged; the partner who wanted it simply packed up the other's belongings and placed them by the door. Remarriage occurred with little interval. The woman in the meantime returned to her family. Adultery was dealt with severely by some tribes and punished by cutting off an ear in females and the penis in males. Some women elected to ensure their own sterility at about 30 years of age by taking a potion made from various roots. Death and burial were treated differently in different tribes and most believed an individual's spirit survived after death and entered various natural objects, but was not reincarnated.

Meso-Americans

Meso-Americans lived in Central and South America and 5,000 years ago, there were about 51 Indian tribes living here. At first they were hunter-gatherers, but this ended once corn was discovered and cultivated.

The Olmecs were one of the oldest civilizations, and like the Mayans, they were polytheistic. However, Olmec women never attained important political or social roles, as did Mayan women (17, p. 193). The Mayans started in the lowlands of Guatemala at the beginning of the Common Era, were reborn in the Yucatan and collapsed before the Spaniards arrived in the sixteenth century. Their society was said to have a more matriarchal structure than any other pre-Columbian culture. In fact, there is 'no other new world civilization in which females reached the degree of power that has been attested for the Maya' (17, p. 193).

The Maya believed in gods who represented rain, thunder, lightning and hail as well as the sun, the moon and corn (18, p. 18). They had a three-class society consisting of priests and nobles, craftsmen, merchants and peasants. After marriage, a new son-in-law usually worked for the bride's family until he had proved himself. Divorce was allowed, particularly if there were no offspring and both could then remarry. Women could own and inherit property, but they could not hold public office or enter a temple.

Many different tribes occupied the Andean highlands in what is now Northern Peru and parts of Ecuador, Colombia, Bolivia, Argentina and Chile. The Inca Empire began in 565 CE with the first Inca, Manco Coapac, and ended with the death of Huascar in 1533, one year after their defeat by the Spaniards (19, p. 53). The Incas worshipped the sun and his wife, the moon. The emperor's claim to divinity came through his descent from the two children of the sun, a son and daughter.

Like the Maya, Inca society was divided into castes, which were established at birth (18, p. 42). When girls were 8 to 10 years of age they were brought before an official who selected some to learn weaving. At 13 to 14, another inspection selected girls to work for the Inca nobles or for the Inca's harem, to become priestesses or to be sacrificed. There was a ceremony for girls when they reached puberty and another when they conceived. Inca rulers married their sisters but they also practised polygyny, selecting girls from other tribes. Girls were married at 18 and boys at 24, in communal weddings (18, p. 31). Divorce was easy to obtain.

The Aztecs were initially a small tribe whose population grew to about 13 million people. They made their capital in what is now Mexico City, about 7,000 feet above sea level. Aztec society was hierarchical with chieftains, priests and warriors (20, p. 137). Girls had to learn household routines, child rearing and weaving, starting when they were four or five years old (20, p. 154). They received no formal education. Boys got some education and then entered the legal profession, the military or joined the priesthood. Aztec women could own property, make business contracts and appear in court, but in general they had fewer rights than men (20, p. 142). They could be priestesses. Girls married in their mid-teens, boys in their twenties, and most marriages were arranged, usually within the same social class (20, p. 144). Weddings were quite elabourate affairs and lasted for several days (20, p. 155). Polygyny was common among the nobles and divorce was relatively easy to obtain. Girls then remained with their mothers, boys with their fathers. Pregnant women were given a lot of attention and care, and those who died in childbirth were honoured as much as fallen warriors (20, p. 149).

In 1519 Cortes arrived and defeated the Aztecs in less than two years. Within ten years, all of Mexico was under Spanish control. The Aztecs had antagonized many other Indian tribes who then collabourated with the Spaniards to defeat them.

The Australian Aborigines

The origin of the Australian Aborigines is not known, but they are believed to have existed for over 40,000 years. Initially there were about 500 tribes, each with its own unwritten language. Each tribe had a religious leader and consisted of hunting groups or bands made up of family units (21). Their mythology depicted a world once occupied by spirits or deities, the Dreaming. There was a father of all spirits and a sun mother. Plants grew wherever the sun mother walked, and streams and rivers appeared where she melted the ice. She gave birth to two children, a god, the sun, and a goddess, the moon. Their two children were the 'ancestors' (21). According to Aboriginal lore, their spirits are transferred to a child before birth, so that all humans contain some part of these ancestral beings (1, vol. 1, p. 531).

Girls were valued as much as boys although men rated themselves as superior. The two sexes had separate duties, roles and rituals (21). A girl was promised to her future husband – who had been selected by her family – at birth (22, p. 40). If he was an adult at the time, he assumed certain responsibilities to her parents. Children were shared and reared by the women of the family unit. When a boy reached puberty, he was taken away from the women to be trained by the men of his tribe in masculine skills such as hunting (22, p. 69). He underwent a lengthy initiation which included circumcision, puncture of his nasal septum, front tooth removal, scarification of his back and sub-incision, all practices which continued over the next seven years (1, vol. 1, p. 533). When his initiation was complete, the young man was admitted to the Men's Business but did not participate in decision-making until he married.

When a girl reached puberty, she was initiated into Women's Business. She remained with the women's group and trained in the arts of healing, childcare, food preparation and in raising and gathering plants (22, p. 76). When she married, a girl adopted the tribe of her husband. She participated in Women's Business in its own secret-sacred place to which men were not admitted. Both sexes celebrated certain rituals and festivals together, some lasting for many days.

Aboriginal society has great respect for its ancestors and older family members. All initiated members have a duty to perform rituals which maintain the life-sustaining power of the ancestors (22, p. 71). Decisions made in the Men's Business are discussed with older family members and are not adopted without their agreement.

Summary

Zoroastrianism and Vedism are two of the oldest religions and appear to have their origins in the early Indo-Eurasians who came out of Southern Russia and overran the Middle East, Northern India and Europe. Their early histories suggest they were initially less patriarchal.

Evidence of the earlier Goddess culture persisted in the ancient civilizations of Egypt and may have influenced the beliefs and practices of the Palaeo-Indians of North and Meso-America. Many of these ancient religions recognized a separate and important role for their women. Some tribes retained their matrilocal and matrilinear cultures, and nearly all afforded women property rights, the right to divorce and rights to the custody of their children.

Some of the ancestral beliefs and practices of these ancient cultures were recalled in the folklore, superstitions, festivals and seasonal events observed by European peasant women and segments of society who were concerned with agriculture and crop-raising. Creation was attributed to one or more supreme powers often associated with the sun, moon and other natural phenomena. Most cultures believed in some mechanism to ensure an individual's spiritual survival after death, either outside the planet or in natural objects such as mountains, lakes or other flora and fauna. Women's essential role in reproduction – through which the tribe or civilization would survive – was revered.

References

1   *Encyclopedia of Religion*. Ed. Eliade Mircea. MacMillan Publishing. Co. 1987.
2   www. duke.edu/~jds17/zoroast.html
3   *Encyclopedia Britannica*. Ed. W. Benton. Chicago University Press. 1968.
4   Simpkins, C. Alexander and Annellen Simpkins. *Confucianism*. Tuttle Publishing Co. 2000.
5   Kelleher, Theresa. 'Confucianism'. In *Women in World Religions*. Ed. A. Sharmer. State University of New York. 1987.
6   Steindorff, George and Keith, C. Seele. *When Egypt Ruled the East*. University of Chicago Press. 1942.
7   Tripolitis, Antonia. *Religions of the Hellenistic-Roman Age*. Grand Rapids, Michigan. W. B. Eerdmans Publishing Co. 2002.

8   Picknett, Lynn. *Mary Magdalene. Christianity's Hidden Goddess*. New York. Carroll and Graf. 2003.
9   Dillon, Matthew. *Girls and Women in Classical Greek Religion*. London. Routledge. *2002*.
10   Lerner, Gerda. *The Creation of Patriarchy*. Oxford University Press. 1986.
11   Mason, Moya K. *Ancient Roman Women: A Look at their Lives*. www.moyak.com/papers/roman-women.html
12   Michener, James. A. *Centennial*. New York. Random House. 1974.
13   www. crystalinks.com/Inuit.
14   Green, Rayna. *Women in American Indian Society*. Ed. Frank. W, Porter. New York. Chelsea House. 1998.
15   Griffin, James. B. 'The Midlands'. In *Ancient North-America*. Ed. Jesse. D. Jennings. San Francisco. W. H. Freeman and Company. 1978.
16   Ronda, James P. *Lewis and Clark Among the Indians*. University of Nebraska Press. 2002.
17   Coe, Michael D. 'Olmec and Maya: A Study in Relationships'. In *The Origins of Maya Civilization*. Ed. Richard E. W. Adams. University of New Mexico Press. 1977.
18   Crow, John A. *The Epic of Latin America*. Berkeley. University of California Press. 1946.
19   de Gamboa, Pedro, S. *History of the Incas*. Tr. and ed. Clements Markham. Milwood, New York. Kraus Reprint. 1967.
20   Fagan, Brian M. *The Aztecs*. New York. W. H. Freeman and Company. 1984.
21   Durkheim, E. *Australian Aboriginal Religion*. www. Geocities.com.
22   Bell, Hannahß R. *Men's Business Women's Business*. Inner Traditions. Rochester, Vermont. 1948.

Additional bibliography

Baldick, Julian. *Animal and Shaman*. New York University Press. 2000.
Gimbutas, Marija. *Goddesses and Gods of Old Europe*. University of California Press. 1982.
Jennings, Jesse D. *Ancient North Americans*. W. H. Freeman and Company. 1983.
Lefkowitz, Mary R. and Maureen B. Font. *Women's Life in Greece and Rome*. John Hopkins University Press. 1992.
Long, G. W. 'The Mixe-Logue as Competing Neighbours in the Early Lowland Mayas. in Olmec and Maya'. Ed. Richard. E. W. Adams. University of New Mexico Press. 1977.
Mehr, Farhang. *The Zoroastrian Tradition*. Element Books. 1991.

Mellaart, James. *Earliest Civilization in the NearEast*. New York. McGraw Hill. 1965.
Muller, Karin. *Along the Inca Road*. National Geographic. 2000.
Spores, Ronald. *The Mixtecs in Ancient Times*. University of Oklahoma Press. 1984.

Conclusions

My reason for writing this book was to answer four questions: when and why did women come to be classed as inferior to men; why did this pattern of human behaviour continue for so long: how did it affect the lives of women?

The results of my research are reviewed in the previous chapters. I found that the major religions accepted the concept of male superiority and incorporated it into their scriptures, together with explanations and excuses. Over a period of time, these religious tracts gained recognition by the faithful of each religion and came to be regarded as sacred and immune to change. They have had a major affect on human behaviour, at least in those societies where each is the major religion. This continues to this day.

When did this concept of male superiority occur? It clearly existed in Hammurabi's time – in the second millennium BCE – but not in the Neolithic age when there appears to have been a period of equality, or even a time of female dominance. Why did it occur? The most likely explanation seems to have been superior male body strength during a period of tribal wars. Lerner contends that the captured females of the losers were allowed to survive while the males were killed (1, p. 77). Manpower was in short supply so the female slaves became reproductive machines for their captors. Then over a period of time, male dominance or patriarchy was established as the pattern of human behaviour.

With the exception of very early Hinduism – the oldest of the major religions – female subjugation was the customary pattern of behaviour in the society where each religion had its start. The holy books and religious laws of each – written by men – include statements to this effect. Women had no power to influence this literature, since they were excluded from the religious bodies that determined the practices of each religion.

Hinduism's excuse was fear of racial and caste pollution. Judaism also feared contamination but of their holy places, the Temple and tabernacle. Women would pollute both. Buddhism – which developed out of Hinduism – accepted females as inherently inferior and therefore nuns ranked below monks and females had to be reborn as males before they could achieve enlightenment. Christians, who borrowed Jewish scriptures, gave credence to their mythical accounts of creation that Eve appeared after Adam and must therefore be inferior to him. For good measure, a second reason was provided: Eve was responsible for misleading Adam. Muslims – nearly 600 years later – accepted these myths and simply wrote that men are superior and women required protection.

The major religions have had a devastating effect on women's progress for nearly 3,000 years. Although changes in interpretation and practice have been made by some of the more recent branches of each religion, in general they have taken no steps to correct these inequities. Changes only occurred when secular governments enacted laws to improve women's rights. India – now a secular democracy – outlawed many of the discriminatory practices of Hinduism. Buddhist countries now generally observe state laws that promote equality, although this does not apply to the *sangha*s. Israel is a democracy, but Orthodox Judaism is its state religion and rabbinic courts there control virtually all aspects of family law. Most Christian countries have established secular governments and abolished the jurisdiction of ecclesiastical courts, but religious authorities continue to control many aspects of Family Law in those states where they are the dominant faith. Islamic countries have in a few cases banned Islamic law, or limited its power, while others continue to allow its practice, in full.

The major tool used to suppress the progress of females has been the denial of education. This continues to be practised to this day; witness the Taliban's actions in Afghanistan, where girls were denied all schooling. The disparity in male and female literacy rates in a state is a measure of the degree of gender inequality in education. Countries with the greatest degree of inequality in education are also some of the world's poorest. There is a direct relationship between the level of female education and the standard of living and prosperity of a state. Women account for half the population and there is agreement that their education is one of the most important reforms a state can make, if it really wants to improve its overall economy. This boosts productivity, increases per capita income, lowers fertility, decreases maternal and infant mortalities, increases life expectancy: improves prospects for the next generation and promotes better management of environmental resources (2). Data from 82 developing countries show that for every year a girl stays in school, the risk of early death in her children is reduced by 7 to 9 per cent (3).

In the past 50 years, nearly all countries have shown marked improvement in the education of its girls. Female literacy in India was only 13 per cent in 1961 (4, p. 238). It is now 48 per cent but still 25 per cent less than for males (5, p. 119). These numbers are higher in urban areas. Education is sponsored by the state in most Buddhist countries, except in villages where *sangha*s are the only resource and they may not accept girls. Israel provides 12 years of education for all its children, except that strict Orthodox Jews may continue to limit the education of girls. Primary school education has been compulsory in most Christian countries since the mid-nineteenth century, but fewer girls attend secondary schools. Islamic countries have lagged in improving the education of its girls and the required segregation of the sexes imposes additional limitations. Nevertheless there have been improvements and in Kuwait for instance, literacy for females is now 91 per cent (ibid.).

Employment opportunities for women depend on their education and her family's economic status. Poor families may limit the education of their daughters and they are forced into low-skill jobs to support their families. The admission of women into the job and career markets has been slow and preference is given to men seeking the same position. The average woman is paid one third less than a man, despite laws in most states requiring equal pay for the same work. Additionally, women tend to occupy lower tier and non-managerial positions. Improvement – although slow – is occurring. In 2009, 15 Fortune 500 companies were run by women (6). India reported 11 per cent of its 240 largest companies had women CEOs (7). Three per cent of the world's top 1,000 companies have women CEOs (8). Some countries like Norway have mandated that women must have 40 per cent of the seats on the corporate boards of their public companies.

The second most important tool for women's progress is the election of female legislators to local and central governing offices. This was long delayed since women were unable to vote in local and national elections until the twentieth century in most countries. Except in Russia – where nearly one half of the parliament is female – relatively few women have been elected to legislatures. This too is changing and at a faster rate than in businesses. A number of countries now mandate that 25 per cent to 30 per cent of legislative seats must be reserved for women. Twenty to 30 per cent of ministerial positions in 15 state governments are now held by women (9). The number is lower in the United States and much lower in Asian countries.

Religious beliefs concerning Family Law have been strongly conserved, particularly in Islamic countries, Israel, Latin America and a few other Catholic countries. These affect marriage, dowries, divorce, polygyny, adultery, child-custody and reproductive rights. Most Protestant states dissolved ecclesiastic courts and placed all aspects of Family Law under civil courts. India abolished Hindu laws after Independence. Israel retained rabbinical courts for marriage and divorce only. A few Islamic countries such as Turkey and Tunisia administer Family Law through civil courts and Egypt abolished Sharia courts in 1956. In most others, Family Law remains under the jurisdiction of Sharia courts.

Most states – other than Islamic ones – have passed laws forbidding the marriage of girls who are younger than 18 years of age, but custom frequently prevails over law. Despite legislation in India, child marriages continue, especially in rural areas. Islam makes no stipulation concerning marriage age and this varies in different states. Reports from Qatar show that one third of all married women were between 15 and 19 years of age (10, p. 258).

Reproductive rights include the right to prevent or terminate a pregnancy. Hindus and Buddhist countries follow state laws permitting birth control and abortion. Israel allows both, although neither is practised by the ultra-Orthodox. The Catholic Church opposes both except by the rhythm method for contraception. Most Protestant Churches permit birth control except for Evangelicals and the Southern Baptist Convention, who also oppose abortion, as does the Mormon Church except in special situations. Infanticide is not allowed by any religion but still occurs, especially in India.

Not long ago, the major religions ruled that the father had a superior right to the custody of all children. India changed Hindu law in 1956 and practice there tends to consider the best interests of the child. Buddhist countries do the same. Israel places children under the age of five years with the mother. There is a difference of opinion concerning older children as to whether Talmudic law or the best interests of the child should prevail. Most courts in predominantly Christian countries base their decisions on the best interests of the child, and custody is usually awarded to the mother, who generally receives financial support. Islamic countries observing Sharia law, give the father custody, after children reach a specific age.

All religions, with the possible exception of the Catholic Church, experience recurring waves of recidivism or fundamentalism. These episodes appear to be cyclic, but one of their goals is to re-establish patriarchy (11, p. 79). The Hindu Radical Right has become more aggressive in its efforts to establish a Hindu theocracy in India, where the model for women is the long-suffering and trusting mythic Sita. Some of its members even support a return to widow burning on the grounds of religious freedom. Orthodox Jewish sects in Israel, have become more strident in their demands for state laws reflecting their own very restrictive views concerning women. Islam is experiencing religious revivals resulting in greater observance of Muslim dress and denouncements against Western democracy, and in their extreme form, have led to the intimidation and abuse of women, as experienced recently in Afghanistan under the Taliban. Evangelical Christians – another fundamentalist group – have become better organized and funded, by using the media for proselytizing, and moving from the pulpit to the political stage in the United States. They are now firmly wedded to the right wing of the Republican party. They include the Southern Baptist Convention which believes in the inerrancy of the Bible, both Old Testament and New Testament: the subjugation of women: and the denial of all their recently won rights including suffrage, employment, birth control and abortion. In addition to promoting their own editions of educational curricula, their goal appears to be the creation of a male-dominated theocracy in the United States.

In the 1970s, during the Decade of Women, the United Nations Women's Convention drafted treaties making states responsible for correcting discrimination against women in the 'political, social, economic and cultural life of their countries' (12, p. 351). This action to improve the lives of women, by a well-respected international organization is just and long overdue, but acceptance does not guarantee fulfilment and some method of regular surveillance is necessary to ensure compliance.

By 1995, 139 countries had agreed to ratify these requirements, but 29 had not. The main stumbling blocks were Article two calling for abolishing existing discriminatory laws, customs, regulations and practices, and Articles 15 and 16 concerning equality in marriage and Family Law. The states entering reservations were mostly Muslim countries, and in many cases this was because they believed these Articles were in contention with the Sharia or their own constitutions. Objections were also raised by predominantly Roman Catholic countries and the Vatican concerning reproductive freedom (Article 16); specifically the right to decide on the number and spacing of children and access to the information and means to do this. There were also reservations concerning the submission of disputes to the International Court of Justice.

President Carter signed the treaty for the United States and it was then sent to the Senate Foreign Relations' Committee who passed it and sent it on to the full Senate. Here, after a long delay, it was sent back to the previous committee who again endorsed it and sent it back to the Senate. It has never been ratified, despite support from 190 religious, civic and community organizations including the American Nurses Association and the National Association of Catholic Nuns (13). Failure by states to enact the Equal Rights Amendment and the denial of funding for international family planning services under some recent administrations, provide additional evidence for antagonism to women's rights in this country. These appear especially hypocritical since these same reproductive rights are legal in the United States.

More recently, the United Nations published its Eight Millennium Developmental Goals for 2015. Three of these especially impact women: universal primary education, gender equality and improved maternal health. Three others affect both sexes: to end extreme poverty – where women are a majority, improve child health and improve the prevention and treatment of HIV/AIDS.

It is tempting to speculate on the course world history and women's lives would have taken if they had always been accepted as equals. Female education became more generally available in the Western world in the last 200 years, following many millennia of denial. Their progress has been remarkable in this short time and five women were awarded Nobel prizes in 2009. National prosperities would almost certainly have been more advanced, birth rates would have been lower and local and national conflicts would likely have been much less frequent. Standards of living and all the advances we have witnessed in the last century in science and industry might well have been realized much earlier. Television and newspaper reports show an increasing number of women are successful economists and financial advisors, chairpersons of legislative committees and hold national ministerial positions. One can only wonder how different the world might have been if they had had these opportunities earlier. Countries that still deny women equality in this day and age, should understand it is unlikely they can compete and make progress while over half of their citizens are unproductive.

All the major religions have the power to reinterpret their scriptures and enact changes appropriate to the times. Although uncommon, some have already started to do this: the state of Israel does not permit Levirate marriage despite words promoting this practice in Leviticus. Most – but not all – Islamic states have stopped stoning adulterers to death and they no longer condone slavery. The Bible, in both the Old Testament and the New Testament's Gospel of Matthew, orders a man to divorce his wife if she commits adultery, but contrary to this, the Catholic Church forbids divorce even for adultery. Religions sometimes add new requirements and dogmas later in their history and then invest them with the authority of scriptural law; examples are the celibacy requirement for priests and rules against contraception and abortion imposed by the Roman Catholic Church in the thirteenth and sixteenth centuries, respectively. Could they not do the same to raise the status of women?

Some changes appear to be relatively simple ones to enact. Surely Theravedan Buddhism could allow the full ordination of its nuns? How about deleting some of the verses in scriptures that are insulting to women or at least omitting them from their liturgies? Reform Jews first changed and then deleted the Benediction with its demeaning statement about women. Most religious leaders have had some education in science and biology; do they still really believe that women are unclean or a source of pollution? Are they inferior and if so, in what way? If not, would it not be reasonable for all to correct phrases saying men are superior? These are after all relics of patriarchy whose goal was to control female sexuality. Ignorance may have been an excuse at the time the scriptures were written but not now. Further, women should be included in the synods, which deliberate about a religion's actions so that the opinion of the other half of the human race can be heard.

Unfortunately, hubris makes it unlikely that any of these changes will occur, and the only alternative is a more clear-cut and strongly enforced limitation of religious authority in all countries and their separation from government. State legislation is necessary to dictate equality across genders with regard to education, Family Law, suffrage, employment, inheritance and reproductive freedom. Strong women's organizations are necessary to promote and maintain these changes and ensure equal numbers of male and female elected representatives, government office holders and representatives on judicial bodies. The ordination of women into the priesthood would then remain as the only domain under the control of religions and a useful indicator of that religion's responsibility for women's subjugation.

References

1   Lerner, Gerda. *The Creation of Patriarchy*. Oxford University Press. 1987.

2   www. BasicEd.org. Basic Education. Coalition
3   Walker, A. R. P. 'Women, how far still to go?' *Journal of the Royal Society of Medicine*. 92. 57. 1999.
4   Sengupta, Padmini. *The Story of Women in India*. New Delhi. Indian Book Company. 1974.
5   Seager, Joni. *The Penguin Atlas of Women in the World*. Penguin Books. 2009.
6   http://www. money.cnn.com/magazines/fortune500/2009/womenceos/
7   http://www. business.rediff.com/ ... / slide-show-1-more-women-ceos-in-india-than-abroadhtm
8   www. infoplease.com/spot/womenceo1.html
9   www. un.org/
10   Fahkro, Munira. 'Gulf Women and Islamic Law'. In *Feminism and Islam*. Ed. Mai, Yamani. New York University Press. 1996.
11   French, Marilyn. *The War Against Women*. New York. Ballantine Books. 1992.
12   Connors, Jane. 'The Women's Convention in the Muslim World'. In *Feminism and Islam*. Ed. Mai, Yamani. New York University Press. 1996.
13   www. aavw.org/About/international_corner/...CEDAWin-the-US./pdf

Index